MAJOR LEAGUE
LOSERS

MAJOR LEAGUE LOSERS

THE REAL COST OF SPORTS AND WHO'S PAYING FOR IT

Revised Edition

MARK S. ROSENTRAUB

BASIC
BOOKS

A Member of the Perseus Books Group

The author wishes to note the following:

The Journal of Urban Affairs for permission to reproduce data from his previously published work co-authored with Michael Przybylski, David Swindell, and Dan Mullins (Tables 5-3 and 5-4, and Figures 5-1 through 5-5).

Thanks is also expressed to the American Society of Public Administration for permission to reproduce data from the author's previously published work with David Swindell that appeared in the Public Administration Review (Tables 9-1 through 9-6).

Tables 7-1, 7-2, and 7-4 are from Mark S. Rosentraub and Sam Nunn's "Sports Wars: Suburbs and Center Cities in a Zero Sum Game," which appeared in the Journal of Sport and Social Issues 21, no. 1, (1997) and appears here with the permission of Sage Publications.

REVISED EDITION

Library of Congress Cataloging-in-Publication Data
Rosentraub, Mark S., 1950-
    Major league losers: the real cost of sports and who's paying for it/by Mark S. Rosentraub.—Revised ed.
       p. cm
    Includes bibliographical references.
    ISBN: 0-465-07143-0
    1. Sports—Economic aspects—United States.   2. Sports teams—United States—Costs.   3. Sports teams—United States—Finance.   4. Cities and towns—United States—Economic conditions.   5. Sports team owners—United States.   I. Title.

99   00   01   02   03   ❖/RRD   10   9   8   7   6   5   4   3   2   1

For Karen

CONTENTS

ACKNOWLEDGMENTS

All those who have undertaken the task of writing a book know the support required from others to complete the work. I was extremely fortunate to have the professional and personal networks that made it possible to write the first and second versions of this book. The Center for Urban Policy and the Environment at Indiana University–Purdue University Indianapolis (IUPUI) provided the intellectual and professional support necessary to write a book on cities and sports. I can only hope that this second edition is worthy of the continuing support I have received from the Center, my colleagues at IUPUI, and Indiana University's School of Public and Environmental Affairs.

Several people were especially important in helping me make the numerous improvements that are to be found in this second edition. Dr. Dennis Zimmerman of the Congressional Research Service of the Library of Congress helped me refine many of my ideas and thoughts. Several others, with whom I was fortunate to be able to discuss sports and economic development, also helped me improve on the first edition. Drs. Robert Baade, Roger Noll, Robert Sandy, and Andrew Zimbalist assisted me more than they know, and I am especially grateful for their insights and thought-provoking questions. Richard Sandomir and I began talking about sports thirty years ago, and now that he is at *The New York Times*, I continue to benefit from his insight and wisdom.

Through the course of the past two years I have also been able to learn a great deal from such reporters as Justin Catanoso and Welch Suggs.

Two colleagues at the Center and Indiana University's School of Public and Environmental Affairs were especially important to me and the completion of this second edition. Teresa Bennett's careful review of each chapter and each sentence helped make this second edition far more readable; she has been of invaluable aid. The task of preparing each chapter fell to Jeannine Smith, who not only did a great job but is now among Indianapolis's experts on cities and sports.

It has been my good fortune to discuss sports issues and develop friendships with public officials who work to attract and retain teams. The debates I engaged in with Stephen Goldsmith, Jim Snyder, Paul Helmke, William Hudnut, Richard Greene, Tom Vandergriff, Steve Soboroff, Brett Mandel, and Tom Chema helped me refine my ideas. Even though I was not able to agree with these fine leaders on every point, I enjoyed all our many conversations. Indeed, Tom Vandergriff and I have been discussing cities and sports for more than twenty years, and his respect is one of my most cherished assets.

My personal debts remain to those who have supported me through my years of work on cities and sports. Michael Carroll, vice president of the Lilly Endowment, died before *Major League Losers* was first published. Although he would have disagreed with some of the ideas presented, he definitely would have enjoyed the conversations that the first edition generated. Mike's intellectual and emotional support framed and helped create the Center for Urban Policy and the Environment. It is my hope that he would have found this second edition worthy of his aspirations for the Center's work.

My father also did not live to see that I can really "study" sports. My greatest disappointment is that I was not able to share *Major League Losers* with him. I have been able to share the book with my brother, and that remains a great source of comfort. Michael is my eternal co-conspirator in our family's love of sports, and my mother, who still must tolerate my sports mania, will have to gauge if this second edition would have burst the buttons on Dad's shirt.

My wife, Karen, has been a rock of support during my "sports wars" and in my efforts to get this second edition completed. Alexa, Natalie, and Sabrina have endured another year of sports wars, but I think they enjoyed it as much as I did. Each family member has become a true sports fan, and we each cried when the Pacers fell to the Bulls in 1998. The excitement we shared at the victories over the Knicks and those three wonderful games against the Bulls in Indianapolis is why I continue to love sports and our Indiana Pacers.

What follows is my responsibility. This work does not represent the views and ideas of the Center for Urban Policy and the Environment or Indiana University. I trust that what has been produced is worthy of all the support I have received. Alexa, Natalie, and Sabrina, thanks for all your help and love. Your love and respect make producing this book for you a father's joy!

Indianapolis
February 1999

1

Introduction

A welfare system exists in this country that transfers hundreds of millions of dollars from taxpayers to wealthy investors and their extraordinarily well paid employees. Who are these individuals profiting from life on the dole? They are the owners of America's professional sports teams and the athletes who play in each of the four major sports leagues (baseball, basketball, football, and hockey). The true welfare kings and queens of America are the players and team owners whose salaries and profits produce sufficient copy for a season's worth of episodes of *Lifestyles of the Rich and Famous*.

The sports welfare system exists—indeed, it thrives and continues to grow—because state and local government leaders, dazzled by promises of economic growth from sports, mesmerized by visions of enhanced images for their communities, and captivated by a mythology of the importance of professional sports, have failed to do their homework. Too many community leaders do not understand—or they choose to ignore—the reams of information describing the minuscule impact of teams on local economies and the ways in which the four major sports leagues control the number of teams and manipulate revenue-sharing programs to victimize taxpayers and sports fans.

1

Many public leaders use clever sound bites to dismiss the idea that professional sports teams are oversold as a magic elixir for redevelopment and job creation. In addition, these same leaders frequently shrug their shoulders when asked why they would increase taxes to raise hundreds of millions of dollars for subsidies instead of challenging the control that the leagues have to regulate the number of teams that exist. Numerous analyses by academicians, consulting companies, and federal and state government agencies are available that describe the paltry number of full-time jobs created by heavily subsidized sports facilities, the low levels of economic development that accompany a team's presence, and the abusive monopoly behavior of the leagues. Yet new sports palaces continue to rise, supported by billions of dollars in extra taxes, and there appears to be no relief in sight. In 1997 and 1998 alone, new subsidized facilities were planned and approved for Cleveland, Dallas, Detroit, Denver, Houston, Indianapolis, San Francisco, and Seattle. The situation was made more absurd when the baseball team with more gross revenues than any other, the New York Yankees, initiated discussions for a stadium in New York that could involve $700 million in subsidies.

Why do public officials who routinely oppose tax increases and may even doubt the economic benefits of teams urge voters to approve subsidies for facilities and leases that give teams virtually all revenues produced by the stadium or arena? These public officials, as well as the voters and sports fans who accede to the demands of team owners, are victims of a monopoly system created by the Congress, courts, and the sports leagues. The original purpose of the protections from market forces granted to the leagues was to ensure the fiscal viability of teams in large and small communities. Franchises in larger markets always have a greater potential to earn more money and attract the best players. In exchange for exemptions from antitrust laws, the professional sports leagues promised to safeguard the competitiveness of all teams regardless of their respective market sizes. Today, the protections from market forces have been manipulated to produce an unfair welfare system that victimizes taxpayers and sports fans alike while protecting the wealth of team owners, players, and the few business interests in each community that are tied to teams.

The acquiescence of public officials to the demands of team owners and the resulting sports welfare system is maintained by the perpetuation of several popular myths. Each time an owner demands a subsidized stadium or arena, taxpayers are told that teams (1) convey major league status to a city, (2) attract businesses and jobs to a community, (3) redevelop downtown areas, (4) improve the quality of life, and (5) provide opportunities for family entertainment. These tales, told and retold in every city, do little more than obscure the workings of each league and the unfair nature of the legalized form of extortion practiced by Major League Baseball (MLB), the National Football League (NFL), the National Basketball Association (NBA), and the National Hockey League (NHL). The primary winners in this welfare game, the owners and their players, have been joined in the retelling of these myths by the national and local mass media, local real estate investors, and some politicians in order to fan the fears that cities will lose their beloved teams if they do not meet the extortion terms specified by owners. Recently, driven by the fear that a team would leave their communities, voters in Washington State, San Francisco, and Dallas begrudgingly approved subsidies that totaled almost $1 billion. These three elections were so contested and divisive that in no instance did more than 51.5 percent of the voters support the subsidy plans. Further, public officials and community leaders in those areas rarely discussed challenging the monopoly system that legitimizes the demands for subsidies. The failure to present this option to voters is made more curious when one realizes that cities rarely lose a battle when challenging the monopoly status of sports. Ironically, Seattle won one such battle and secured a new baseball franchise; but in 1997 the city and Washington State agreed to provide more than $700 million in subsidies to ensure the continued presence of teams.

The existing welfare system that leads cities to subsidize wealthy team owners and multi-million-dollar athletes and creates bitter local political battles can be dismantled. I will identify the changes required to eliminate the need for broad-based taxes paid by lower- and middle-class families to generate the high salaries and profits enjoyed by athletes and owners. The factors that produce the political battles that have defiled local politics in San Diego, San Francisco, Seattle, Dallas, Houston, Minneapolis, St. Paul, and Columbus can be eliminated. Simply put, there is a far more equitable way to finance the facilities needed by professional sports teams, and there are several easy ways to eliminate the need for tax-supported stadiums and arenas.

To end the perverse and unfair welfare system, the mystique of sports and the mythical benefits of the business must be understood and unraveled. MLB, the NFL, the NBA, and the NHL each enjoy special protections from market forces because of these myths. If market pressures were allowed to influence the supply of sports teams, admission prices and taxes would decline. Sports fans would enjoy more high-quality entertainment—not less—and taxpayers would enjoy lower taxes. Deregulating professional sports will not destroy the value of sports in our culture and society. Indeed, it will lead to more sports at a lower premium. The sports welfare system and the leagues' stranglehold on America's cities can be changed to benefit players, owners, sports fans, and taxpayers. This book has been produced in the hope of accomplishing that goal.

Why Does the Sports Welfare System Exist?

The modern sports welfare system is sustained by three separate powers. First, the leagues control the number of teams that exist. This guarantees that there always will be fewer teams than the number of cities that want one. This artificial scarcity assures owners of continued competition; cities seeking teams will offer substantial inducements to move the teams, and cities that fear the move will provide substantial counteroffers to keep them in their home city.

Second, the leagues also restrict the number of teams in any market including the continent's largest urban areas. This guarantees that teams in smaller markets will be at an economic disadvantage, permitting their owners to demand extra financial assistance from taxpayers to attract and retain the best players. Without subsidies, how could the Indiana Pacers or San Diego Chargers ever hope to match the salaries paid by teams in New York and Chicago and those owned by media conglomerates (Atlanta Braves, Anaheim Mighty Ducks, and Los Angeles Dodgers)?

Third, each of the sports leagues has adopted guidelines with regard to revenue sharing between large- and small-market teams to make sure that the sports welfare system will be maintained. For example, although the NFL points to the equal shares given to each team from its very lucrative television contracts ($17.6 billion across eight years, or $73.3 million per team *each* year), incomes from luxury seating, in-stadium advertising, in-stadium food and beverage purchases, and parking fees are not shared. Teams in larger markets usually earn substantially more money from these revenue sources, creating a division of class into "have" and "have-not" teams. Teams with less potential to earn in-stadium revenues demand subsidies from their host cities in the form of subsidized stadiums to reduce these income differences.

How Does the Sports Welfare System Work?

How are these powers used to persuade cities to provide subsidies? To maximize their revenues, owners seek to form unusual and rather unique partnerships with state and local governments. The goal of each of these partnerships is to build a new stadium or arena replete with luxury seats, suites, and trendy restaurants. Each of these amenities is expected to enhance revenues, but it is here that the partnership becomes bizarre. The team generally retains all the revenues or profits earned from the operation of the facility. If the public sector receives even a small portion of the revenues from the operation of a stadium or arena, these funds are counted as part of the private sector's contribution to the partnership. In this manner the public sector does not receive a monetary return on its investment; fiscal returns on investments are reserved for the team owners, while the public sector's investment—through taxes—does not generate direct financial returns from the operation of the facilities.

How do teams develop partnerships like this? Why do cities accept the terms? The steps taken are so familiar and the scripts so well known that the play has been acted and reenacted from Baltimore to Nashville, from San Antonio to Oakland, from Detroit to Tampa Bay, and from Minnesota to the Dallas/Fort Worth area.

Act I: The Portrait of a Noble Victim

The sports drama or community soap opera begins with a team owner generally seated alone, bemoaning the current and unfair state of the economics of his or her sport. Our hero or heroine decries the state of the world and describes the litany of problems now all too familiar to sports fans and community leaders: Player salaries are escalating, travel and hotel costs keep rising, and large-market teams are amassing huge cash reserves of unshared revenues that they use to buy the best players and win repeated championships. If help is not forthcoming, how will it ever be possible to save the family business, build a winner for the city, and defend the community's pride?

The victim's opening monologue also contains the obligatory observation that he or she will have to leave the community, as unpleasant and repulsive as that thought is, if a satisfactory facility is not built that has the potential to increase revenues (profits) substantially. In other versions of the play, a team owner promises to come to your city if an acceptable public/private partnership can be developed. Regardless of the setting—the team will leave your community or come to your city—the first act always ends with a vivid description of the need for a new stadium or arena because players are demanding high salaries and large-market teams earn far more money from which they can pay the best players. The first act, then, paints the players as culprits or greedy rascals. The heroes or heroines never suggest that they should reduce their profits or wealth by paying the players higher salaries. It also is never suggested that there should be broader revenue-sharing programs that would offset differences in market sizes or that more teams should be created in the largest markets. Outcomes of that nature could avoid subsidies and higher taxes. These options are never part of the soap opera.

Act II: The People Deserve a Champion: Who Will Stand with Me?

With good and evil clearly defined in Act I, the team owner then declares that if the new facility is not built, if substantial public subsidies are not provided, and if additional revenues (from luxury seating, advertising, and the sale of food and beverages) are not earned without increasing the costs supported by the team, the franchise is destined to be mediocre and unable to win the championship that the fans deserve. Since the owner wants to build a winner, a pliant public-sector partner is sought who shares this championship dream and fervor and who is willing to spend tax dollars to increase the team's revenues. The owner also frequently suggests that the fans deserve a more comfortable stadium with the modern conveniences common in the newest facilities. Act II ends with a call to arms—actually a call for cash to build a new facility—to permit a championship team to exist so that all the fans can see the championship banner flying proudly over a new first-class stadium or arena that has all the modern conveniences the fans deserve.

Act III: We All Can Be Winners: One for All and All for One?

Once the challenge to help build a winner through the construction of a publicly subsidized first-class facility is presented, reports circulate describing the economic and image benefits to a city and region of having a major league team and a "winner." These benefits are identified as the "returns" to the public sector from its "investment" and its commitment to building a winning team, a first-class facility, and a first-class image. (The fiscal or money returns will, of course, accrue to the owners and the players. The city's benefits will be the "winning image.") This information is then used to counter any studies or stories that suggest that the direct economic benefits of a team are relatively small. At the end of Act III, our hero or heroine cries, "If only the stadium or arena could be built, we all could live in Titletown, U.S.A."

Act IV: The Nobility Joins the Visionary Leader

In the fourth act of this drama, community leaders emerge who proclaim the proposed arena or stadium as a potential civic asset and monument worthy of the public's support. In some instances this chorus proclaims the proposed stadium or arena as a "signa ture statement" for the community, an edifice or landmark for the ages that will proclaim the city's greatness and centrality in American life. These leaders also discuss the enhanced economic development that will result from the team's presence and the building of a new facility. Newspaper reports usually follow these discussions, and these articles always discuss the extensive "feelings" of community solidarity that the team will foster in their new home. Frequently reporters are dispatched to other cities to describe the resurgence in civic pride that took place there after a team arrived or won a title or pennant. It is within this act that coalitions form, comprised of individuals and businesses (newspapers, land developers, etc.) in the local community that will benefit from the team's presence. The fourth act concludes with a reading of these tributes and an enumeration of the achievements of the communities that were wise enough to build a stadium or arena.

Act V: The Answer Is Provided and the Word Is Given

With a relatively friendly political environment established by the stories published in Act IV, an elected official—not desiring to be the one in office when a team moves or fails to come to town—develops a public/private partnership proposal for a new facility. The proposal sometimes is voted on at a general election; other times a council or legislature simply ratifies the agreement.

Regardless, the debate or vote is always accompanied by large cash donations from facility and team supporters (and sometimes the team and its owners) that help secure the needed votes.

Where does all this typically lead? Generally it ends with the building of playing facilities that cost far more than initially projected and with most, if not all, revenues from the facility belonging to the team. Conversely, much of the responsibility for cost overruns is left to the public sector. Other inducements are frequently given to owners to compete with the largesse that others have received. For example, some cities have provided "moving expenses" to team owners that were so large that the funds given to the team owners amounted to nothing more than a bounty or one-time welfare payment for relocating their teams. Other owners have received land, special investment opportunities, offices, luxury suites at the new stadiums and arenas, and practice facilities for their teams. Most of these inducements, of course, are paid for by the public's taxes.

Does the Sports Industry Need Welfare to Exist?

This welfare system is not needed. By virtually any measure, professional sports is an extremely successful business. The players—once underpaid and abused—now enjoy princely salaries, and the vast majority of teams earn profits and generate substantial wealth for their owners through the escalating value of most franchises. Although owners continue to bemoan the impact of free agency and player salaries, teams "fetch" unreal values whenever they are sold. In 1998, for example, the Minnesota Vikings were sold for more than $200 million; in 1997 the Seattle Seahawks also were sold for $200 million. Both teams' previous owners earned handsome profits. Ken Behring purchased the

Seahawks in 1988 for a "reported $89.7 million" (Much and Friedman, 1998). Less than a decade later Mr. Behring received $200 million when the Seahawks were sold to Paul Allen. Adjusting for inflation, Mr. Behring earned a 79.4 percent return on his investment. Governor George Bush of Texas paid $606,000 for a share of the Texas Rangers and then sold his interest in the team for approximately $15 million. The value of the Texas Rangers increased as a direct result of a $130+ million tax subsidy received by Governor Bush and his partners. New NFL franchises now cost investors more than half a billion dollars.

Sports as a business also has no problems attracting consumers. Fan interest, as measured by attendance, though declining in baseball and hockey from earlier levels, still is robust. And for some baseball teams it has never been stronger. In 1995 the Cleveland Indians became the first MLB team to sell all tickets to all its games four months before the 1996 season started. This feat was also accomplished for the 1997, 1998, and 1999 seasons, making the Indians the first MLB team ever to play their home games before more than 300 consecutive sell-out crowds. During this period the Indians hosted several playoff and World Series games that also were sold out. Many football teams routinely sell all tickets to their games, and NBA teams also are playing before sold-out arenas or near-capacity crowds in numerous cities. Does such a business really need a public subsidy or welfare to exist?

One report for the U.S. Congress evaluated the state of MLB when a congressional committee discussed the sport's exemption from antitrust laws during the 1994 strike and lockout. This report found that seemingly profitable and unprofitable teams alike were increasing in value, thus generating substantial returns on the investments made by owners.

Franchise revenues grew by nearly 12 percent per year from 1970 to 1991, a 6.3 percent annual growth rate over and above the rate of inflation. . . . The Baltimore Orioles, a profitable team, were sold for $12 million in 1979, $70 million in 1989, and again for $173 million in 1993 (with the benefit of a new stadium complex financed by Maryland taxpayers). The Seattle Mariners, long a financially weak team, were sold in 1981 for $13 million and again in 1988 for $89.5 million ($77.5 million changed hands, with the buyer taking over $12 million in liabilities). In 1992 they were sold again for $106 million to a group of local businesses that offered to invest an additional $19 million in the team. The Texas Rangers, also a weak team, were sold for $10.5 million in 1974 and for $79 million in 1989 (Cox and Zimmerman, 1995: 4).

Wealth has been growing for team owners not only in terms of the value of their franchises but from the fees charged to individuals or groups who seek expansion teams. The successful bidders for these few scarce franchises pay an extremely large and arbitrarily defined fee for the right to have a franchise. These franchise fees then are equally divided among the existing owners, generating more income. The owners of the Florida Marlins and Colorado Rockies each paid $95 million in 1991 to join MLB. The owners of the Arizona Diamondbacks and the Tampa Bay Devil Rays each paid $130 million to join the major leagues. In three years, then, the value of a new MLB franchise increased 37 percent. How were these franchise fees chosen? There is at least some evidence to suggest that these numbers were literally picked "out of the air" by other owners, and the funds received were then divided among the existing team owners (Whitford, 1993).

The owners of the latest entries to the NBA, the Vancouver Grizzlies and the Toronto Raptors, paid US$125 million "to be where the action is." For Toronto's owners this was another case of "pay me now or pay me (lots) later." The Toronto Huskies were part of the Basketball Association of America in 1946. That team folded at the end of its inaugural season. The surviving members of the Basketball Association of America merged with the National Basketball League to form the NBA in 1949. After World War II, basketball franchises in any league were available for nominal sums ($300). Had Toronto stayed in the NBA, the team's owners would have earned a substantial return on their investment.

It also costs a small fortune to join the NFL. The owners of the Carolina Cougars and the Jacksonville Jaguars each paid the NFL $140 million to become league members. These funds, of course, were distributed to each existing owner. Today the cost of joining the NFL is in excess of $500 million, given the large television contract negotiated by the league in 1998. And NHL team owners saw their teams' values increase 80 percent from 1992 to 1997 (Much and Friedman, 1998). With assets of this value it is hard to justify that any team owner deserves welfare or the subsidies they have been receiving from state and local governments.

The players also reap substantial benefits from these subsidies. In the past, athletes did not receive a substantial share of the wealth produced by professional sports. Today, the situation is quite different from the world Bob Cousy, Willie Mays, Andy Bathgate, Johnny Unitas, Lenny Moore, Frank Gifford, and Ray Felix knew. Players in each of the four major sports are very well paid for their work, with "star" players receiving unimaginable amounts of money. In 1997 the average salary of a MLB player was in excess of $1 million unless the player was on the Milwaukee Brewers, Minnesota Twins, Oakland A's, Montreal Expos, or Pittsburgh Pirates. The median salary of an NBA player is in excess of $1 million, and it is common for a team to have several players earning more than $3 million. It is safe to conclude that a great deal of money is being earned by both owners and players. At a result, it is impossible to find any evidence that team owners or players need subsidies or welfare support. Sports is a very successful business for all involved, with the only real issue being who deserves a larger portion of an expanding pie—the owners or the players.

The four major professional sports have the best of all worlds. Team owners can use their control over the supply of teams to extract subsidies from taxpayers while reaping huge profits and contracts from the national networks. At the same time, the players, once oppressed and underpaid, are now real partners in this process. They receive virtually half of all revenues, so the taxes paid to build the modern sports palaces make both players and owners the true welfare kings in America.

The subsidies paid to build sports palaces are even more difficult to explain if one takes even a casual look at the political landscape. During virtually every election, candidates from both parties present platforms and make promises to "privatize," "downsize," and "marketize" governments at all levels. From the U.S. Congress to every state legislature, Republicans and Democrats alike call for reduced welfare payments and smaller governments through the utilization of private firms to deliver services. At every turn in the political world one finds increasing calls for a reliance on free markets and market-based solutions to all our policy dilemmas. Yet when it comes to sports, both Republicans and Democrats endorse larger welfare packages. From areas as politically different as Maryland and Tennessee, state and local governments are willing to shower hundreds of millions of dollars on millionaire ballplayers and owners. We may demand that the elderly spend down their wealth before they can receive Medicaid benefits, but we shudder to ask team owners and players to do the same before they receive subsidies. Politicians who promise never to raise taxes routinely agree to join partnerships that require higher taxes to build these big boys their big toys.

Moving Across State Lines for More Welfare

Legislatures across the country debate welfare-for-work programs, reduced welfare payments for poor people, and the need to discourage people from moving to their state to receive welfare. But few elected officials raise a voice to protest hundred-million-dollar welfare programs for wealthy team owners and rich athletes, and most states seem eager to encourage teams to move to their borders to receive public subsidies. Seattle (with Washington State) and Cleveland (with the assistance of Cuyahoga County and the state) have provided more than $500 million in subsidies for sports. Baltimore (with the help of the State of Maryland), Cincinnati (and Hamilton County), Phoenix (and Maricopa County), and Nashville have provided at least $300 million in subsidies to sports teams. More than a score of state and local governments have each provided over $100 million in subsidies to professional sports teams, and several of these subsidies will amount to almost $200 million.

The welfare system that now exists in professional sports actually encourages team owners to move their franchises to communities where more robust subsidies will be provided. Although some teams move as a result of a loss of fan support or out of a desire to locate in a larger market, increasingly the movement of teams has very little to do with fan support but a great deal to do with the subsidies or welfare that teams receive from different communities and the amount of revenue the teams are permitted to keep from the tax-supported facilities built for them. What is now taking place that makes the recent moves of teams different from those in the past is that teams with substantial levels of fan support are drawn to other communities as a result of welfare packages. Local fan support is no longer the sole factor responsible for securing a home team. Now taxpayers have to be willing to contribute to a team's financial success.

Two recent moves illustrate this process. The Oakland Raiders regularly sold out their home games at the Oakland-Alameda Coliseum, but that did not stop the team's owner, Al Davis, from moving the team to Los Angeles in 1982. The driving force behind this move was the commitment Los Angeles was willing to make to have a NFL team. Why was Los Angeles interested in subsidizing professional football? The Los Angeles Rams had just left for Anaheim, and Los Angeles County and the city of Los Angeles wanted another team.

Los Angeles County lured the Raiders with promises of renovations to the aging coliseum. The Los Angeles market never fully embraced the Raiders as the fans in Oakland had, however, and the Los Angeles–area governments were not willing to respond to Al Davis's increasing requests for additional assistance. As a result, when Oakland increased the size of the subsidy it was willing to provide to the team, the Raiders returned home for the 1995 season. The Raiders' return to Oakland has not brought a financial boon to the city or created unending joy for sports fans. The Raiders, one of the most successful teams in the AFL and the NFL through the mid-1980s, have not qualified for the playoffs for five years. The cost of all the incentives provided to the team by the city was far greater than anticipated, even though the team has an average ticket price among the highest in the NFL. The cost of hosting an NFL team has been quite substantial for both the city of Oakland and its sports fans. To make the matter even worse, in early 1998 Oakland and Alameda County had to endure speculation that the Raiders would try to return to Los Angeles as that city sought to attract a football team.

The Cleveland Browns provide another example of a team moving to another state to take advantage of a better welfare program. From 1986 through 1994 the Cleveland Browns averaged more than seventy thousand fans for each of their home games despite several losing seasons (1990 through 1993). Few teams had fans more loyal than the followers of the Browns. And the Browns' most loyal fans regularly filled the ground-level seats in the end zone, nicknamed the "Dawg Pound," to dress in costume and toss "dawg bones" onto the field to reward their favorite players. This level of fan support, together with the city of Cleveland's commitment to spend $175 million to improve Cleveland Stadium, did not stop Art Modell from taking his team and its five decades of history to Baltimore (Rushin, 1995). Baltimore, of course, had been left with its thirty years of memories of Alan Ameche, Johnny Unitas, Lenny Moore, Don Shula, and two Super Bowl appearances when the Colts moved to Indianapolis in 1984. What attracted Art Modell to Baltimore? The Maryland Stadium Authority promised to build a brand-new stadium replete with luxury seating and let the team retain all revenues generated at this new palace. Art Modell would not only receive revenues generated by his team but would keep a substantial portion of the revenues generated from concerts and other events held at the new stadium.

Table 1-1 describes the facility demands and outcomes for some one hundred professional sports teams. These franchises and their owners frequently threatened to move or have moved in an effort to secure a facility that would generate more income and that included a larger welfare bonus than they were currently able to secure. Teams now are moving across state lines to get better welfare deals, and this process shows no signs of abating unless public officials do their homework and understand what sports mean and do not mean for their communities.

TABLE 1-1
The Status of Teams Seeking New Facilities

League/Team	Situation	Resolution
Major League Baseball		
Anaheim Angels	Requested stadium improvements	$100 million renovation (30% public), 1996
Arizona Diamondbacks	New stadium for expansion team	$238 million public subsidy, **1998**
Atlanta Braves	Demanded new stadium	Received 1996 Olympic stadium for $23 million
Baltimore Orioles	Demanded new stadium	Camden Yards, $200+ million subsidy, 1992
Boston Red Sox	Discussing new stadium	Planning a privately financed facility for 2001
Chicago White Sox	Threatened move to Florida	New stadium, 1991, 100% public subsidy
Cincinnati Reds	Threatened to move	New stadium approved, 1996
Cleveland Indians	Threatened move out of region	New stadium, public subsidy in excess of $150 million, 1994
Colorado Rockies	Received new stadium	$215 million public subsidy, 1995
Detroit Tigers	Threatened move to the suburbs	New stadium approved, 1997; $240 million subsidy
Florida Marlins	Demanding new stadium	Team sold; unresolved
Houston Astros	Threatened to leave the region	New stadium approved, 1997; $180 million subsidy
Milwaukee Brewers	Threatened to leave the region	New stadium approved, 1997; $232 million subsidy
Minnesota Twins	Threatened to move to North Carolina	Remaining in Minnesota for 2 years; unresolved
Montreal Expos	Low levels of fans support, revenue	Unresolved
New York Mets	Demanded equal treatment with Yankees	New stadium "promised," 1997; no plans yet
New York Yankees	Threatening to leave New York City	Unresolved; plans being debated
Philadelphia Phillies	Requesting new stadium, tax support	Unresolved; state subsidy approved
Pittsburgh Pirates	Threatening to leave the region	New stadium proposed; financing incomplete
San Diego Padres	Demanding new stadium	$250 million public subsidy; $495 million private investment for redevelopment
San Francisco Giants	Threatened move to Florida	New private stadium under way
Seattle Mariners	Threatened to leave the region	New stadium approved, 1997; $360+ million public subsidy
Tampa Bay Devil Rays	Renovations to existing dome	Public cost in excess of $150 million, 1998

(continues)

TABLE 1-1   *(continued)*

League/Team	Situation	Resolution
Texas Rangers	Threatened to leave Arlington	New stadium, public cost $135 million, 1994
Toronto Blue Jays	New stadium in 1989	Public subsidy $262 (Canadian); new financial crisis in 1998
National Basketball Association		
Atlanta Hawks	Requested new arena	$62 million in public infrastructure, $213+ million facility opens in 1999
Boston Celtics	Built new arena—largely private	$16+ million public infrastructure, 1995
Charlotte Hornets	Requested changes to existing arena	100% public financing, $52 million in 1988; renovations unresolved
Chicago Bulls	Privately built arena	Property tax abatement, 1994; private financing
Cleveland Cavaliers	New arena to move to downtown	Public investment in excess of $100 million
Dallas Mavericks	Threatened to move to Arlington, Texas	Public subsidy of $125 million approved, 1998
Denver Nuggets	Proposed new privately financed arena	Building opens in 1999; public subsidy less than $20 million
Golden State Warriors	Renovation in 1997	Public subsidy in excess of $20 million; team paid in excess of $80 million
Houston Rockets	Demanding new arena	Team expects new arena in 2002/2003
Indiana Pacers	Requested new arena	New facility opens in 1999; $107 million subsidy
Los Angeles Lakers	New arena in downtown Los Angeles	Public investment limited to approximately $8 million in redevelopment funds; other public funds, $70 million, repaid through user fees and guaranteed by teams
Miami Heat	Requested new arena	Public sector pays annual operating expenses of $6.5 million; public sector paid $34.7 million for land; team builds arena; public sector 1 guarantees naming rights, 1996
Milwaukee Bucs	New arena in 1988	Public paid a substantial portion of the $90 million cost
Minnesota Timberwolves	New arena part of expansion bid	Public sector now responsible for majority of $100 million cost

TABLE 1-1 *(continued)*

League/Team	Situation	Resolution
New Jersey Nets	New arena drew team to New Jersey	Public paid $85 million for arena; team pays rent; some early discussions of improvements, 1998; team wants new arena
New York Knicks	Renovations in 1991	Privately financed
Orlando Magic	Requesting renovations in arena	$60 million subsidy to be provided
Philadelphia 76ers	New arena in 1998	Privately financed; public sector paid for infrastructure
Phoenix Suns	New arena in 1992	Public subsidy exceeded $45 million
Portland Trail Blazers	New arena, the Rose Garden	Public subsidy of $34.5 million for infrastructure; team paid for arena, 1995
San Antonio Spurs	Threatening to move to New Orleans	Tax increment financing plan proposed
Seattle Super Sonics	Threatened to leave the region	Remodeled arena, users fees to pay bonds
Toronto Raptors	New arena in 1999	Privately financed Air Canada arena opens February 1999
Utah Jazz	New arena in 1991 *ues)*	Public sector paid for land, infrastructure; team paid for arena
Vancouver Grizzlies	New arena in 1995	Privately financed
Washington Wizards	New arena in downtown Washington	Privately financed; $60 million in public infrastructure costs
National Football League		
Arizona Cardinals	Discussing new facility	Unresolved
Atlanta Falcons	New stadium in 1992	State provided land; public authority and team shared all other costs
Baltimore Ravens	Received new stadium to relocate	Public subsidy in excess of $200 million
Buffalo Bills	Threatened to move	Received public subsidy of $180 million for renovations, operating subsidy, 1997 & 1998
Carolina Panthers	Expansion team	City provided land; county provided $10 million; stadium was privately financed
Chicago Bears	Threatening to move to Indiana, suburbs	Unresolved
Cincinnati Bengals	Threatening a move	New stadium approved, 1996
Cleveland Browns	New franchise with new stadium	Public subsidy exceeds $200 million, 1999
Dallas Cowboys	Threatening to move to Arlington	Unresolved

(continues)

TABLE 1-1   *(continued)*

League/Team	Situation	Resolution
Denver Broncos	Demanding a new stadium	New stadium approved, 1998; public subsidy of approximately $260 million
Detroit Lions	Threatened a move within the region	New stadium in Detroit approved; $240 million subsidy
Green Bay Packers	Sought renovations to stadium	Privately financed
Houston Oilers	Moved to Nashville	New stadium in 1999; $292 million subsidy
Indianapolis Colts	Discussed revenue needs with city	New lease, remodeled stadium, 1998; expanded public subsidy
Los Angles Raiders	Moved to Oakland	New stadium lease, remodeled stadium, $100 million subsidy
Los Angles Rams	Moved to St. Louis	New stadium in St. Louis; $280 million subsidy
Miami Dolphins	New stadium in 1987	Privately financed
Minnesota Vikings	Demanding new stadium	Unresolved
New England Patriots	Move planned to Hartford, Connecticut	Public subsidy in excess of $350 million
Pittsburgh Steelers	New stadium discussed	Final details pending
San Diego Chargers	Sought increased stadium revenues	Stadium remodeled, ticket guarantee provided
San Francisco 49ers	Sought new stadium	Plan approved, $100 million+ in public subsidies; problems have delayed project
Seattle Seahawks	Threatened to move	New stadium approved, $325 million public subsidy, 1997
Tampa Bay Buccaneers	Threatened to move	New stadium, 1998, $300 million subsidy
Washington Redskins	Built new stadium in Maryland	Public subsidy of $70+ million for infrastructure; facility paid for by team
National Hockey League		
Boston Bruins	Sought new arena	See Boston Celtics
Buffalo Sabres	New arena in 1996	Public subsidy less than $25 million
Calgary Flames	Moved to Phoenix	Seeking modifications to America West arena; considering new arena in suburbs
Chicago Blackhawks	New arena	See Chicago Bulls
Colorado Avalanche	New arena	See Denver Nuggets
Columbus Blue Jackets	New arena	Public responsible for infrastructure, environmental clean-up of site; private financing for arena
Dallas Stars	Threatened to move to suburbs	New arena approved (see Dallas Mavericks)

(continues)

TABLE 1-1   *(continued)*

League/Team	Situation	Resolution
Detroit Red Wings	New arena in 1979	$57 million; 100% public funding
Florida Panthers	Threatened to move within region	New arena in Broward County, approved in 1997 with public subsidy of $180+ million
Hartford Whalers	Moved to North Carolina; became Carolina Hurricanes	New arena opens in 1999; $70 million public subsidy
Los Angeles Kings	Moving downtown	See Los Angeles Lakers
Mighty Ducks of Anaheim	Disney Corporation owns team	Ogden, Inc. assumed responsibility for city bonds for construction
Minnesota Wild	New arena part of expansion bid	Public subsidy of at least $95 million
Montreal Canadiens	New arena in 1996	Privately financed
Nashville Predators	Arena part of expansion bid	100% public subsidy for arena
New Jersey Devils	Threatened to move	New lease in New Jersey; threatening to move within state
New York Islanders	Demanding new arena	Unresolved
New York Rangers	See New York Knicks	See New York Knicks
Philadelphia Flyers	See Philadelphia 76ers	See Philadelphia 76ers
Pittsburgh Penguins	New arena in 1961	$22 million in city costs; team pays rent and needs new arena
Québec Nordiques	Moved to Denver	See Denver Nuggets
St. Louis Blues	New arena	Privately financed; public infrastructure
San Jose Sharks	New arena in 1993	Public subsidy of $132.5 million
Tampa Bay Lightning	New arena	Public subsidy in excess of $100 million
Toronto Maple Leafs	New arena in 1999	Moving into privately financed Air Canada arena
Vancouver Canucks	New arena in 1995	Privately financed
Washington Capitals	New arena downtown	See Washington Wizards

Who Pays for the Public's Support of Professional Sports?

Do these welfare issues affect you? If you live in most places in North America, they do. It is likely, no matter where you live, that you will be confronted with demands for a subsidy to help a "struggling" sports franchise. There are now 132 major league teams in fifty-six different cities in North America. Additional football teams may be added to fill the voids that exist in Los Angeles following the moves of the Rams and Raiders and in Houston to replace the Oilers. NFL expansion into Canada appears likely in the not too distant future. European divisions for the NHL and NBA are now a distinct possibility. If your county or province has a population of three hundred thousand people, you likely will deal with at least one professional sports team. If you live in a larger community, be prepared for demands for welfare from multiple teams.

Arlington Makes the Deal

In the early 1990s the Texas Rangers wanted a new stadium. Arlington Stadium, a remodeled minor league park, had almost 50 percent of its seats in the outfield. As a result, the team's revenues were among baseball's lowest. Although the old field had good sight lines and everyone was close to the action, there were no skyboxes, club seats, or restaurants.

When the team began discussions for a new stadium, they were quick to cast a roaming eye toward Dallas and St. Petersburg, Florida, where the unoccupied Sun Coast Dome beckoned. To convince the team to stay in Arlington a "partnership" was created to build the ballpark in Arlington. During his campaign for the governorship of Texas, George Bush, Jr., a minority owner of the Texas Rangers, proudly described the partnership as an example of his experience as an entrepreneur and in building successful partnerships for economic development. A close examination of the partnership reveals why national columnist George F. Will noted, "The safest way to gauge baseball disputes is to assume the owners are wrong" (Will, 1994).

To build the new facility, a structure that is an architectural masterpiece, a public/private partnership was developed. The city's investment was supported by a sales tax increment. The 0.5 percent increase in the sales tax will expire when the bonds are retired. Because of the explosive growth of the economy in north Texas, the city will be able to pay off the bonds sooner than expected. Since Arlington is a retail, convention, and entertainment hub, the comptroller's office estimates that more than half of the sales tax income earned by Arlington is from nonresidents.

The investment by the Rangers consisted of its short-term commitment of lease revenues from luxury boxes. The city received 115 percent of the luxury suite revenue in the first year of the stadium's operation. In the second through fourth years of operation, the city received 5 percent of the luxury suite revenue. Corporations that leased luxury suites paid a rental fee in addition to the cost of the tickets.

To recoup its commitment of revenue from these various leases, the Rangers and Arlington agreed the team would charge a $1 per-ticket fee on all seats sold. The revenues from this fee would repay the team for its cash commitment to financing the stadium. The team, then, committed revenues in the form of taxes from fans to build the stadium and then "recouped" this investment by increasing the price of the tickets. In addition, the team also committed the land it owned for the new stadium. However, this land was part of the original inducements given to attract the Rangers from Washington, D.C., and to retain the team over the years. The stadium land (site of the present and previous stadiums) was purchased through bonds that taxpayers had approved previously and supported with tax dollars. In this sense, one part of the team's investment took the form of the previous inducements it had received to relocate to Arlington and to remain in the city.

The team also received other benefits from the new stadium deal. The stadium included office space for the team and additional space that the team could rent to tenants. The baseball team would retain all profits from any leases it negotiated and from any development of the land surrounding the stadium that the team owned.

What's wrong with this deal from the city's perspective? After all, the Rangers are a private business, and if they can get their consumers (fans) to purchase their product at rates sufficient to cover the cost of the stadium, is there a problem? The problem rests with increasing a local sales tax to improve the profitability of the team without the city's sharing in the profits. In other words, if the city of Arlington is investing tax revenue that increases the wealth of the team's owners and its players, what return should it earn on these funds? It is true that the Rangers do pay rent for the use of the stadium, and the team is responsible for maintaining the stadium. Further, if the Texas Rangers are a successful business, able to pass along their share of the cost of the stadium to fans, why should the city subsidize any portion of the stadium's cost without sharing in the wealth created for team owners and players?

Lastly, in 1998, when the Rangers were sold, Governor George Bush netted $14.9 million on his investment of $606,000 in the team. Arlington's sales tax or welfare program for professional sports helped produce a 2,460 percent return for Governor Bush. Does that sound like "good business"?

ENDING WELFARE AND SURVIVING SPORTS:
THE CHAPTERS THAT FOLLOW

Will the subsidy game ever end? As this is being written, Connecticut has broken all subsidy records with a grotesque offer to move the Patriots to Hartford, San Antonio is considering a new home for the Spurs, and Houston, Los Angeles, North Carolina, and northern Virginia are trying to secure new teams for their communities. Negotiations also are under way between the city of New York and the Yankees and Mets for new facilities, and subsidies for these teams in the hundreds of millions of dollars have been discussed. The Phillies, Pirates, Steelers, and Eagles received $80 million each from the State of Pennsylvania but now want more from the cities of Philadelphia and Pittsburgh. Each year it seems that the "ante" expected from the public sector increases. More than one civic leader interviewed for this book responded that it was a good idea to subsidize an existing team to avoid the escalating costs of attracting another team after you have lost one. Both St. Louis and Baltimore paid far more to get an NFL team back than they would have paid to save their original teams. The need for this book is probably best underscored by the number of civic leaders who accept the notion that subsidies for professional sports are very much a case of "pay me a little now or pay me a great deal later."

Why Do So Many People Support the Sports Welfare System?

Although the Republicans' "Contract with America" called for limits on welfare and prompted calls in several states for no additional support for moms on welfare who had another out-of-wedlock child, there is considerable support for providing welfare to wealthy team owners and their ballplayers. Why is this taking place? Why do voters and elected officials endorse welfare packages for teams but reject support for education, unwed mothers, and the homeless? Chapter 2 provides some answers to this question through an analysis of "Why Is Sports So Important to So Many People?" Ending the sports welfare system will not be easy. A mind-set exists among many that sports are so important, even critical, to a city's image and development that they deserve the public's support and welfare. Yet the myths that drive this mind-set must be challenged and exposed.

There is probably no better example of the extent to which sports manipulate the political agenda than the events that took place in early December 1995. During the days after Thanksgiving the United States had to decide whether or not to send troops to Bosnia to help support a peace treaty negotiated in Dayton, Ohio, between all parties to the dispute. During this same time, the president and Congress were locked in a difficult battle over the U.S. budget that had already forced one partial shutdown of the federal government. A second shutdown loomed as both sides sought an acceptable balanced budget proposal. Meanwhile, what was the U.S. Senate doing? Indeed, there is some special irony or perhaps a warped sense of priorities in noting that while the United States was committing troops to maintain peace in Bosnia and the president and Congress were battling to define the parameters for balancing the federal budget, the Senate was holding hearings on the move of the Cleveland Browns to Baltimore. A budget accord did not exist, but drafts of proposed legislation to remedy the NFL's inability to stop Art Modell from leaving Cleveland were being prepared. The rights of Cleveland to subsidize the Browns and their wealthy owner and players were being jeopardized by a $270+ million proposal from Maryland and Baltimore. Indignantly, Cleveland's Mayor White, testifying before a U.S. Senate committee, demanded a "fair" hearing or level playing field from the NFL and Art Modell for his $175 million welfare proposal. The mayor proclaimed, triumphantly

"Cleveland will not just go away." He never added "until someone accepts our welfare proposal and gives us an NFL team," but he could have. The subtle ways in which sports cultivate their welfare status are discussed in Chapter 2.

Why Do Sports Cost So Much?

Chapter 3 reviews the evolution of the leagues as cartels that control the number of teams and the revenue-sharing rules that are at the heart of the sports welfare system. Ironically, neither Congress nor any state legislature or attorney general seem particularly interested in changing or challenging this system. As a result, teams demand and receive subsidized stadiums and arenas. The way in which the sports welfare system victimizes elected officials and taxpayers alike probably is best illustrated by events in Indianapolis. In 1996, Indianapolis's Market Square Arena, built in 1974, was the third oldest facility serving as a home for an NBA team. During the 1993–94 season there were repeated calls from the Indiana Pacers for improvements and enhancements to the arena so that the team could close the revenue gap between itself and several larger market franchises. By the 1994–95 season, Stephen Goldsmith, Indianapolis's fiscally conservative mayor, was convinced that the Indiana Pacers would lose money even if every game were sold out. The Indianapolis market is one of the smallest with an NBA franchise, and without a new and publicly subsidized arena, the team could not attract the best players. Goldsmith, a mayor renowned for his opposition to taxes and his fervor for shrinking government, reluctantly agreed to raise taxes not for better schools, roads, or sewers but to save a professional team for a small market.

Measuring What Cities Get from Teams

Much of the debate over the use of tax dollars for facilities involves a consideration of the returns to the public sector. How to analyze the economic and intangible gains from teams is discussed in Chapter 4. In many ways this is the most critical part of this book. The leagues may have an unfair control over the economics of sports. However, if taxpayers receive a fair return on the funds used to build today's sports palaces, then everyone could win in the sports game. If the teams generate precious little for a community, then the taxes spent on facilities are nothing more than welfare for the rich.

After this exploration of the economic and intangible benefits from teams and sports in Chapter 4, Chapters 5 through 8 focus on the commitments made to teams by ten different cities. These case studies focus on the amount of money committed, the goals or expectations each community had for their sports program, and the outcomes from the investments. The case studies identify several important lessons that should guide any attempt to reform the sports welfare system. Chapter 5 details the extensive sports and downtown development policies and programs developed by Indianapolis. The building of two sports facilities by Cleveland to reshape its identity is also analyzed. No city has had a more defined and articulated sports program for downtown development than Indianapolis. If sports could have any economic effects or impact on a city's economy, it would have happened in Indianapolis. Cleveland's extensive investments in Jacobs Field and Gund Arena involved a public/private partnership designed to save the Indians and to bring the NBA's Cavaliers back to the downtown area from the suburbs. These facilities were designed to redefine Cleveland and reestablish its national identity. More than $300 million in taxes was pledged to the effort. What did Cleveland get, and what lessons for cities and sports can be learned from the experiences of both of these midwestern cities?

Chapter 6 focuses on three cities that emphasized sports in an effort to enhance their images and ended up with more than $1.7 billion in public subsidies for professional teams. These investments represent some of the largest subsidies ever provided. St. Louis's desire to get an NFL team at any price provides an opportunity to analyze the ability of a member of a sports cartel to dictate terms, demand and receive subsidies, and provide very little in return. In addition, St. Louis's largesse undermined the financial health of every city as a new benchmark for subsidies was established. Canadian cities also are engaged in subsidies for professional sports. Montreal's and Toronto's experiences with MLB detail the hopes, success, and failure of two of Canada's largest experiments with the American pastime. Separately and together, Montreal and Toronto spent more for a single facility than any other city in North America, and both cities saddled their taxpayers with astounding levels of debt. How not to do sports is probably best underscored by the experiences of St. Louis, Toronto, and Montreal.

Chapter 7 looks at how cities within the Dallas/Fort Worth area bid against one another in a cutthroat manner that did nothing but raise the level of subsidy to an MLB team. The lack of regional cooperation in the area set the stage for a second bidding war involving the Stars and the Mavericks. The Dallas/Fort Worth region's lack of cooperation and the costs to taxpayers provide a poignant lesson for civic leaders everywhere. In Chapter 8, the problems of small-market cities are placed in the very real context of Pittsburgh's battle to save the Pirates and Indianapolis's effort to retain the Colts. The ways MLB and the NFL victimize small-market cities are graphically illustrated in Chapter 8 through the struggles of these two communities to save their teams.

Future Choices: How Cities and Their Taxpayers Can Avoid Subsidies and Become True Partners in the Sports Business

Chapter 9 details a plan for eliminating unneeded subsidies and welfare payments for professional sports teams. This chapter provides a set of guidelines and strategies to help local communities survive and benefit from professional sports. Having established why sports are so important in our culture, I present in Chapter 9 a strategy for building real partnerships between teams and their communities—a simple but effective way to permit all cities, even those that lose teams, to have new franchises as well as a plan for effectively using market solutions to stop the spiraling subsidies. Cities as well as team owners and players can benefit and prosper from professional sports. To accomplish this objective, however, community leaders must learn what team owners know and what players learned in the last twenty years: the real economics of cities and professional team sports.

2

Why Are Sports So Important to So Many People?

The sharpest memory of my first week in college is of walking toward the Purdue football stadium on a sunny, cool September afternoon, the noise of the marching band and the huge crowd in the distance, the anticipation of seeing the Boilermakers play Notre Dame. That event, over a generation ago, began a personal love affair with college sports.

Murray Sperber, College Sports, Inc.

When asked to define the greatest days of his life, Billy Crystal's character in *City Slickers* describes his first Yankee Game, at age eight, "The beauty of the grass, the red clay running track, the smell of Yankee Stadium, my father holding my hand. . . ."

The subsidies (or welfare) given to professional sports teams are a result of two factors: (1) the privileged position accorded to and the importance placed on sports by our society, and (2) the artificial scarcity and the control owners have over the number of teams that exist. If the subsidies provided to teams are ever to be

33

curtailed or eliminated, sports will need to be seen only as the interesting diversions and the small businesses that they are. Their romanticized and overemphasized qualities need to be diminished in the minds of negotiators who represent cities in their discussions with teams and the professional leagues. Further, the authority that the professional sports leagues have been given to control the number of teams that exist must be changed, and that, too, will require a recognition that sports are not deserving of the special treatment and reverence they are accorded. Both of these alterations in the modern psyche will occur only if taxpayers and legislators place the mythology of sports in its proper perspective. Before dealing with the evolution of the sports leagues and their acquisition of the power to control the number of franchises (Chapter 3), it is important to understand the roots and extent of the romanticized elements of sports.

Sports have been a vital part of most societies and Western civilization for at least three thousand years. This emotional and cultural attachment to sports does not mean, however, that governments should or need to provide subsidies to professional teams. It is possible to recognize the central role of sports in our society and still understand that professional teams do not require a welfare system to provide the substantial joy and excitement that games and athletes generate for a substantial portion of our population.

CAN ANYONE SEE THE MAN
BEHIND THE CURTAIN?

Preparing for negotiations with a professional sports team or league requires more than just doing your homework on the business of professional sports. Developing a "game face" for the negotiations necessitates a clear understanding of how sports became so popular and how the importance of professional teams to our society and communities is exaggerated. This does not mean that one does not like or enjoy sports or wants to see any community deprived of the cultural importance of a team. Sports, and professional teams, are icons in our communities. But their meaning and relative worth is constantly overvalued by the media and league officials to protect the existing welfare system. Like Dorothy and Toto, you have to look at what is behind the curtain or facade of sports to understand the forces that have made teams a modern-day Wizard of Oz. But be warned: Just as the residents of Oz believed that the Wizard could do anything, there are large numbers of people who believe sports, teams, and athletes are the elixirs for any number of social, economic, and political ailments. But as Toto, Dorothy, the Lion, the Scarecrow, and the Tin Man learned, our modern Wizard of Oz relies on smoke and a bombastic display of revelry to illustrate its abilities and power. Is there any substance to this imagery, romanticism, and mysticism? Just what is it that makes sports so important to so many people, and why do people believe that sports have a magical quality that can transform communities and their social settings?

At one level there are few parts of life, from language to holiday celebrations, that are not touched, affected, and even partially defined by sports. This pervasiveness builds a number of emotional attachments to sports for men (and for many women, too) that are exploited to justify taxes and subsidies for sports teams. Indeed, sports have been a central element of societies for thousands of years. Greek society emphasized athletics through its celebration of the Olympics. The Romans built stadiums throughout their empire for sporting events, and some of these facilities in Turkey and Israel are still used. The Hippodrome in Istanbul served as a convening point for chariot races and political rallies for the Ottoman Empire long before the NBA established its Dream Teams for the modern Olympics and the Super Bowl became the unofficial end to the winter holiday season that begins with Thanksgiving.

Individual teams and the professional leagues, as well as their advocates, use these psychological and sociological attachments as ploys to engender excitement and "tug at the hearts" of enthusiasts and nonenthusiasts when negotiations occur. This excitement or emotionalism often prevents cities and their citizens from remembering that the imagery and emotionalism of sports are part of the "show." Spectator sports as a form of escapism and entertainment can captivate and divert attention from the dreary aspects of life. As a form of entertainment, sports have the ability to create memorable events that mark the passage of time and bond generations through shared activities. This romantic bond, coupled with opportunities to escape from the worries of the day, is what owners and leagues manipulate to get what they want from governments, fans, and taxpayers, even in an era of repeated calls for smaller governments and lower taxes.

Just How Popular Are Sports?
Some Important Examples

Although the protracted labor problems that have plagued professional sports in recent years have undoubtedly tarnished their image and reduced their meaning for some fans, overall support and interest remains incredibly robust. Attendance levels at games, despite rising ticket prices, remain at or near record levels. As already noted, for four consecutive seasons the Cleveland Indians have sold every seat for every game they play. In 1990 nearly 55 million tickets were sold by MLB teams. In 1998 the twenty-eight MLB teams played before 70.5 million fans.

Despite the fact that basketball teams in several cities play before near-capacity crowds, overall attendance still has increased for the NBA from 17 million in 1991 to 20.4 million in 1997–98. In the NFL, where most teams also sell out all their games, league attendance levels now surpass 15 million. In the NHL, when all expansion teams are included, attendance has increased from 13 million in 1990 to more than 17 million in the 1997–98 season.

There also has been an unprecedented growth in the demand for minor league teams from small- and medium-sized cities. Erie, Pennsylvania, population 108,718, recently spent $8.7 million to become a home for a minor league team. Some medium-sized cities have been able to successfully support even major league hockey and basketball teams.

Likewise, the media's interest in broadcasting and telecasting games has not waned despite an amazing proliferation of coverage. In 1997 and 1998 the NFL and the NBA each received record contracts to telecast their games. Each team in the NFL will receive approximately $73 million per season from 1998 through 2005. In the NBA each team will receive approximately $24 million from the broadcast of games. In 1995, ESPN signed a commitment to televise all the games for the NCAA's women's basketball championship tournament. The nation's colleges have organized themselves into large blocks or leagues to negotiate profitable media packages, and Notre Dame University was able to negotiate its own contract with NBC to telecast its football games. Pay-per-view and other changes in the cable television industry continue to create exceptional opportunities for teams and leagues as they seek to reach households in North America, Europe, and Asia. The NFL and the NBA regularly play games in Europe and Asia, and MLB will likely add Asia to its market very soon.

Has the popularity of sports diminished? Not at all!

SPORTS, CULTURE, AND IMAGERY

Many members of my generation can remember where they were and what they were doing when they heard that President Kennedy and Dr. King had been killed. Neil Armstrong's moon-landing proclamation is similarly etched in our minds. Unfortunately for community leaders who deal with professional sports teams, many people also romanticize their memories of the 1980 U.S. Olympic hockey team's upset of the Soviet Union (probably no sports broadcast is replayed as often as the ending of this hockey game, when ABC's Al Michaels declared, "America, do you believe in miracles?") and the Amazing Mets of 1969. Most baseball fans also know what they were doing on any number of days when the Boston Red Sox collapsed.

My defining moments in life include my first visit to Yankee Stadium; I was eight and can recall that entire day, together with my first sight of that green grass and red-clay running track circling the field. Like Billy Crystal, I have never seen grass so green or clay so red since. My father also held my hand as we descended closer and closer to our seats. I still remember that Yogi Berra had failed to shave before the game and had quite a shadow. Such are the things that eight-year-olds remember.

I also remember a warm November Saturday in the Los Angeles Coliseum. The University of Southern California's football team was trailing Notre Dame 24–6, but as the sun set over the coliseum on one of those glorious fall afternoons in southern California, the Trojans, led by Anthony Davis, Pat Haden, and J. K. McKay, scored seven straight touchdowns to defeat the Irish. I remember USC's band and horse, and the song girls celebrating the most improbable end to the game. Such are the things twenty-two-year-olds remember.

These cherished memories, like those enjoyed by Murray Sperber and Billy Crystal, do mark my relationships and sense of time.

It is emotions like these that frequently lead public officials to conclude that sports teams deserve subsidies because they create powerful and positive memories. If the welfare system that creates large profits for team owners and players is to end, taxpayers and community leaders must understand the psychological grip that sports have on our society and decide not to let these emotions rule our pocketbooks. Sports play on the psyche of taxpayers and community leaders through (1) their image as a romanticized ideal, (2) their integral role in everyday life, (3) their importance to the media, (4) their political symbolism, and (5) their imagery for economic development. These powerful emotional forces must be demystified if the welfare system is to end.

SPORTS AS A ROMANTICIZED IDEAL

The romanticized view that many people have of sports has two primary threads. First, people are fond of telling one another that there are a number of positive values that can be taught (or taught more easily) only through sports. These values include the merits and payoffs from hard work and practice; the importance of leadership; the meaning and benefits of team efforts to accomplish or reach a group's goal; and the value of individual sacrifice for group achievement. If these worthy attributes are not sufficient to create a sympathetic environment in which to discuss a sports subsidy, the second thread of the romanticized ideal of sports can be touted: Sports provide a complete set of activities in which parents and children can play together. As a result, for many people a number of their memories of parents and childhood are intertwined with these shared activities. Whether it is attending a game together, playing games together, or watching other family members play in their games, family life is not only interwoven with many dimensions of sports but is at least partially defined by sports.

To be sure, in recent years we have become all too keenly aware of some of the negative psychological factors that sports can impart. Many male athletes, exposed to levels of violence that are integral parts of certain sports, have had difficulty finding the appropriate boundaries for this physical violence in their lives. From excessive drug abuse to rape and spousal abuse to inappropriate risk-taking, promiscuity, and gambling, there is ample evidence that sports have contributed to several of society's pathologies (Lipsyte, 1995). But these extremely critical and important elements of the dark side of sports should not detract from the many positive outcomes that emanate from athletics and athletes.

Sports do teach the very positive values of teamwork, hard work, and sacrifice to attain goals. One cannot become a winner or champion without a substantial commitment to practice, and it is through that commitment that sports teach the value of working hard to achieve a goal. Sports also can teach people to challenge themselves, set goals, and work with others to reach objectives or goals that, without teamwork, could not be achieved. The commitment sports can require and the team effort involved with all sports (coaches and players in nonteam sports make up a team as well) also form a set of powerful emotional relationships that affect people. It is these memories and the feelings of accomplishment and success that come from working with others that create many of the positive values or impressions of sports that many people reference for their entire lives. Anything that supports these memories or underscores these positive values is seen as very desirable. That desirability is what team owners and the professional sports leagues rely on to increase the support they receive from cities and state governments. After all, without a team, what role models would a community use to extol the positive attributes of teamwork, hard work, and achievement?

The romanticized ideal of sports extends from these positive (and negative) role-model issues to the memories that sports create for parents and children. Sports, much like Disney World, create opportunities for parents and children to enjoy the same set of activities. From playing games together to watching games together, sports create a level of bonding that is quite powerful. Whether it is a boy or girl remembering a game of catch or passing a soccer ball with a parent, games played through school years, or spectator events, sports are a powerful force that binds generations together. This emotionalism can affect people's desires to "land a team." Federico Peña, Denver's mayor during its successful drive to get an MLB team, cited his desire to take his children to baseball games as part of the reason for bringing baseball to Denver. Leaders carry their youthful emotions into their decisionmaking roles. Denver committed large amounts of the public's money to indulge and subsidize Mayor Peña's bonding needs.

So why is it important to remember these facets of sports as no more than a mythical ideal when negotiating for a team? First, each of these elements that I've described is overly romanticized. It is certainly true that one can learn the value of teamwork, hard work, and sacrifice from sports, but those lessons can also be learned from many other activities and events. And they can be learned without subsidizing professional teams to play in your city. Nor does a city need to subsidize a professional team to teach values to children through sports. Even though professional teams and athletes usually are fine examples of success as a result of hard work, good habits can be taught to children through their own participation in sports. Further, given how few jobs there are in professional sports for players, focusing the attention of young people on sports can distract them from their education and other goals that can create a more stable economic future.

Second, parents and children can do things together without public subsidies for sports teams. Playing catch, shooting hoops, passing a soccer ball, and other such activities do not require taxes to support stadiums and arenas. And there is no guarantee that the existence of these facilities will actually encourage parents to do anything with their children. With the current prices charged for tickets to many games, parents may have fewer opportunities to bond with their children at sporting events than they realize.

Finally, although there are positive values in sports, there are also negative ones as well. It may not be impossible to determine the balance between the good and bad, but it is necessary to recognize that both exist. As such, when your city's leadership says a team is needed to provide recreation for families or to generate memories, remember that you are being taken for a walk down memory lane. In sports, this stroll translates into a subsidy for teams and the passage of new taxes.

SPORTS AND EVERYDAY LIFE

If you think about events in the United States at almost any point in recent history, other than when our attention was temporarily deflected by a national crisis, sports and the activities of its participants have been a dominant preoccupation. For example, for more than a year America was gripped by the trial of O. J. Simpson, and the public's interest in his life and the trial was much more than media hype. True, the trial provided an opportunity for the mass media to produce relatively inexpensive "filler" for numerous tabloid television shows. However, America wanted much more coverage, especially from the "mainstream" of America's media. Each network's evening news shows included daily updates on the trial; on many nights, CNN provided expanded coverage of issues and events associated with the trial. The early morning network shows such as *Today* and *Good Morning America* also included frequent updates on the trial through the use of special reporters. On the Internet there was even an "OJNet" that included daily updates on the trial's progress and tidbits on O. J.'s life.

The media's attention was out of proportion to the crime; other spousal abuse cases and trials are virtually ignored by the media unless there is a bizarre twist (such as in the Bobbitt case). But O. J. Simpson, as a sports star, was an American icon, and Americans wanted to know every detail of his private life. Lost amid the details of his life was the death of another victim of spousal abuse, a young man who may simply have been in the wrong place at the wrong time.

The sensational events of the Simpson trial were interrupted briefly by Michael Jordan's return to basketball. Newspapers across the country carried front-page stories of the "Second Coming of His Airiness," and residents of Chicago were enthralled. During this same time period, Mike Tyson, a boxing champion convicted of rape, was released from prison, and his initial activities and press conference were reported by the media with a level of intensity even greater than that given visiting leaders of foreign countries. Indeed, it is safe to say that Americans probably were more interested in the trial of O. J. Simpson, Michael Jordan's decision to return to professional basketball, and the life of Mike Tyson than they were in the statements and opinions of these leaders. All these events involving sports stars, along with the substantial public attention directed by the mass media, underscore the importance of sports and help establish the environment in which subsidies can be demanded and supported.

Sports and Language

To discover the importance of sports in everyday life one does not have to focus on the celebrity status of Michael Jordan or the notoriety of O. J. Simpson and Mike Tyson. The first way that sports define our culture and lifestyle is in the use of language. Sports metaphors can be found in our everyday language, and we even define ourselves, events, situations, and outcomes in sports terms. Are you a "winner" or a "loser"? Can you "go the distance" and make your city "major league," or do you want to be the mayor that "lost" the team? As you can see, we can even use sports metaphors to convince you that you should want a team in your city.

The use of sports in our language is seemingly endless. Deadlines and the need for critical actions or decisions are frequently described as "ninth-inning" decisions or actions, while the need for a major effort in a hopeless situation may be described as "fourth and long." Midlife crises are described as "halftime" in the game of life. By extension, midlife crises may be nothing more than a form of halftime entertainment engaged in while waiting for the older team to take the field. Unlikely but favorable outcomes are "long shots" or "three-point shots" from "downtown." Keeping people updated on items is to give them a "heads up," as in looking for a fly ball or pass. And we all know how "to play hardball" and make an aggressive argument that is "in your face." Loyal employees are "team players," and much of the thinking that has dominated administrative reform, from Ford's Quality Circles to all aspects of the total quality management concept, emphasizes the "team approach" to problem solving and getting to be "number one." National leaders, corporate leaders, civic and community leaders, citizens, students, men and women, rich and poor—all of us have probably, at one time or another, used sports metaphors. Senator Richard Lugar of Indiana, when discussing his candidacy for the Republican presidential nomination, said as follows:

> I am the Cal Ripken candidate if people are interested in performance, consistency, a person they can trust . . . winning the devotion of people who revere the idea of a person constantly being there to witness goodness to his family, to witness faithfulness to a lifetime of work and striving for excellence, to witness fair play and enthusiasm for the achievement of others, to witness the healthy example of a leader who says no to personal vices and to marital infidelity (Stuteville, 1995).

What does it mean when the language of a culture begins to include metaphors from something such as sports? It means that at one level, maybe subconsciously, the importance of sports in life and for communication is being emphasized. If we are using the terminology of sports to communicate our ideas, then aren't sports deserving of public support, subsidies, and special attention? Shouldn't we treat sports differently from other items that the public must consider? Aren't sports the way we shape values and mold people to be successful adults? As a form of public education, don't sports warrant a subsidy?

Sports and Schools

By way of alumni reunions, homecomings, parents' days, and other ways of establishing school spirit, sports are part of our educational experiences from grade school through graduate school. Residential colleges have turned sports into an industry filled with ritual, bands, midnight practices, school planes and buses, and tutors who help athletes balance academic life with sports life. But the pageantry and excess found in college sports do not begin with college life. They begin with grade school teams, with basketball, cheerleading, and the band camps that are part of the life of youngsters across North America.

Books and movies abound to highlight high school sports and their importance for young people, their parents, and their communities. During one's high school years, Friday nights are dominated by high school events that encircle "the game." Sports are intertwined with the entire process of dating; the weekly games become the activities during which young men and women learn about the opposite sex and how to relate to them. Romantic relationships sometimes begin at a school's athletic events or the events organized to complement them. As a result, it is not uncommon to find people believing that sports are very important to their lives.

Sports and Holidays

Sports are intrinsically linked to life-cycle events because "key" sporting events are placed around holidays. What do most families do on Thanksgiving? Eat turkey and watch professional football. What do they do on the Friday after Thanksgiving? Eat leftovers, shop, and watch college football. What do we do on national holidays such as the Fourth of July, Memorial Day, Labor Day, New Year's Day, and Martin Luther King Day? We go to the ol' ballpark or arena or watch the games on television. We have baseball games on the Fourth of July, with fireworks afterward, and on Memorial Day and Labor Day. And on Martin Luther King Day there are special afternoon basketball games.

The largest spectator event, the Indianapolis 500, is scheduled for Memorial Day weekend, on Sunday to give its organizers an extra day for the race in the event of rain. What would New Year's Day be without a college bowl game—or, actually, eight college bowl games? Only parts of Christmas Day have remained protected from the domination of sports. The NBA's Christmas Day present to fans includes two games between contending teams. There is no holy day, Sabbath (Jewish or Christian), or holiday that is not defined by sports. How many ministers in Texas have been advised to keep their sermons short to avoid conflicting with Cowboy kickoffs? As a team that plays in the central time zone, Cowboy games frequently begin at noon. I still remember one Yom Kippur service, the holiest day in the Jewish calendar, when the "buzz" in the congregation was so intense that an orthodox rabbi agreed to announce the score of the World Series if we would then return to prayer.

Just how extensive is sports programming on the holidays? Here is a partial listing for a typical Christmas Day, but it could also be Thanksgiving or New Year's Eve or Day (all times eastern standard):

Christmas Day, 1995

Noon   Kelly Tires Blue/Gray College All Star Football Classic
3:30   Jeep Eagle Aloha Bowl, College Football, Kansas v.
          UCLA
3:30   NBA Basketball Doubleheader, Game 1: San Antonio v.
          Phoenix
6:00   NBA Basketball Doubleheader, Game 2: Houston v.
          Orlando
9:00   NFL Football, Dallas at Arizona

As you can see, the schedule has sports programs available from noon to midnight, eastern time, or from nine in the morning until nine in the evening, pacific time.

What do all these sporting events, which are part of our natural life cycle, mean for state and local governments that are negotiating with teams? It means that many civic and community leaders, whose holidays and life cycles are defined in part by sports, might believe that sports are of such importance that they deserve subsidies from the government and subsidies from taxpayers.

Emotionalism and a City's Negotiating Style: Denver Gives Away the Store

David Whitford, in *Playing Hardball*, provides an excellent description of how the emotional commitment to sports can affect community leaders when they "try to make the deal." This emotionalism produced a lease for the Colorado Rockies that the team's president, Carl Barger, described in the following terms: "Ha Ha Ha Ha! It's a great lease. I gotta hand it to those people who negotiated it, it's a hell of lease, boy! In fact, it's unbelievable" (Whitford, 1993: 87).

The taxpayers in the Denver metropolitan region voted to provide up to $100 million, or 70 percent of the cost, for a stadium if a team was awarded to the area. Voters approved a 0.1 percent increase in the regional sales tax to extend for as long as necessary to retire the bonds for this investment. It was known that the stadium would cost more than $100 million. The measure was written so that voters were assured that 30 percent of the cost of the stadium would be supported by private money—from such sources as parking, private investment, advertising at the stadium, concessions, and so forth. However, the citizens never got what they voted to support.

When the time came to submit Denver's bid to MLB for a team, problems emerged with the proposed ownership group. A great deal of money was needed to secure the team. MLB required a $95 million fee from the prospective owners to receive the franchise. To operate the team until revenues began to accrue, each potential ownership group was reminded that another $20 million in cash was needed.

With more than $100 million required from private investors, "flexibility" in the financing of the stadium was required to attract investors or companies who could pay what MLB demanded for a new team. Led by the governor of Colorado, the planning group for the future franchise found that unless potential team owners were given all of the stadium's revenues, investors would not be found. The mayor of Denver, Federico Peña, who had already invested substantial political capital to secure a team, was eager to provide whatever was necessary to attract the team and an acceptable ownership group. After hearing of the financial problems faced by an emerging ownership group, he wrote, "I assure you the city and county of Denver will cooperate with franchise owners to make Mile High Stadium available on terms that are fair and reasonable" (Whitford, 1993: 99).

For the first and second year of their existence, and while a new stadium was being built, the Colorado baseball team would have to play in Mile High Stadium. This stadium was built for the Denver Broncos of the NFL. As a result, two leases were actually developed: one for the use of Mile High Stadium for two years and one for the new stadium.

The mayor was true to his word. For the two years during which the team would need to use Mile High Stadium, they paid no rent. In each of these years the team drew approximately 4 million fans. The city also gave the team 92 percent of the revenues from concessions.

In terms of the new ballpark, it was agreed that the public sector would pay the entire cost of construction, $156 million. The Rockies were to be responsible for all operating and maintenance costs, and were to make payments of $550,000 each year to a capital repair fund. The team also agreed to pay the district that oversees the stadium 25 cents for each ticket sold between 2.25 and 2.5 million; 50 cents for each ticket sold between 2.5 and 3 million; and $1 for each ticket sold over 3 million. The seating capacity of the new stadium is fifty thousand, so more than 4 million tickets may be sold each year. If 4 million fans attend games in any season at the new stadium, the government receives $1,312,500.

To calculate the percentage of the costs for the new stadium paid by the team and the public sector, assume that the team always draws 4 million fans and that it continues to make payments of $550,000 to the capital fund. If this is done for twenty-two years, at a 6 percent discount rate, the contribution by the Rockies to the ballpark, in 1995 dollars, would be $21,157,986, or an amount equal to 13.6 percent of the construction cost. If an 8 percent discount rate is used for the twenty-two-year revenue stream, the contribution by the team would be $17,591,560 in 1995 dollars. This would represent 11.3 percent of the cost of the stadium. Each of these figures is below the 30 percent anticipated by the voters who supported the tax increase to build the stadium and is dependent on the team's selling 4 million tickets every year. Although the team's contribution never matched what was originally expected, this did not stop the public sector from providing even more revenue for the owners. The city permitted the team to retain the $15 million fee for naming rights charged to the Coors brewing company.

Why did Denver "have" to enhance its original commitment for the new stadium? The lease made a big impression on the existing MLB owners, exactly as it was intended to do. During the question-and-answer period (after the presentation of Denver's proposal to MLB), Warren Giles of the Phillies was moved to ask Jacobs, "Will you come to Philadelphia and negotiate my lease? This is the best lease I've ever read." Later, National League president Bill White, after he had had a chance to fully digest its terms, would label Denver's lease "the prototype of what we ask our teams to look at" (Whitford, 1993: 130). Federico Peña can now take his children to an MLB game in Denver.

SPORTS AS THE MEDIA'S BREAD AND BUTTER

A great deal of the public's attention on sports is driven by mass media, which argue that they simply are responding to consumers who have an enormous appetite for sports. However, sports are a critical asset for the mass media and directly contribute in several ways to the profitability of newspapers, television stations, and radio stations. Sports fans have an almost insatiable desire for news and information about their teams. Even those fans who attend a game or watch on television want to read about it in the paper. As a result, advertisers, eager to reach people interested in sports (males between the ages of eighteen and fifty-four), purchase space or broadcast time. Most important for the media, however, is that the cost of producing these stories is very low. Athletes and coaches frequently talk to the media (to increase their own visibility), and if they will not talk to the media, that fact can be covered by journalists. Sports are an inexpensive source of news. Information and news about sports accounts for approximately 20 percent of the material included in newspapers (Stevens, 1987).

Sporting events are both a drama and a form of escapism. For the broadcast media, games represent an almost endless supply of live entertainment with unknown outcomes. Each game includes limitless examples of success and failure, triumph, despair, ecstasy with risk, and just rewards for hard work. All of this is graphically portrayed in a neatly packaged two- or three-hour time period with sufficient commercial "breaks." Indeed, where additional opportunities for advertisers are needed, extra "time-outs" are added to the game. The mass media, then, want people to crave sports. Inexpensive dramas and copy are produced for which advertisers will pay handsomely as long as the demand for sports remains high. A never-ending and mutually reinforcing network or linkage exists between sports and the media.

Civic leaders also must remember that television stations pay the teams for the right to transmit games. Since the television industry is paying for entertainment, it is not surprising that broadcast stations want entertainment and not news. As a result, hard news issues or topics may be avoided. For example, when there was some controversy about the death of Celtic star Reggie Lewis and a possible connection to cocaine abuse, it was the *Wall Street Journal* that reported the story; it was not any of the major networks that broadcast NBA games for their entertainment value or newspapers with sports sections whose revenues are vital to the fiscal success of the paper. With several of the major television networks now paying $17.6 billion to broadcast NFL games, and NBC and TNT paying $2.6 billion for the rights to NBA games, it may well be time to ask if these networks can report sports news that might diminish the luster of the prized broadcast jewels.

There are at least six attributes or facets to any sporting event that account for its appeal to fans. These attributes also assure television and radio programmers of ever-changing dramas. First, there is a level of competition with a winner and a loser. From both winners and losers there are emotional reactions. Fans can enjoy their own emotional reactions and observe others from a safe distance, realizing that the outcomes really do not create lasting positive or negative consequences. (Of course, for gamblers such outcomes may produce very real consequences; but for this illustration I am talking about fans who do not gamble to the point of risking their financial stability.)

Second, no two games or events are ever identical. Every contest is different, with separate nuances and possible outcomes, so there is never a "rerun." For the programmers this means a constant source of new mini-dramas that can be endlessly reviewed and discussed.

Third, there are frequent upsets in which an underdog or modern-day David overcomes obstacles to conquer a Goliath. This creates, for fans who may be Davids in their own lives, a sense of hope that they, too, might overcome some large obstacle. Even if a fan does not need to see a David beat a Goliath, the possibility of an upset creates a constant drama for each event or game. Northwestern University's improbable arrival at the 1996 Rose Bowl permitted NBC to focus everyone's attention on the Cinderella season of this highly regarded academic institution. Northwestern's stellar academic achievements were the "sidebar," however, to the fact that its team was the Big 10 football champion. The university had placed fifty-five players on the Academic All-American team in the past decade, but this had not brought it the exposure it received for its first Big 10 football championship in several decades.

Fourth, most games end with a winner and a loser (though ties are possible in some sports), so there is a finality or clear-cut outcome, which is produced in a relatively short period of time. Ties are unlikely even where possible, so fans are virtually assured of a clear-cut drama with an ending.

Fifth, there is always hope for the losers because there is always a tomorrow in the form of a new season or another game that might be won. This provides hope at the end of every drama.

Sixth, although participants are rarely seriously hurt as a direct result of events in a game (this is changing at an alarming rate in the NFL), there are sufficient injuries to create appeal, for these represent badges of courage to be seen, witnessed, and analyzed through innumerable replays. In addition, physical injuries become the random and uncontrollable events that can affect a team's fate. This establishes a strong parallel with each fan's life. Events sometimes happen in our lives that cannot be controlled and that change what is likely to occur. In a sense, injuries provide this random element and give both hope (as when an opponent's players are injured) and fear (one of our players might be hurt and cause a loss). The endless variety of outcomes, the emotions produced, and the bounded time frame within which these dramas take place are perfectly designed for the mass media.

The profitability of sports means few newspapers or broadcast stations have much interest in the politics and economics of sports. Most media prefer to focus on the entertainment value of sports. Howard Cosell was the first, and clearly the best, of a very small group of hard news reporters who concentrated on the broader issues defined and interlaced with sports. *The New York Times, Wall Street Journal, Washington Post, Los Angeles Times,* and selected other papers do have reporters (such as John Helyar, Mike Lupica, Richard Sandomir, Murray Chass, and Robert Lipsyte) who detail the politics and economics of sports; so do a few of the networks. But these examples, together with *Sports Illustrated,* are the exceptions, not the rule. The media has discovered a "golden goose" in sports, and that goose is rarely analyzed for local officials who must decide whether or not a subsidy is needed.

The financial importance of sports to the media is probably best illustrated by the impact that sports have on the sale of newspapers. During the 1994–95 labor disruption in the NHL, the daily circulation of newspapers in both Montreal and Toronto declined by at least four thousand copies. The *Dallas Morning News* also reported that its largest daily sales were on the Sundays that the Dallas Cowboys played in the Super Bowls and the Mondays after their victories.

Sporting events comprise more than half of the most watched television programs of all time. By rating points, sports programs account for half of the most watched programs, but by households, sports programs account for six of the eleven most watched programs (see Table 2-1). With the fragmentation of viewership brought by the proliferation of stations available through cable and satellite systems, sports programs may well be the last remaining event where advertisers can reliably count on attracting a large number of viewers to see their commercials.

The importance of sports for the print and broadcast media means that when state and local officials negotiate with teams, the media will (1) likely be strong supporters of any deal needed to bring a team to a community, (2) be unlikely to critically report or investigate the negative implications or aspects of any partnership that brings a team to a community, (3) provide substantial coverage of the positive impacts or benefits from a team's presence in the community, and (4) provide substantial coverage of any lost opportunities or events that surround the movement of a team from one city to another community. As a result, substantial pressure is likely to be generated by the media to support any effort to secure a team's location. Elected officials know well the power of the media to highlight negative outcomes. As such, they may be unwilling to "take on" the media, and they may be very receptive to supporting sports issues if it means favorable exposure in the media.

In some communities, major media sources have a direct financial interest in the success of a team. This results from their ownership of the team or the stadium or arena in which the team plays. Although arrangements of this nature are a clear example of media firms participating in the building of their communities, they also establish an important, if not critical, conflict of interest. If the newspaper or a broadcast station has a direct

TABLE 2-1
The Most Watched Television Programs Through 1998

Program	Event	Network	Year	Rating	Millions of Households
M*A*S*H	Final episode	CBS	1983	60.2	50.2
Dallas	"Who Shot J. R.?"	CBS	1980	53.3	41.5
Roots	Part 8	ABC	1977	51.1	36.4
Super Bowl XVI	49ers 26, Bengals 21	CBS	1982	49.1	40.0
Super Bowl XVII	Redskins 27, Dolphins 17	NBC	1983	48.6	40.5
17th Winter Olympics	Women's skating	CBS	1994	48.5	45.7
Super Bowl XX	Bears 46, Patriots 10	NBC	1986	48.3	41.5
Gone with the Wind	Part I	NBC	1976	47.7	34.0
Gone with the Wind	Part II	NBC	1976	47.4	33.8
Super Bowl XII	Cowboys 27, Broncos 10	CBS	1978	47.2	34.4
Super Bowl XIII	Steelers 35, Cowboys 31	NBC	1979	47.1	35.1

Source: Brown and Morrison, 1998.

financial investment in a team or the playing facilities built in a city, how can that same community expect the media to provide a balanced appraisal of the benefits, costs, liabilities, and alternatives to any financing program presented by the city or region's political leadership? How can elected leaders and citizens be confident that the media will provide a balanced and fair review of issues if a particular newspaper or station is also an owner of an arena or stadium?

SPORTS AND POLITICS

Attention is, of course, power, luring those who would appropriate that attention to different ends than those which generated it in the first place.
John MacAloon (1987: 116)

The importance of sports for the public sector and as something governments should support is repeatedly underscored by the use of sports in politics. Most members of my generation grew to adulthood amid images of Adolf Hitler's use of the 1936 Olympics to illustrate the virtues, values, and triumph of Nazi society. (This was reemphasized in the movie *Contact.*) When groups in the 1960s wanted to highlight the contributions of African Americans, many recalled with great joy the triumph of Jesse Owens over the athletes from the Third Reich and Hitler's inability to acknowledge graciously Owens's accomplishments. Of course, one does not have to return to the 1930s to see examples of the use of sports for political messages and efforts.

In 1980, President Jimmy Carter used the Olympics to protest the Soviet Union's invasion of Afghanistan when he refused to send the U.S. team to the Moscow games. The Soviet Union retaliated later by refusing to participate in the 1984 Olympics in Los Angeles. China sought to attract the 2000 Olympic games to Beijing to showcase a new China in a new millennium. Virtually every nation that hosts the Olympics uses the events to portray a favorable image of their country and society. Large events have always served this purpose, but often the attention that sports command makes them showcases for political statements.

Beyond the international politics associated with sports, participants in both domestic and regional confrontations use sports as a vehicle to deliver messages. Because of the attention they attract, sports create a forum within which regional, national, and international politics are played; this was evidenced by the protests against racism in the United States by African Americans at the 1968 Olympics and the capture and murder of Israeli athletes by Palestinians at the 1972 games in Munich.

Sports also are used to validate cultures and establish both prestige and image. This was very important to the Communist nations during the Cold War when they tried to counter the West's consumer lifestyles with a lifestyle that focused on national prestige and not consumption. Capitalists wanted to see their athletes win to vindicate or validate the lifestyles and governance systems in the West. Roone Arledge, ABC Television's director of sports for many years, once noted that at the height of the Cold War he could have televised any event involving a Russian and an American and had a solid audience. Americans rejoiced when the U.S. hockey team defeated the Soviet Union in 1980, and Americans basked in the glory of the NBA's "Dream Team" after having seen collegians lose to foreign basketball teams in several Olympic and Pan American contests.

The use of sports to celebrate or validate a culture is not a new phenomenon; most of us can call to mind the gladiators and the chariot races in the film *Ben-Hur*, showing an important part of the Roman culture. Greek culture gave the world the concept of the Olympic Games. Some might argue that we are more familiar with the Roman Coliseum and the concept of the Olympics than we are with the Roman Senate or any of the other achievements of Greek society. Finally, the importance of sports to ancient cultures is not limited to European societies. Mexico's native tribes used sports to celebrate their culture and holidays. A basketball-like game played at Chichén Itzá on Mexico's Yucatán Peninsula was part of ritual celebrations within the Mayan culture. The Islamic world also has had its notable fascination with sports. For centuries the Ottoman Empire focused great attention on the chariot races at the Hippodrome, located adjacent to Istanbul's great religious monuments, the Blue Mosque and the Hagia Sophia.

Why is the association or linkage between politics and sports important in terms of the subsidies that teams receive? Because sports are used to make political statements, establish identities, and achieve a certain status. Sports are used in national and international politics to gain prestige. If our athletes beat their athletes, our town, our culture, or our country is somehow better.

Winning teams and athletes validate cultures, economic systems, and value systems, and for many people they establish an external identity. But if you don't have a team, do you have an identity? Better pay what it takes to get a team, right?

SPORTS, IMAGE, AND ECONOMIC DEVELOPMENT

Without them, we're a cow town.
Christopher Flores, *Sports Illustrated* (commenting on
the importance of St. Louis attracting the Los Angeles Rams)

Sports represents a significant opportunity to generate economic development for a city. Leveraging sports to create jobs and expand business paid off handsomely for Indianapolis during the 1980s.
William H. Hudnut III,
four-term mayor of Indianapolis

During D'Alessandro's three terms as mayor (1940s and 1950s), Baltimore built new schools and roads, public housing, a major airport, and, of course, Memorial Stadium. He wanted to bring baseball to the city to show that Baltimore was a big league town.
Miller (on the importance of the move of
the Orioles to Baltimore in 1954)

The media's attention to sports has encouraged many cities to reshape or establish their images and reputations through sports. Indianapolis is frequently mentioned as a city that used its reputation as the "amateur sports capital" to undo its image as a sleepy city that came to life one day a year. The resurgence of Buffalo, New York, involved the building of new facilities for its football and minor league baseball teams. Cleveland attempted to overhaul its image and redevelop its downtown with more than $400 million in sports-related construction. Both St. Louis and St. Petersburg built domed stadiums in an effort to attract sports teams to their cities. Oklahoma City's redevelopment of its downtown area involved a minor league baseball stadium, a twenty-thousand-seat indoor facility for an anticipated NHL team, and a renovated convention center. These efforts have been described as the most significant events in Oklahoma City's history since the land run (Hamilton, 1995). Gary, Indiana, and the surrounding county were willing to consider a special income tax to attract the Chicago Bears, who would play only ten games a year in the new stadium.

Cleveland's recent investments in new homes for the Indians and Cavaliers were not the first attempts by this city to try to use sports to "jump-start" economic development. In 1928 city officials asked voters to approve a $2.5 million bond to build a municipal enterprise known as Municipal Stadium.

City officials, in this case led by city manager William R. Hopkins, viewed sports as an economic benefit for the city. A city-owned facility would generate rental revenues from sports teams. In addition, the Mayor also promised that a large, modern facility would attract conventions and other programs to Cleveland, which in turn would generate economic growth. The supposed ability of sports to drive a service economy has been part of our mythology for decades. Despite cost overruns and setbacks caused by the depression, the stadium was completed on July 1, 1931 (Grabowski, 1992: 46–47).

Many college presidents and officials also are convinced that the only way to become a "real university" is to have a sports program that attracts attention and students, and maintains alumni. The mythology of the importance of sports is pervasive in the halls of academia.

Making the University of Texas at Arlington a Real University

Ryan C. Amacher served as president of the University of Texas at Arlington (UTA) for several years in the early 1990s. Located in the center of the Dallas/Fort Worth region, the largely commuter campus has faced continuing challenges in establishing its identity. Home to several fine schools and more than twenty thousand students, UTA lacked name recognition and identity. As president, Amacher sought to develop the university's image through sports. The following is an excerpt from an open letter he sent to alumni shortly before his resignation.

Let me explain why I believe Division I NCAA athletics can contribute to the development of universities in general and of UTA in particular. Another major college president recently told me: "Real universities do athletics." This seems obvious to me, but perhaps we should ask the question: Why do (real) universities do athletics?

First, universities do athletics because athletic programs attract many good students. Students are drawn to universities for various educational and leadership enhancing programs besides the regular offerings: theater, student newspapers, band, debate, and athletics. At present UTA has about 325 student-athletes. These students would not be here if we did not play Division I athletics. They would instead be at Texas Tech or North Texas or another school that recruited them. These same students are going to be successful, loyal alumnus.

Second, student athletes have a work ethic sought by employers. Recently, I asked many Metroplex human relations personnel what they found most lacking in recent university graduates, ours and others. The most common response was a lack of competitive spirit and commitment to the teamwork of the company. Those are the very skills developed by participation in athletics. . . .

Third, athletics are good for alums and students. They develop a sense of spirit and camaraderie. Many universities build their development efforts around this spirit. When I visit community alumni groups, they ask about UTA athletics more frequently than anything else. In our society, athletics provide a place where we can all come to-gether regardless of career interest or race. They create a common bond. . . .

Finally, let's return for a moment to the proposition that real universities do athletics. Let's play the wannabe game. List five public universities that you would aspire for UTA to challenge. Write them down. Now that you've done that, think of their athletic programs. My guess is that the univer-sities you listed have invested significantly in athletics. Per-haps you even know of them because of their athletic programs. . . . In ten years, return to your list of five public universities you wish UTA could be "more like." My guess is that you will agree with my presidential colleague who said "real universities do athletics." I think she is correct.

Many of the points made by Dr. Amacher are valid in the sense that they represent perceptions rampant in our society. What Dr. Amacher ignores are the negative issues associated with sports. First, many athletic programs lose money for their colleges and universities (Blum, 1994). Second, there is no certainty that win-ning sports programs, or sports programs in general, are associ-ated with increased alumni donations and activities (Lederman, 1988). Third, college sports programs have generated a myriad of management and ethical problems (Sperber, 1990). Fourth, as noted by Sperber (1990: 1), when considering the educational mission of college sports: "The main purpose of college sports is commercial entertainment. Within most universities with big-time intercollegiate programs, the athletic department operates as a separate business and has almost no connection to the educa-tion departments and functions of the school; even the research into and teaching of sports is done by the physical education de-partment. The reason elite athletes are in universities has nothing to do with the educational missions of their schools. Athletes are the only group of students recruited for entertainment."

Fifth, virtually every year there are sports programs placed on probation as a result of recruiting and other program administration violations.

Consider the problems that emerged within the last few years. The University of Georgia admitted to manipulating grade reports to permit players to compete (Bowen, 1986). At least three Texas universities—Texas Christian, Southern Methodist, and Texas A&M—were placed on probation because student-athletes received illegal payments (McNabb, 1986). Barry Switzer resigned from his head coaching position at the University of Oklahoma amid reports of illegal activities by several football players. Despite placing programs on probation and forcing SMU to abandon its football program, neither the NCAA nor selected university administrations have been able to control certain athletic programs. In 1995, *Sports Illustrated* reviewed in great detail the excesses of the University of Miami's football program. The problems were so severe that the magazine's story called the program "Broken Beyond Repair" and called upon its president to terminate the football team (Wolff, 1995). Point-shaving scandals have emerged at Northwestern University and cheating was recently disclosed at the University of Minnesota. Are these problems and issues worth the gains that UTA's former president hoped to achieve? Are sports needed to develop a "real" university?

Sports and imagery can be a sort of double-edged sword even if one believes that hosting winning teams does attract economic development. James Edward Miller, in his wonderful history of the Baltimore Orioles, noted that longtime sports scribe Roger Angell frequently described a "deep pessimism" that was part of the city of Baltimore during its teams' repeated losses to New York baseball, football, and basketball teams (1990: 153). Residents of Boston long have had to live with the repeated failures of the Boston Red Sox, which many link to the trade of Babe Ruth to the hated

Yankees in the 1920s. That legacy, however, has had little negative impact on the rise and fall of Boston's economy over the years and the (continuing) staggering importance of its educational, health, and finance centers. Boston's redevelopment and revitalization also seem to have continued without many sports championships.

The facilities built for sports teams and events, because of their size and the number of people they attract, also have become defining elements or architectural statements for many cities and regions. While the Roman Coliseum remains one of the important legacies of Imperial Rome, the facilities built by cities throughout the world generate substantial levels of civic pride. Popular author James A. Michener was among the first to emphasize the levels of civic pride generated by these new facilities. Maybe public stadiums are even a required part of the definition of a city. In *Sports in America* Michener noted:

> The real reason is that a city needs a big public stadium because that's one of the things that distinguishes a city. I would not elect to live in a city that did not have a spacious public building in which to play games, and as a taxpayer I would be willing to have the city use my dollars to help build such a stadium, if that were necessary. I am therefore unequivocally in support of public stadiums.

Ah, but isn't that the heart of the matter? Is it necessary? Michener continues:

> My reasons are not all pragmatic. I believe that each era of civilization generates its peculiar architectural symbol, and that this acquires a spiritual significance far beyond its mere utilitarian purpose. First we had the Age of Pyramids in which I would include such edifices as the ziggurat in Babylon, Borobudur in Java, and Angkor Wat in Cambodia. . . . Those societies which built well in this age of mas-

sive structures are well remembered. . . . Then came the Age of Temples, symbolized by the Parthenon, followed by the Age of Stadia, symbolized by the Coliseum (Rome). Then came the glorious Age of Cathedrals, and much later the Age of Bridges when flying arches were thrown across all the rivers of the world. One of the best periods, architecturally, was the Age of the Railroad Stations.

Michener's observations may ring with more truth today when cities across North America use sport facilities to establish their identities, anchor development, and lead redevelopment efforts. For more than twenty-five years sports facilities have been presented to voters and taxpayers as packages to "establish identities," "make us big league," "define our city," "give character to our city," and to "redevelop," "invigorate," "stimulate," or "rebuild" downtowns, declining areas, or faltering economies.

In 1974, Indianapolis launched the redevelopment of its downtown area with the building of Market Square Arena (home to the NBA's Pacers) to anchor the eastern edge of the then-new downtown. Slightly more than two decades later, Indianapolis completed its redevelopment with a new baseball stadium for its minor league team on the downtown's western edge and across the street from the RCA Dome, home of the NFL's Colts. Likewise, Cleveland's Gateway Economic Redevelopment Corporation led efforts to rebuild downtown Cleveland with two new sports facilities, a restaurant and entertainment district, and a mall. Temple University's president and Philadelphia's mayor were both interested in redeveloping north Philadelphia in 1995 through the construction of at least one new sports facility for the university's teams.

Basking in the architectural and critical acclaim for the "Ballpark in Arlington," a facility cast in the nostalgic mode of Baltimore's Camden Yards and home to MLB's Texas Rangers,

Arlington, Texas's civic leadership was eager to build another facility for an NBA team, Dallas's Mavericks, and for the NHL's Dallas Stars. The city's leaders wanted to build this second facility to continue to foster Arlington's reputation as a sports and recreation capital. The watershed for the latest round of sports as a redevelopment tool was Oriole Park at Camden Yards, which capped that city's redevelopment of its Inner Harbor. Baltimore's effort may have been a particularly significant factor in continuing society's preoccupation with sports and encouraging teams to push cities to build architectural statements for their new home-court advantages.

How Far Will a City Go for Civic Pride?
The St. Louis Rams

St. Louis lost its football team, the Cardinals, to Phoenix in 1988. In 1993 the NFL decided to add two new teams, and many believed St. Louis would receive one of these franchises as compensation for the Cardinals. Problems with the establishment of a local ownership group in St. Louis encouraged the NFL to award its new franchises to Charlotte, North Carolina, and Jacksonville, Florida. That left St. Louis with no hope for a team unless they could persuade an existing franchise to relocate. To establish itself as a potential home for an existing team, the city of St. Louis and St. Louis County, with help from the state, built a $260+ million domed stadium.

To entice the Rams from Anaheim, the city and county of St. Louis offered the team a wonderful lease for use of their new dome. The St. Louis Rams would receive 100 percent of all concession revenues, 75 percent of advertising income from the facility, and 90 percent in any year that more than $6 million in advertising income was earned. A local corporate group guaranteed that 85 percent of the luxury boxes and club seats would be sold for fifteen years and the Rams could keep all of this income. Through the sale of seat options to prospective fans, the city and county of St. Louis also agreed to provide the funds to pay the team's indemnity to Anaheim, all moving expenses, and the costs associated with building a practice facility. The Rams received twelve hundred parking spots for each game at a cost of $2 per spot as well, and could distribute or sell these as they desired.

For all these incentives or provisions, the Rams pay an annual rent of $250,000 and between $250,000 and $300,000 for game-day expenses associated with the use of the facility. There is the potential for the Rams to "cover" the annual cost of their lease from the advertising they sell in the stadium built for them with taxpayers' funds.

If the present value of the Rams' costs for use of the stadium through 2016 are calculated in 1995 dollars, their investment ranges from $39.1 million (using a 6 percent discount rate) to $30.6 million (using an 8 percent discount rate). This amounts to either 15 percent of the public sector's investment (at the 6 percent rate) or 11.8 percent (at an 8 percent discount rate). Some have estimated the total cost to state and local taxpayers for attracting the Rams to St. Louis to be $720 million (Burstein and Rolnick, 1995).

SPORTS AND A GROWTH COALITION

On one philosophical point I am adamant. Ninety-nine out of the hundred greatest buildings in world history—pyramids, Parthenon, Chartres Cathedral, Rockefeller Center—would never have been built if approval from the general public had been required. You cannot construct a beautiful city by plebiscite; someone with vision must force the issue, override trivial objections, and ensure that the job is finished artistically. Therefore, I would not want the building of great stadiums to be subjected to picayune supervision by the general public. Let the project be explained,

justified, and funded honestly, then let the men and women of vision proceed with the actual work.

James A. Michener, *Sports in America*

Cleveland entered the 1980s having just come out of fiscal default (in 1978
it was the first major American city to default on its fiscal obligations since
the Depression) with the realization that its old industrial economy was no
longer viable. Service industries such as banks, hospitals, restaurants, entertainment facilities, and hotels would now be the core of the economy.
Sports would be a critical ingredient in two ways: a winning team would
boost the city's image through its national exposure, and also bring needed
revenues to the community. The place of sports in civic life had come 180
degrees from its origins. Play was now work, and sporting pastimes were
economic products of greater or equal value than previous products such
as agricultural crops, or the iron and steel produced by Cleveland's once
vast mills. By the end of the decade many believed the city had achieved a
renaissance as it escaped default. New construction projects filled the
downtown area, and Cleveland earned national recognition as an "All
American City."

John J. Grabowski, *Sports in Cleveland*

There is a great deal of money to be made from the stadiums and
arenas that cities and states build to attract and retain teams.
There are bonds to be sold that create income for lawyers and the
financial community. There is land to be purchased and developed, and that means money for banks, real estate developers,
landowners, and lawyers. When facilities are built, frequently the
land adjacent to the arena or stadium escalates in value. There is
profit to be made here, too. As already noted, the local media also
will benefit from the location of a team. And then there is the increase in value that the team owners enjoy. When new facilities
are built, the value of teams usually increases, and the increases
are quite substantial. The value of the Texas Rangers, as estimated
by *Financial World*, increased from $106 million to $174 million
(1997) after the Ballpark in Arlington opened. This represented a
64.2 percent increase in the wealth of the team's owners. The
ownership of the Cleveland Indians enjoyed a similar return after

Jacobs Field opened. In 1993 that team's value was estimated to be $81 million; it was $100 million in 1994, an increase of 23.5 percent, and then jumped to $175 million in 1997. The owners of the Phoenix Suns saw the value of their investment increase from $71 million to $108 million after the opening of the America West Arena, and then to $220 million in 1997. This represented a 209.8 percent increase in the value of the team. The value of the Dallas Mavericks and Dallas Stars also increased substantially after the city of Dallas agreed to provide a subsidy of $125 million to build a new arena for the teams. According to John Wilson in *Playing by the Rules:*

> As capitalist firms grow in size and strategic importance, they become more public than private, forcing the state and local governments to consider them more as partners than as private actors. . . . This convergence of interest explains why, despite the fact that many businessmen are apprehensive about the expansion of government, they can be quite tolerant of government action when it serves their interest. Their support of the ideology of free enterprise does not prevent them from occasionally seeking help from the government when profits are endangered. The ideology of the free market does serve a purpose, however; for it allows businessmen to reject the idea of quid pro quo for government assistance. . . . Sport capitalists have learned these lessons well, lobbying for government protection (and assistance) when profits are threatened, appealing for more market freedoms when opportunities for gain arise.

The collection of financial interests that stands to benefit, even if the investment does not generate substantial economic growth or new tax revenues for state and local governments, is sometimes referred to as a "growth coalition" or "growth machine"

(Molotch, 1993). These coalitions or machines consist of the people who will benefit politically or economically from the team's presence and who use their political, social, and economic connections to facilitate, encourage, and even lead the effort for the development of a sports facility. It is also possible that the elected leaders who negotiate with teams and the professional sports leagues are themselves members of the growth coalition. This is most common in areas where mayors are part-time officials who also have other jobs. If the elected officials are not a direct part of the growth coalition, they are frequently dependent on these economic participants and their institutions for campaign funds.

Growth coalitions do provide important leadership for the development of many cities, and without such influence many medium-sized cities would find their developmental efforts seriously hampered. Yet when it comes to sports and ensuring public guarantees for professional teams, taxpayers and civic leaders would be wise to question the proposals made by growth coalitions.

The frequent refrain when cities and states are approached for subsidies is that the team cannot afford to operate without tax support. However, consider this point. In 1994 the Milwaukee Bucs gave Glenn Robinson a multi-year $68 million contract. Some NBA players, just three years later, received $100+ million contracts. If someone can afford to pay a player these huge sums of money, you can be sure someone or a group of people, other than the player, is able to earn a profit from this investment. Who? The owners of teams, those who own land in the area near the location of the arena or stadium, and the businesses that prosper from the location of a team. All these "winners" from professional sports are part of the growth coalition that pressures for tax support for stadiums and arenas. This group may include the same people who contribute to the campaign coffers of elected officials, or the business tycoons who whisper to mayors about the need to be a "major league city." We all need to be cautious when the siren's song is sung by a growth coalition.

THE IMPORTANCE OF SPORTS

Why do citizens accept and support the subsidies provided to teams? The emotional attachments to sports, cultivated by institutions that also profit from sports, have clouded their judgment and established a set of unrealistic priorities. *Consumer Reports* always advises their readers to avoid emotional attachments to any one car when negotiating with dealers. That is good advice to taxpayers and their community leaders when they deal with professional sports teams. Understand the emotional attachments to sports; be sensitive to the ways in which these bonds affect decisionmaking and logic; and try to remember that sports, as entertainment, is but one way a city can establish its image and civic reputation. As enjoyable as sports are, there is no need to subsidize them. Be aware of the growth coalition that emerges to support sports. From the media to developers you will hear calls to be major league. Understand why they make these calls and the profits they are likely to earn.

Sports are important, but nothing that has been described here could or should be used to justify a subsidy or welfare payment to the owners of teams. Nevertheless, when negotiating with teams or leagues, it is critical to understand the range of emotional issues that can surface and the institutions that will capitalize on these feelings to secure a team. The first step toward reducing the welfare that is paid to professional sports teams involves a pulling back of the curtain and an understanding that the people manipulating the smoke and pageantry of sports are presenting an illusion steeped in the traditions and culture of our society. Just as the Lion learned that he had always had all the courage he needed, despite the Wizard's admonishments we need to remember that the professional sports wizards cannot give us anything we already possess. Sports can teach valuable lessons, but so can any number of other institutions. Sports can provide entertainment, but so do movies, concerts, nature trails, bicycle paths, and countless other activities. Sports can bring people to downtown areas, but so can other civic events. Sports can be a helpful and beneficial diversion, but they do not have the power and abilities ascribed to them by the wizards and their believers. Why did we give these wizards who own teams the power to control where teams will play and where they will not?

3

The Courts, Congress, and Development of the Sports Welfare System

Professional sports teams demand and receive subsidies from local communities because the leagues, not markets, dictate how many teams will exist, where they will play, and which revenues will be shared between large- and small-market teams. For most goods and services consumers dictate the number of businesses that will exist to supply products or services. When it comes to the supply of sports teams in the four major leagues, small groups of owners, not consumers, with the help of court decisions and the U.S. Congress, have established cartels able to:

1. create an artificial scarcity of teams;
2. eliminate the possibility of other teams moving into large markets that could support more than one or two franchises; and
3. retard the development of competing leagues.

These powers lead to the subsidies that have been granted by communities that fear the loss of a team if the demands or financial whims of owners are not indulged. When St. Louis, Houston, Cleveland, Hartford, Winnipeg, Quebec, Los Angeles, and Anaheim failed to meet an owner's demands, they did lose a team. While communities spend billions of taxpayers' dollars in virtual capitulation to the whims of the leagues, Congress, the antitrust mechanisms of the Department of Justice, and most state attorney generals have chosen to ignore the antimarket behavior of the leagues. As a result, state and local taxes in most areas are higher because liberals and conservatives alike have refused to alter the market control of the four professional sports leagues.

The unilateral authority to decide which revenues collected by teams will be shared with other franchise owners and which will not be shared is also an essential underpinning of the sports welfare system. This power ensures that large-market teams always have a far greater ability to pay the salaries demanded by the best players unless the governments in the small-market areas agree to provide their teams with subsidies to offset the revenue differences. Each of the four major sports leagues has experimented with salary caps and various revenue-sharing programs to limit the ability of large-market teams to attract and retain the best players. Yet, as will be discussed in greater detail, because of the loopholes in these procedures, small-market teams operate at a substantial fiscal disadvantage. These teams then demand a subsidy so that they will have the additional revenues necessary to attract and retain the best players. Larger market areas are forced to provide subsidies because a team can move and then the leagues can refuse to grant an expansion franchise for the city.

During the last few seasons sports fans and team owners in Green Bay, Indianapolis, Pittsburgh, San Diego, Minneapolis, Montreal, Miami, Orlando, Hartford, Quebec, and Winnipeg have become very familiar with these options. After winning the World Series in 1997, the Florida Marlins reduced their player payroll by more than $30 million because local governments would not build a new subsidized ballpark for the team. During their championship season the Marlins' payroll was greater than $53 million, but the owner wanted the public sector to build him a new stadium. When his demands were not indulged he slashed the team payroll by trading the best players. In 1998 the Marlins finished the season in last place, fifty-two games behind the Atlanta Braves. If the public sector was not going to subsidize the Marlins, the team's owner had no interest in fielding a championship team. Indeed, with a payroll below $15 million at the season's end the Marlins actually generated more profits than they had in 1997. The team's fans, of course, bought tickets to see a championship team. The brazen action of dismantling a championship team through trades went unchecked by the league. This sent a very clear message to all communities: If subsidies are not provided, the baseball commissioner's office will not protect fans and taxpayers from owners who seek to destroy a team. MLB's de facto policy has become one of supporting an owner in his or her effort to secure a subsidy without regard for the quality of the team and its competitiveness.

While this scenario played itself out in the Miami area, the Yankees continued to amass more money than any other team. "Also rans" in the race for the World Series in 1997, the Yankees collected $47.4 million from their local broadcast contracts. In 1998 the Yankees' gross revenues approached (or may have exceeded) $200 million, a figure $100 million greater than at least six teams and twice as large as half of all teams in MLB. MLB did nothing to stop the fire sale of Marlins' players, and with the severe revenue imbalances between teams, more than half publicly and privately conceded that they had no chance to win a pennant in 1999.

The Green Bay Packers are another small-market team that required a subsidy even with the sharing of all national media revenues by teams in the NFL. After winning the Super Bowl in 1997 the Packers sold additional shares of stock to increase their revenues. These shares had no market value and represented nothing more than a tax willingly paid by the team's loyal supporters to offset the disadvantage of the Packers' location in the NFL's smallest market. The Denver Broncos won the Super Bowl in 1998, and then in the midst of a charge toward an undefeated season and another Super Bowl championship threatened to leave the area if taxpayers did not agree to provide them with a subsidized stadium. In November 1998 the community agreed to build a new palace for the Broncos. Despite the team receiving more than $73 million in annual payments from the NFL's media contracts, if the taxpayers did not pony up more than $250 million in subsidies, the Broncos were prepared to gallop to Houston. The Montreal Expos and Pittsburgh Pirates also regularly trade or sell their best players to larger-market teams; in years past some thought that the San Diego Padres permitted higher-priced players to move to other teams to lower costs and increase revenues. Fans of the Orlando Magic, another small-market team, endured the loss of one of their "franchise" players, Shaquille O'Neal, to the megamarket Los Angeles Lakers.

As these examples illustrate, the power to control the supply of franchises and the sharing of revenue between large and small markets ensures the continued existence of the very profitable sports welfare system. Communities are told to "pay up" or watch as their teams are dismantled or the franchises moved to another city. Thomas A. Piraino Jr., an antitrust lawyer, summarized the legal status of the four major sports leagues by noting:

> Professional sports are one of the last refuges of unchallenged monopoly power in America. . . . Although the courts have allowed

antitrust challenges to certain aspects of league behavior (such as restrictions on the free movement of players or franchises), they have not directly challenged the means by which the owners of professional sports teams achieve their monopoly profits. The owners have successfully conspired to keep the number of franchises substantially below that which would exist in a free market. They have enforced this conspiracy through super majority voting requirements in the leagues' bylaws which have prevented the leagues from expanding to meet the demand from cities capable of supporting professional sports franchises. The resulting artificial scarcity of franchises has given owners the leverage to force fans and taxpayers to provide them with billions of dollars in subsidies (Piraino, 1677–1678).

How did the four major sports leagues acquire the power to create the sports welfare system that victimizes small- and large-market cities? At a time when deregulation and open markets have become the accepted path for economic development, how is it that professional team sports remain a protected cartel? Microsoft may be required to allow programs from its competitors to use its Windows operating system, but the Yankees and Knicks can block the creation of another MLB or NBA team in the lucrative New York City market. How have the four major sports leagues been able to create virtual monopolies in the midst of the world's most powerful open-market economy? This chapter charts the creation and maintenance of the power of the four major sports leagues and how this ability to manipulate markets has been used to extract subsidies and welfare from America's taxpayers.

IN THE BEGINNING . . .

When the first team owners initially formed leagues, it is likely that few imagined these fledgling and fiscally weak associations would become powerful and profitable cartels. In less than half a century, leagues that had teetered on the brink of bankruptcy would receive unimaginable subsidies from taxpayers and completely thwart a free-market system. In a similar vein, it is unlikely that the U.S. Supreme Court believed that protection from antitrust acts for MLB would contribute to the building of an extraordinary welfare system. When Congress permitted competing football leagues to merge, few thought this would lead to higher state and local taxes.

The four sports leagues were originally formed to ensure competition and to attract other investors who might be willing to assume the risks associated with team ownership. Sports teams require the formation of leagues to survive regardless of the size of any single market. No team can continue to attract fans unless there are other teams with which to schedule competitive and exciting games. In this regard, sports is unlike any other business in that sports teams need competitors to survive. As has been repeatedly demonstrated, the most successful leagues are those that have some degree of competitive balance. Leagues in which a handful of teams dominate year after year often face declining attendance levels. The emergence of the American League and its merger with the older National League was at least partially related to a competitive pennant race at a time when the Pirates were twenty-seven games in front of all other teams in the senior circuit (Quirk and Fort, 1992).

The NFL, NBA, NHL, and MLB each sought a stable base of competitors that respected one another's local markets and were willing to stage games according to established rules and regulations. To succeed it was believed that league members had to agree to three basic principles. First, league members would play games only with each other to minimize the possibility that competing leagues would emerge. Second, no owner would move a franchise into a market area claimed by another league member. Third, new teams would be admitted to the league only with the agreement of a super-majority of the existing clubs. This gave the league members extensive control over their market area.

To control labor costs the owners in each league also attempted to limit the mobility of players. When players are bound to a specific club, salaries do not escalate because players cannot have several owners bid for their services. The concept of a sports league, then, was initially established to ensure competitive integrity (a sufficient number of teams from different areas) and to regularize the competition and the game itself. However, early entrepreneurs learned that financial success could be substantially enhanced if monopoly control over the number of teams that existed and players' salaries was achieved.

At first these initial objectives for the sports leagues seemed reasonable. Professional sports leagues were extremely fragile enterprises. When some players earn in excess of $9 million for a single season, when television networks pay $17.6 billion to telecast games, and when franchises sell for more $500 million, it is hard to imagine that teams ever lost substantial amounts of money and ceased operations. Yet the history of each of the four major sports leagues is filled with examples of teams being unable to pay their players and going out of business . Although few believe the refrain from some owners that these unfortunate and bleak fiscal times will return if the structure of sports is changed or if rising player salaries are not controlled, teams did go bankrupt and entire leagues disappeared in the formative years. This past has been used to justify the special protection the leagues have sought from market forces and antitrust laws.

Major League Baseball. There are several excellent histories of the early days of baseball. Harold Seymour's *Baseball: The Early Years* and James Quirk and Rodney Fort's *Pay Dirt: The Business of Professional Team Sports* each chronicle an early history of teams losing money and moving from city to city seeking a supportive fan base of paying customers. Indeed, one may conclude that an early goal of the professional leagues was to recruit and attract individuals who could be persuaded to invest in a sports team. In reviewing the early years of professional sports, Gerald W. Scully noted:

> Most of the National League clubs lost money in the early years, and many of them folded. Some clubs were thrown out of the league and others folded for financial reasons. . . . Of the original clubs, only Chicago and Boston survived. Measured over the longer time period from 1876 to 1900, when the National League faced competition from other leagues, the failure rate of the franchises seems high. Of the twenty-nine clubs created by the National League or absorbed from the American Association, twenty-nine failed. On an annual basis, however, about one team failed per year, a business failure rate of about three percent per year.
>
> In modern times a similar percentage of small businesses fail each year.

National Basketball Association. Early failure and franchise instability also characterized the founding years of professional basketball. Teams formed, reorganized, went out of business, and moved to other cities. The American Basketball League was formed in 1925 but collapsed in the wake of the Great Depression. In 1937 the National Basketball League was formed, but five of its thirteen member teams ceased operations in 1938 and another team folded during the World War II years. The league expanded after World War II and competed with the eleven-member Basketball Association of America. The NBA emerged in 1949 with seventeen members, but by the 1954–55 season there

TABLE 3-1
The Early Years of the NBA: The Fate of the 17 Founding Members

Formation of the NBA

1949–50 Season	1954–55 Season	1963–64 Season
Anderson Packers (Indiana)	Defunct	Defunct
Baltimore Bullets	Baltimore Bullets	Defunct
Boston Celtics	Boston Celtics	Boston Celtics
Chicago Stags	Defunct	Defunct
Denver Nuggets	Defunct	Defunct
Fort Wayne Zollner Pistons	Fort Wayne Zollner Pistons	Detroit Pistons
Indianapolis Jets	Defunct	Defunct
Minneapolis Lakers	Minneapolis Lakers	Los Angeles Lakers
New York Knicks	New York Knicks	New York Knicks
Philadelphia Warriors	Philadelphia Warriors	Golden State Warriors
Rochester Royals	Rochester Royals	Cincinnati Royals
Sheboygan Redskins	Defunct	Defunct
St. Louis Bombers	Defunct	Defunct
Syracuse Nationals	Syracuse Nationals	Philadelphia 76ers
Tri Cities Blackhawks	Milwaukee Hawks	St. Louis Hawks
Waterloo Hawks	Defunct	Defunct
Washington Capitols	Defunct	Baltimore Bullets[1]

[1]The Chicago Zephyrs entered the NBA in 1961 as the Chicago Packers. They were renamed the Zephyrs in 1962 and became the Baltimore Bullets for the 1963–64 season; the Chicago Bulls entered the NBA in 1966.

were just eight teams. Table 3-1 illustrates the fate of the seventeen franchises that joined together in 1949 to form the NBA at the league's initial meeting in Fort Wayne, Indiana. From that original group, only two teams were playing in the same city fifteen years later. Financial success for the NBA is a phenomenon of the past two decades. Prior to the 1970s, the NBA was still a small organization without a national television contract. In the 1960s, for example, the city of Chicago was unable to support a team, and until Michael Jordan's appearance, basketball in the Windy City seemed to be a risky proposition.

The National Football League. George Halas established the first stable league in 1920, but it would expand, contract, expand, and teams would move from area to area before the league emerged as the modern-day NFL. From 1926 through 1949 four other football leagues arose, but each of these enterprises failed. Just two teams from the last venture, the San Francisco 49ers and the Cleveland Browns, survived to join the NFL. In 1960 a new American Football League began play and its eight original members joined the NFL in 1966. In later years, the World Football League (1975) and the United States Football League (1985) formed to challenge the NFL, but these leagues and their teams folded.

The Chicago Bears, Chicago (now Arizona via St. Louis) Cardinals, and the Green Bay Packers are the only founding members of the American Professional Football Association playing today. Between 1920 and 1929, numerous struggling teams played in thirty-three different cities. From the teams that tried to survive in the 1920s, only one, the New York Giants, endured to join the three others as founding members of the NFL (Scully, 1995; Meserole, 1995).

The growth in popularity of the NFL began in the 1960s, and many tie the increase in fan interest to the legendary overtime championship game between the New York Giants and the Baltimore Colts in 1958. The NFL added the Baltimore Colts in 1953 and but did not expand again until 1960. In that year a new American Football League appeared, and with its successful television contract, this expansion league was a real threat to the NFL. Eventually the NFL absorbed the AFL. The combined or merged NFL added the New Orleans Saints in 1967 and the Tampa Bay Buccaneers and Seattle Seahawks in 1976. It did not expand again until the mid-1990s when the Carolina Cougars and Jacksonville Jaguars joined the league. In 1995 both the Raiders and the Rams left the Los Angeles market. As of this writing, the NFL still has not returned to Los Angeles, but the Seattle

Seahawks and Buffalo Bills have used the threat of moving to this market to receive subsidies from the states of Washington and New York. After the Cleveland Browns moved to Baltimore in 1996, the NFL agreed to provide a replacement team in Cleveland. The new Cleveland Browns will begin play in a new stadium in 1999.

National Hockey League. Professional hockey had its origins in Canada and was always much smaller in scope and scale than the other professional sports leagues. Four teams formed the NHL in 1917, but only two, the Montreal Canadiens and the Toronto Maple Leafs (originally Arenas) survived. Numerous teams joined the league over the next decade, but only four of these still exist: the New York Rangers, Boston Bruins, Detroit Red Wings, and Chicago Blackhawks. These six teams formed the NHL prior to World War II, and it would be more than four decades before the NHL would add other cities. In a battle with the expansion World Hockey League, the NHL would expand and absorb many of the more successful teams from the upstart league.

The early history of each of the sports leagues is a tale of unstable teams developing, folding, and moving, with only a few surviving. Leagues developed, collapsed, and then reemerged. Some owners, fearful of a possible return to an unstable past, have sought to maximize their options. Harking back to earlier unstable years, owners seek to limit the number of teams to preserve the possibility of moving to other locations if fan support erodes. But as Scully noted, sports franchises probably have a survival rate similar to that of many enterprises in new industries. Scully's work would suggest that the sports leagues need no special protection from market forces, yet when the Supreme Court was asked to review the economic status of MLB, the Court concluded that special protection was required.

PROTECTION FROM THE FREE MARKET AND
THE FORMAL ESTABLISHMENT OF CARTELS

The deepest roots of the sports welfare system are to be found in the arguments and logic used by the U.S. Supreme Court in its 1922 decision in the *Federal Baseball Club v. National League* case (259 U.S. 200). The Federal League had emerged to compete with the more established American and National Leagues, which had merged in 1903. The National League was Major League Baseball's first league, formed in 1876. The American League was born as a result of the National League's abandoning a vibrant market, Cleveland, which the Western League, a minor league, attempted to fill. In 1901 the Western League placed a team in Cleveland and several teams in other cities, changed its name to the American League, and began to recruit players from the National League. Two years of legal and economic competition followed, but in 1903 the two leagues joined together and agreed to stop bidding against each other for players (effectively reducing players' salaries) and to respect each other's markets. The leagues also agreed to a common championship, the World Series, first played in 1903 and won by the upstart league's Boston Red Sox. The following year, John McGraw refused to permit his New York Giants to play the "inferior" Red Sox. But in 1905 the series resumed, with the Giants defeating the Red Sox.

In 1913 the Federal League was formed to compete with the now established combination of the National and American Leagues known as MLB. In 1914 the Federal League began play with eight teams. Indianapolis won the initial pennant, finishing just ahead of the Chicago Whales. Baltimore, Buffalo, Brooklyn, Kansas City, Pittsburgh, and St. Louis also had franchises in the new league. With attendance levels matching those in the American and National Leagues, the Federal League escalated its pursuit of stars. The 1915 season began with the franchise from Indianapolis playing in a larger market—Newark, New Jersey—and the two leagues suing each other in Judge Keneshaw Landis's court. Judge Landis, soon to become commissioner of MLB, urged the leagues to resolve their differences. Since both leagues were suffering from rising player costs and feared declining attendance if a war did occur in Europe, a compromise was reached in December 1915. The owner of the Federal League's Chicago franchise was permitted to purchase the Chicago Cubs, and the owner of the St. Louis franchise purchased the Browns. The owners of clubs in the National and American Leagues also agreed to pay large sums of money to the owners of Federal League franchises in exchange for dissolution of the league and the auctioning of players to the remaining teams.

This settlement did not satisfy the owners of the Baltimore franchise. As the remaining Federal League franchise, the plaintiff was known as Federal Baseball Club. The plaintiffs argued that owners of clubs in the National League conspired with some owners in the Federal League to both monopolize baseball and convince other Federal League franchise owners to abandon the league. The trial court found the defendants in violation of the Sherman Anti-Trust Act and awarded the Baltimore franchise owners the $80,000 requested, which was trebled under the provisions of the act. The defendants appealed, and a higher court reversed the original decision, arguing that baseball was not commerce as defined by the Sherman Act. The Baltimore club appealed this ruling to the U.S. Supreme Court, which affirmed the decision of the appellate court. Justice Oliver Wendell Holmes wrote the fateful words that baseball was not subject to the reach of the Sherman Act. Interstate commerce, it was argued, was not required for the commerce of baseball but was ancillary to the primary purpose of baseball. The primary purpose of MLB was the provision of exhibitions that were purely state affairs and "not a subject of commerce." Speaking for a unanimous Supreme Court, Justice Holmes wrote:

The fact that in order to give the exhibitions the Leagues must induce free persons to cross state lines and must arrange and pay for their doing so is not enough to change the character of the business. . . . Transport is a mere incident, not the essential thing. That to which it is incident, the exhibition, although made for money would not be called trade or commerce in the commonly accepted use of those words.

Thus, MLB was established as a legally protected cartel able to establish its own rules outside the bounds of free-market pressures. Justice Holmes's arguments also spoke to the need for teams to work together to obtain balance and maintain the existence of competitive teams. The idea that a league actually was comprised of rivals on the field who had to cooperate to ensure exciting on-the-field contests and pennant races was firmly planted in the psyche of jurists and legislators alike.

Congressional Inaction

With MLB protected by a broad U.S. Supreme Court ruling, the only way for market forces to influence the supply of baseball teams would be for Congress to amend the Sherman Anti-Trust Act and define baseball as a form of commerce. Congress's failure to act was interpreted by lower courts as evidence of its explicit acceptance of Justice Holmes's opinions and the logic that defined professional sports as a special and peculiar business unlike any other. In a 1953 case, *Toolson v. New York Yankees* (346 U.S. 356), the Supreme Court clearly put the ball in Congress's court. Referring to Justice Holmes's opinion declaring that professional baseball did not fit Congress's definition of commerce, the majority declared (346 U.S. 357):

Congress has had the ruling under consideration but has not seen fit to bring such business (Major League Baseball) under these (Sherman Anti-Trust) laws by legislation having prospective effect. The business has thus been left for thirty years to develop, on the understanding that it was not subject to existing antitrust legislation.

If Congress misunderstood Justice Holmes's message in 1922, the Court did not mince any words in 1953. If MLB was to be placed under the framework of an open market as were other businesses, then Congress needed to enact legislation that specifically defined baseball as commerce. The Toolson case was decided in favor of the Yankees and MLB.

Legislation to create a free and open market for professional sports has never been passed by Congress; in fact, when Congress has acted, it has been to extend protections to the sports leagues despite more recent Court decisions to limit the market exemptions given to the leagues. Ironically, although it was the Supreme Court that first created the anti–free market problem, Congress has emerged as the key obstacle in the development of an open-market concept to protect taxpayers and sports fans. Although no court has completely reversed the logic used to establish sports as a peculiar business deserving of special legal protections, numerous judges have noted that current circumstances dictate that professional sports share far more similarities with other businesses than Justice Holmes believed.

The Courts and a Free Market for Sports

Judicial support for a free-market concept for sports has been underscored through subsequent decisions that have (1) refused to extend protection from antitrust actions that MLB enjoyed to other leagues and (2) limited the scope of matters related to MLB that were exempt from the Sherman Anti-Trust Act. Despite these judicial actions during the last forty years, Congress has refused to pass any laws protecting taxpayers, sports fans, and cities from the antimarket behavior of the sports leagues.

The first effort by the Supreme Court to restrict the extent to which sports leagues would be exempt from the provisions of the Sherman Anti-Trust Act involved the NFL. In 1957, *Radovitch v. National Football League* (352 U.S. 445) tested the application of the antitrust laws to the NFL. Justice Tom C. Clark, writing for the majority, noted that Congress still had failed to act in terms of limiting the antitrust exemptions given to MLB. However, the Supreme Court did not intend for its continued recognition of the exemption first given in 1922 to be extended. *"Federal Baseball* (the 1922 case) held the business of baseball outside of the (Sherman) Act. No other business claiming the coverage of those cases has such adjudication" (352 U.S. 451). In no uncertain terms, then, the Supreme Court put all other sports leagues on notice that it had no intention of giving any business protection from antitrust laws unless specific legislation was passed by Congress. Fourteen years later professional basketball would test these waters again. In *Haywood v. National Basketball Association* (401 U.S. 1204, 1971) the Court declared, "Basketball . . . does not enjoy exemption from the antitrust law" (401 U.S. 1205).

Congress Creates Another Cartel

The courts have asked Congress to reform the rules governing the marketplace for sports, but this advice, as well as the admonitions of congressional committees, have been insufficient to create a majority of members who would protect taxpayers. Instead, key actions by Congress have made sure that owners and players would enjoy a gilded existence at the expense of taxpayers. For example, in 1966 the two competing football leagues, the National

Football League and the American Football League, asked Congress for special legislation that would permit the older NFL to absorb the upstart challenger. Owners from both leagues feared that a merger would become the focus of a legal challenge because there would be less competition for players, thus reducing their salaries.

During the congressional hearings held to discuss an antitrust exemption for a single football league, questions were raised about the implications for cities if one league had complete control over the supply of professional football franchises. Representatives of the NFL and AFL made two commitments to reduce this concern and eliminate opposition to the proposed merger. The first commitment was to add several teams over the next few years. This promise secured legislative support from those delegations representing areas that were to receive new teams. Indeed, one of the sponsors of the proposed merger was Representative Hale Boggs from Louisiana. If the merger was approved, New Orleans was promised a new franchise, and this commitment was sufficient to convince Mr. Boggs that a "great mandate" existed for this merger (U.S. House of Representatives, 1966: 102). In terms of the commitment to add several teams, the NFL added only one franchise immediately after the merger was approved, the New Orleans Saints, as promised to Mr. Boggs. The NFL did not add any additional teams until 1976, ten years after making its commitment to the Congress.

The second commitment was to keep teams in their existing markets. Some members of Congress were concerned that without the existence of a competing league, a community that lost a team would have no option but to pursue an existing team. Owners assured Congress that they would not move their teams. Representatives Dingell and Morris reported to the committee reviewing the proposed bill that they had been told the teams franchised in each league would continue to play in the same cities (U.S. House of Representatives, 1966). Bob Dole, then a member of the House of Representatives and coauthor of the proposed legislation, reported that he, too, had received a guarantee that the existing teams would stay in their present locations. "According to their testimony, professional football operations will be preserved in the 23 cities and 25 stadiums where such operations are presently conducted" (U.S. House of Representatives, 1966: 109). The owners of the Oakland Raiders, Los Angeles Rams, Houston Oilers, St. Louis Cardinals, and Cleveland Browns would refuse to honor this commitment, but Congress did not threaten to remove the authorization to permit the merger.

The NFL and Its Commitments to Congress

The Oakland Raiders moved to Los Angeles in 1982, sixteen years after the two leagues merged. The Raiders' move was made possible because the Los Angeles Rams decided in 1980 to leave the city for suburban Anaheim. This move, though leaving a county with more than 7 million residents without a football team, conformed to the NFL's policies since the Rams' market area of seventy-five miles included Anaheim. Although the move was a minor relocation within an existing market area, the residents of Los Angeles County were now without a football team less than fifteen years after the NFL had made a commitment to Congress that its teams would remain in their existing locations and stadiums. Without a competitive league able to place a team in Los Angeles, local leaders turned their attention to existing teams that might be interested in moving to the county's Memorial Coliseum.

The Oakland Raiders accepted an offer by Los Angeles and moved into the coliseum in 1982. The NFL opposed the move by the Raiders, but the team prevailed in a long legal battle. The Raiders argued that the league and the other team owners did not have the authority to refuse their right to relocate even if they were moving within the boundaries of another team's market. On subsequent occasions the NFL's leadership would suggest that Congress should grant it the authority to restrict team movements to protect cities and taxpayers from unjustified moves. While such power would indeed constrain movement, a free market for football also would protect Los Angeles without the creation of detailed and complex laws to constrain market behavior. For example, if an NFL owner wished to leave a vibrant market, a competing league could place a new team in that area. Indeed, the American Football League existed because the NFL had failed to award franchises to several large cities. The lack of monopoly control offers far more protection for cities than any set of rules and regulations to expand the powers of a professional sports league. In addition, with no competitive league from which it could hope to secure a team, Los Angeles's leadership had no option but to lure an existing team to its vacant stadium by offering greater subsidies than the Raiders received from Oakland.

The Raiders' move illustrated the profits that could be earned by simply moving to cities that had yet to receive a new franchise. St. Louis lost its team to Phoenix in 1988, and when the NFL denied St. Louis's application for a new franchise in the early 1990s, the city had no option but to pursue an existing team. The Los Angeles Rams decided to fill that void and moved to Missouri. The Rams received an extraordinary lease for use of a new domed stadium built by the public sector in downtown St. Louis and even secured additional monetary inducements.

The Cleveland Browns and Houston Oilers were the next to follow the example of the Rams and Raiders. Art Modell, owner of the Cleveland Browns, opposed awarding an NFL franchise to the city of Baltimore and then accepted a spectacular set of incentives to move his team to the city (Morgan, 1997). Denied a new franchise, Baltimore had no option but to offer an existing NFL team an extraordinary set of incentives to relocate. Nashville, also denied a franchise in the 1990s, made a similar offer to encourage the Oilers to move from Houston. Currently, Birmingham, another city denied a franchise by the NFL, is preparing to build a facility that will become the next viable option for an NFL team seeking to use the league's failure to expand to increase its revenues. Houston and Los Angeles were bidding to be home to the NFL's thirty-second team. The city ignored in this round of franchise expansions would likely become interested in providing a subsidy to induce an existing team to relocate.

The NFL Cartel and the Media

The 1966 merger also left the NFL with two television partners, CBS (NFL games) and NBC (AFL games). If ABC, the third network at that time, could be part of a "television package," the opportunities for a start-up league would be virtually eliminated. Television revenue is essential for a team to earn the funds needed to attract and retain high-quality players; if all networks preferred to work with the NFL, then there never would be an environment in which a new league could challenge the NFL's monopoly position. After both CBS and NBC refused to accept a weeknight telecast each week of an NFL game, ABC was brought into the league's television fold with the Monday Night Football game. In later years, following the emergence of new cable television networks, TNT and ESPN would be drawn into the package. The Fox network replaced CBS as the home of NFC games in the early 1990s, and four years later, CBS unseated NBC for the rights to the AFC. ABC and ESPN, now owned by the same entity, joined together to eliminate TNT from the package. Although NBC and

TNT could be identified as possible network homes for a new football league, the fiscal strength of the NFL, as a result of its media contracts, makes the development of a new league an unlikely outcome.

The NFL's new television contract assures *each* league member more than $73 million each year. Approximately two thirds of these revenues are dedicated to player salaries, substantially raising the costs for any investors wishing to start a new league. With revenues of this magnitude for salaries, few, if any, high-quality athletes would elect to join a new league that would struggle in an effort to raise funds that would match those available to NFL teams and their players.

In the late 1980s, when the NFL worked with just three networks, some investors did try to challenge the NFL through the creation of the United States Football League (USFL). At first the USFL played their games in the spring to avoid direct competition with the NFL. Americans prefer their football in the fall, however, and a move toward direct competition was made when the USFL planned to play its games at the same time as the NFL. Since the revenue earned by the NFL from its television contracts gave it greater resources to attract the best players, the USFL needed television revenues to compete for them. But with the major networks enjoying a profitable relationship with the NFL, there was no incentive for them to deal with an upstart league. In addition, with inferior players because of a lack of funds, the USFL could attract neither fans nor substantial network interest. This situation created an unfair advantage for the NFL that the new league sought to change through a legal challenge to the NFL's contracts with the major networks.

The USFL's claim for a summary judgment was denied. In reaching its decision the federal court noted that previous actions by Congress gave the NFL the right to have contracts with more than one network. The court noted that a proposal to amend legislation involved with the telecast of games so that a league could not enter "into a package with more than one network" was rejected by Congress *(United States Football League v. National Football League,* 634 F. 1155, 1986: 7). When the USFL was unable to prove a conspiracy existed to restrain its success, it was not awarded any punitive damages from the NFL. The USFL then folded and left the NFL with its protected market position intact.

The NBA As a Cartel

The National Basketball Association (NBA) and the American Basketball Association (ABA) were the next leagues to seek permission to merge. The situation confronting these competing organizations was quite different from the environment in which the AFL and NFL sought to merge. The NBA's players, fearing the loss of income from a merger, sued to prohibit the competition for athletes. The judge hearing the case issued a preliminary injunction to stop any discussions of a merger, and then relaxed this order under the condition that the players' representatives be part of the negotiation. A bill to permit the merger was introduced in Congress in 1971, and before action could be taken, the parties involved came to an agreement. Four teams from the ABA would join the NBA and the players would receive sufficient protection of their interests. Several communities, however, including Louisville, St. Louis, and Richmond (Virginia), lost their teams.

With the players and owners satisfied, Congress dropped its consideration of the bill, believing that the merger was in the best interests of the sport and the fans. A prime issue in the merger discussion was the financial health of professional basketball. For years several ABA franchises had encountered substantial financial problems, and the overall fiscal health of the ABA and professional basketball dominated the discussions in Congress. Roger Noll and Benjamin Okner testified before the Senate Judiciary Committee that the proposed merger would not address any of the fiscal problems confronting professional basketball. The key to basketball's fiscal future involved a sharing of revenues between large- and small-market teams. Although legislation was drafted proposing that revenues be shared so that visiting teams would receive 30 percent of all ticket revenues, no such plan was developed by the team owners and players. Senator Sam Ervin's committee thought that the "merger should do more than simply create lucrative monopoly rights beyond the reach of the antitrust laws or public regulation" (U.S. Senate, 1972: 5). The NBA permits home teams to retain all revenues, and the merger plan accepted by the court included no revenue-sharing program. Currently, teams in the NBA do not share revenues, and there is no protection for small-market teams from the inherent market size advantages granted to teams in New York, Chicago, Los Angeles, and other large population centers. As Noll and Okner noted more than twenty-five years ago, "Each additional one million population in a team's home area is worth 58,000 additional spectators" (U.S. Senate, 1972: 401). When Congress refused to take any action, revenue sharing in the NBA died. Taxpayers in small-market cities later would learn the cost of Congress's de facto acceptance of the agreement between the players and owners, and the formation of the NBA as a cartel.

THE EFFECTS OF THE LEAGUE'S POWERS

The Supreme Court established MLB as the first sports cartel. Congress then permitted the AFL and the NFL to merge, and a court-approved plan, fully endorsed by Congress, established the NBA as the third of the great sports cartels. Have there been any negative consequences from the market protections given these leagues? For example, do the leagues actually constrain the supply of teams? If they do not, then no city or sports fan is any worse off with the market protections given to the leagues. The sports leagues also were given certain protections from market forces to ensure that small-market teams could be both profitable and competitive. Have the leagues developed policies to fulfill these commitments to protect the interests of cities, their sports fans, and taxpayers?

There are clear incentives for all owners to restrict the supply of teams. As long as the supply of teams is less than the number of cities that want one, owners can bargain for the best possible deals from different communities. With the leagues having both incentives and unlimited power to limit the number of franchises, it is reasonable to expect that fewer franchises would exist under market-controlled conditions than would exist in a free market. Does theory predict reality?

The ability of any community to support a team is a function of its population size and the wealth of its residents. Preferences for different sports also are quite important. In 1995, *The New York Times* performed an analysis of the number of baseball teams that could be supported in the United States. This examination focused on four criteria for each area: the number of men between the ages of eighteen and fifty-four, per capita incomes, population growth, and the potential for the sale of luxury suites. The *Times* found nine areas without MLB teams that definitely could support a team, five areas that possibly could support a team, and as many as five areas that could support at least one *additional* team. With twenty-eight teams based in the United States, the analysis by the *Times* would suggest that MLB should have at least thirty-seven teams and possibly as many as forty-seven (Ahmad-Taylor, 1995).

In 1997 the Cleveland Indians earned a pretax profit of almost $10 million, with gross revenues of approximately $140 million. The Indians play in a metropolitan region of 2.9 million people (July 1994 population estimate). If 3 million is the population base needed for a very profitable and successful team (the Indians won the American League pennant in 1997), both the New York City and Los Angeles metropolitan regions could support as many as five or six teams. Currently, MLB has twenty-eight teams in the United States. With too few teams relative to the number of cities able to support teams, and with an adequate supply of talent, an *undersupply* of teams exists, increasing the competition for franchises and raising the level of subsidies that cities are willing to provide.

If one focused only on the increased population in the United States, there also would appear to be too few teams. There are nine metropolitan areas with populations larger than the smallest area with an MLB baseball team. This would suggest that the current U.S. population is large enough to support at least thirty-three major league baseball teams. In the NFL, Buffalo is the smallest market with an NFL team, but fourteen other metropolitan areas with larger populations are without teams. As many as forty-two NFL teams could be supported if population was the only factor considered. The increased population of North America, combined with the participation of minority athletes as well as those from South America, the Caribbean nations, and Europe, in each of the major sports leagues also has added to the supply of talented players. There actually are fewer professional athletes today per one hundred thousand people than there were fifty years ago; there is more than an adequate supply of talent to fill rosters of new teams in each of the four major sports leagues.

The Distribution of Revenue

The distribution of revenue is as important as the supply of teams to the issue of subsidies for sports. If the leagues fail to adequately share revenues among large- and small-market teams, then fans in smaller areas either will have to pay far higher ticket prices or pay taxes to subsidize a playing facility. These additional funds will provide the smaller-market team with the revenues needed to attract and retain the best players. To level the financial playing field between large- and small-market teams, each league has experimented with a variety of revenue-sharing programs. The NFL shares income from its substantial national television and radio contracts and NFL properties. In addition, gate revenues are shared, with 60 percent retained by home teams and 40 percent given to visiting teams. However, incomes from luxury seating and other in-stadium activities (naming rights, advertising, sale of food and beverages, and so forth) are not shared. In MLB prior to 1997, visiting teams received 10 percent (National League) or 15 percent (American League) of gate revenues. In 1997 a new revenue-sharing and luxury tax program was implemented as part of the collective bargaining agreement with players. This plan involves the dedication of 39 percent of each team's total revenues contributed to a pool that is shared equally and a luxury tax on the five teams with the highest player payrolls. In the NHL and NBA, visiting teams do not share in any revenues with home teams, but all national media contracts are shared, as is income from the sale of souvenirs, clothes, and so forth. How well have these plans worked to protect small-market teams?

Major League Baseball. In 1996, prior to MLB's new revenue-sharing program, teams averaged $66 million in total revenues (see Table 3-2). Half of all the teams in MLB, however, had revenues below this average, and seven had revenues that were at least 33 percent larger. The high-revenue teams either played in large-market areas (New York, Boston, Chicago) or played in facilities where the public sector provided a subsidy equal to at least one-half of the costs for the new stadium (Texas, Cleveland, Chicago). In these heavily subsidized facilities the teams frequently retain the vast majority of the revenues generated. (It is somewhat surprising that a large-market area like Chicago provided a completely subsidized stadium for the Chicago White Sox.) In 1996 the teams that went to MLB's playoffs had total team revenues that were $23 million larger than the teams that did not make the playoffs. The average earnings of the six teams that spent the most for players were $22.1 million above MLB's 1996 average.

The 1997 MLB season was played with a new revenue-sharing plan, but when the smoke had cleared in 1998 from this redistribution effort, not much had changed since the 1998 season began. In its annual baseball season preview issue, *Sports Illustrated*'s Tom Verducci (1998: 68) noted:

> The five biggest spenders last year all made the post season leaving just three playoff spots for the remaining 23 teams. The three clubs who got those spots . . . were gone from the post season quicker than footprints in the sea at high tide.
>
> "It may not seem that long ago that Oakland, Minnesota, and Kansas City were World Series teams," says Athletics president Sandy Alderson. "But that's ancient history. The dynamics of the game are drastically different from what they were ten years ago—even five years ago. The change is easily explained. It was the construction of stadiums with public money coupled with the drop in TV money after the last CBS contract." Almost overnight the poor [teams] got poorer and the rich [teams] got a lot richer."
>
> As the gap between the haves and have-nots widens, those clubs in between are the most foolhardy. They are the ones spending enough money to dream of a pennant but not enough to compete with the big-revenue clubs. . . .

TABLE 3-2

Team Revenues and Expenditures and Selected Community Characteristics:
MLB Teams in 1996
(all figures in millions of dollars except population)

Team	Revenues				Player Salaries	Income	1996 Population (in millions)	Public Investment
	Gate	Media	Facility	Total				
New York Yankees	42.6	69.8	17.5	133.3	63.0	38.3	19.8	Note 1
Baltimore Orioles	51.0	30.6	21.4	105.3	55.8	19.0	7.8	$200 million
Colorado Rockies	46.0	22.8	23.9	95.6	41.6	23.0	3.8	$215 million
Cleveland Indians	48.0	21.6	22.9	95.4	51.4	15.6	5.9	Approximately $215 million
Los Angeles Dodgers	31.9	31.8	22.0	88.6	39.1	13.5	15.6	Note 2
Boston Red Sox	39.0	30.9	16.4	88.4	42.2	16.3	7.3	Private facility
Texas Rangers	35.5	24.3	25.5	87.7	42.8	18.9	5.1	$135 million
Atlanta Braves	40.1	30.3	6.3	79.1	55.4	-0.4	4.4	Note 3
Chicago Cubs	28.3	29.3	16.9	76.6	32.2	18.3	8.8	Private facility
Chicago White Sox	22.2	24.3	20.9	70.3	47.5	-5.2	8.8	$150 million
Toronto Blue Jays	36.3	28.4	3.1	70.2	30.7	14.5		Can$609 million
St. Louis Cardinals	27.3	25.7	14.9	69.8	42.6	3.2	3.0	Private facility
New York Mets	18.2	30.9	16.8	68.3	26.2	11.0	19.8	Note 4
Houston Astros	21.8	22.3	14.4	62.4	28.4	11.5	4.6	Note 5
Seattle Mariners	31.0	17.2	7.5	57.6	44.3	-1.7	4.0	Note 5
Florida Marlins	21.5	23.9	7.3	55.8	30.0	2.8	3.7	Note 5
San Diego Padres	21.7	16.5	12.1	52.8	33.3	2.5	2.7	Note 5
San Francisco Giants	14.3	25.5	9.6	51.8	37.8	-6.0	6.5	Note 6

Philadelphia Phillies	18.7	21.4	8.0	50.0	31.9	-6.5	7.7	Note 5
Oakland A's	12.5	25.2	9.8	49.4	21.4	11.3	6.5	$130 million
Cincinnati Reds	14.9	21.5	7.0	45.3	45.3	-14.0	9.4	Note 5
Detroit Tigers	12.4	24.7	5.4	44.4	21.6	3.8	6.0	Note 5
Kansas City Royals	14.5	16.5	10.2	43.1	20.9	4.7	3.3	Note 7
Anaheim Angels	15.0	18.3	7.1	42.5	27.7	-2.4	15.6	Note 8
Milwaukee Brewers	14.9	15.1	9.7	41.6	17.5	6.6	2.2	Note 5
Minnesota Twins	13.8	20.4	5.0	41.1	23.4	-1.3	3.9	Note 5
Montreal Expos	14.8	19.4	4.8	40.9	17.7	6.2		Note 5
Pittsburgh Pirates	12.3	17.7	7.7	39.9	20.5	1.4	2.9	Note 5

Average revenues of MLB teams in 1996, $66 million; average revenues of 1996 playoff teams, $89 million.

Average revenues of six teams with highest player payrolls, $88.1 million.

Population, in millions, refers to media markets.

Notes: (1) Yankee Stadium was remodeled at the public's expense more than ten years ago. (2) The public sector provided land to the Dodgers; the team paid for their ballpark. (3) Atlanta Braves paid approximately $50 million for the remodeled 1996 Olympic Stadium. (4) New York City built Shea Stadium in the 1960s. (5) Seeking new stadium, or new stadium approved. (6) Building privately financed stadium; (7) Team is now community-owned. (8) Private financing for remodeled public stadium.

Source: Much and Friedman, 1998.

> Over the past decade MLB has tried to prop up its low-revenue
> franchises with innovations . . . but these changes haven't been
> nearly enough to compensate for the unprecedented revenue of
> the elite clubs. . . . One American League general manager says the
> next logical move will be to split the season into halves. "The
> small-revenue clubs stand a better change of hanging in" for 81
> games than for 162, he explains.

With the transfer of some of the money from the new revenue-
sharing program taking place in 1998, some of the hoped-for
equalization may take place over time. However, there was little
evidence as the 1998 season began that teams anticipated substantial relief or substantial penalties. The Yankees not only
signed Bernie Williams to an extraordinary $8 million contract
for one year, but they acquired Chuck Knoblach, a $6 million-a-
year player, and signed Orlando Hernandez from Cuba and Ri-
cardo Aramboles from the Dominican Republic. This spending
spree boosted the players' payroll past $60 million. In addition,
the Yankees paid other teams in excess of $3 million to acquire
the players they wanted. In a similar fashion, the Braves, Orioles,
and Indians were not reluctant to create player payrolls that exceeded $50 million in an effort to win the World Series. The five
teams that paid the "luxury tax" in 1997—the Yankees, Orioles,
Indians, Braves, and Marlins—paid a total of $12 million to offset
the revenue differences in baseball. Such a small sum is virtually
unable to change the economics of baseball.

In 1998, *Forbes* magazine published an analysis of MLB team
values, and the data in this article further underscored the differences in revenues received. Three teams had gross revenues in excess of $130 million while eleven franchises earned no more than
half of this total. Five teams had gross revenues in excess of $100
million while half of all MLB teams did not earn $80 million (see
Table 3-3).

TABLE 3-3

MLB Team Values, Revenues, and Operating Income in 1997
(all figures in millions of dollars)

Team	Market Value	Revenues	Operating Profit
New York Yankees	362	144.7	21.4
Baltimore Orioles	323	134.5	18.7
Cleveland Indians	322	134.1	15.4
Colorado Rockies	303	116.6	38.3
Atlanta Braves	299	119.6	18.2
Texas Rangers	254	97.6	9.1
Seattle Mariners	251	89.8	11.4
Los Angeles Dodgers	236	94.3	0.9
Boston Red Sox	230	92.1	7.7
Chicago White Sox	214	82.3	-4.2
Chicago Cubs	204	81.5	8.1
New York Mets	193	80.5	8.1
Houston Astros	190	68.0	2.3
San Francisco Giants	188	69.8	0.2
St. Louis Cardinals	174	82.9	2.4
San Diego Padres	161	57.6	-6.7
Florida Marlins	159	88.2	-5.5
Anaheim Angels	157	62.6	-9.6
Toronto Blue Jays	141	67.1	-20.5
Detroit Tigers	137	50.6	-0.4
Cincinnati Reds	136	50.2	-19.9
Pittsburgh Pirates	133	49.3	7.5
Philadelphia Phillies	131	57.1	-2.5
Milwaukee Brewers	127	46.9	-4.8
Oakland Athletics	118	56.4	7.5
Kansas City Royals	108	51.2	-11.8
Minnesota Twins	94	46.8	-16.5
Montreal Expos	87	43.6	-3.7

Source: Ozanian, 1998.

The financial disparity between teams was then dramatically underscored after the 1998 season. The Yankees, Dodgers, Mets, Diamondbacks, Rangers, Orioles, Angels, Red Sox, Indians, and
Rockies dominated the free agent market. Each of these teams
either plays in a large market, receives a huge media contract, plays

in a subsidized stadium, or is owned by a media conglomerate. Regardless of the source of revenue, these teams can afford to attract and retain the best players while the other owners merely assemble glorified minor league teams. The Dodgers shattered all player compensation records in December 1998 by agreeing to pay pitcher Kevin Brown $105 million across seven years. In addition to his annual compensation of $15 million, Brown also receives use of a corporate jet to transport him to his home in Georgia twelve times each season, and when on the road Brown will sleep in a suite. Reacting to the news of the signing, Sandy Alderson, executive vice president of baseball operations in the commissioner's office, was "alarmed by the terms." In fact, he was so distressed that he told columnist Bud Collins three times that he was alarmed "as a former general manager . . . as a member of the commissioner's office . . . as a fan of course" (Collins, 1998: 43). Mr. Alderson went on to note that the deal accentuates the problems between large- and small-market teams in baseball. These differences of course were not limited to the problems between the Dodgers and Brown's former employer, the San Diego Padres. The Yankees agreed to pay Bernie Williams $12.5 million per year while the Diamondbacks and Angels broke the $13 million plateau for Randy Johnson and Mo Vaughn. The rich got richer in 1998, and the poor were merely consigned to the second division. As these differences continued to grow, Commissioner Selig did not intervene to protect baseball fans in smaller markets from seeing their stars leaving for greener pastures. As teams prepared for spring training 1999, the competitive balance in MLB had been effectively destroyed.

As the 1999 baseball season began, the domination of MLB by large-market, media-owned, and highly subsidized teams was completely evident. The Yankees resigned each of their star players after winning the 1998 World Series. In addition to Bernie Williams's seven-year contract, the Bronx Bombers will pay Scott Brosius $5.25 million for each of the next three seasons. Derek

Jeter's new salary as a result of arbitration will be $5 million for 1999, and Mariano Rivera, another victor in the arbitration process, will earn $4.25 million in 1999. When the Yankees traded David Wells to the Toronto Blue Jays for Roger Clemens, the Yankee team payroll was pushed beyond the $83 million mark for 1999. Reacting to the news that the Yankees had enhanced their formidable pitching staff with Clemens, the Cleveland Indians announced that their trading days were not over; they were still going to do what was necessary to catch the Yankees.

Indeed, to win the American League pennant, any team is going to have to spend a great deal of money, as the Yankees were not the only large-market team active in the months after the 1998 World Series. The Anaheim Angels gave Mo Vaughn a six-year contract, paying the slugging first baseman $13.33 million per year. The Baltimore Orioles, in an effort to challenge the Yankees and Angels for supremacy in the American League, gave Albert Belle a $13 million per year contract for five years. The Dodgers' contract with Kevin Brown not only set a new record in terms of a player's salary but effectively destroyed the confidence in the partnership the San Diego Padres had built with local taxpayers. In November 1998, San Diego's voters had approved a $200 million public investment in a large redevelopment plan largely centered around a new ballpark for the Padres that would produce enough revenue to allow the team to compete for the best players. Within three months of the vote, San Diego's taxpayers and team owner realized that the inequities in MLB's revenue-sharing plans would still leave the team at an extreme disadvantage in the effort to attract and retain the best players.

National Basketball Association. In the NBA in 1996, twelve teams earned more than the league average of $57.4 million (see Table 3-4). The teams with the largest revenue bases played in the largest

TABLE 3-4

Team Revenues and Expenditures and Selected Community Characteristics: NBA Teams in 1996

(all figures in millions of dollars except population)

Team	Revenues				Player Salaries	Income	1996 Population (in millions)	Public Investment
	Gate	Media	Facility	Total				
New York Knicks	41.2	30.0	19.6	99.9	45.9	22.9	19.8	Private facility
Chicago Bulls	38.0	27.3	12.2	86.8	25.2	33.2	8.8	Reduced taxes
Portland Trail Blazers	40.9	22.6	15.2	86.1	25.6	33.5	2.6	Infrastructure
Los Angeles Lakers	31.0	36.5	6.8	81.3	34.9	19.9	15.6	None in new arena
Phoenix Suns	27.5	32.5	10.9	78.8	39.0	15.3	4.4	At least $50 million
Detroit Pistons	24.4	33.1	24.5	77.3	25.6	25.7	6.0	Private facility
Boston Celtics	29.8	22.6	7.4	64.6	27.6	16.4	7.3	Private facility
Cleveland Cavaliers	25.7	19.5	13.4	64.5	29.6	11.9	5.9	At least $100 million
Houston Rockets	27.9	25.0	4.4	62.8	27.4	13.4	4.6	New facility planned
Orlando Magic	27.6	25.1	4.8	62.8	39.1	8.5	2.7	$98 million
Utah Jazz	27.2	15.6	11.5	61.4	24.0	14.8	2.2	Land was provided
San Antonio Spurs	29.4	20.2	6.0	59.7	28.0	15.2	3.1	$186 million/note 1
Seattle Supersonics	26.6	19.5	3.9	55.7	27.7	12.0	4.0	Note 2
Charlotte Hornets	23.5	19.8	6.2	53.7	24.2	14.9	6.8	$52 million/note 1
New Jersey Nets	19.2	24.7	5.3	52.9	24.6	7.3	19.8	$85 million/note 1
Sacramento Kings	19.9	15.8	9.4	50.4	26.1	4.3	3.2	$70 million loan
Toronto Raptors	23.7	17.0	4.5	49.4	18.1	14.4		Private
Golden State Warriors	18.6	20.9	4.9	48.2	24.7	7.8	6.4	$28 million
Indiana Pacers	22.4	16.8	4.7	47.8	25.6	9.1	3.2	$107 million

Team								
Washington Wizards	17.5	16.2	7.0	45.9	23.8	4.6	7.8	$60 million infra.
Philadelphia 76ers	14.1	24.5	2.3	44.6	27.1	2.1	7.7	Infrastructure only
Miami Heat	17.2	18.8	4.4	44.3	23.5	4.8	3.7	$6.5 million/year;
Minnesota Timberwolves	13.6	19.9	6.8	44.0	23.9	6.7	3.9	At least $50 million
Denver Nuggets	16.2	18.6	4.6	43.6	24.8	4.4	3.8	$20 million
Vancouver Grizzlies	17.8	14.5	3.8	42.3	19.4	5.4		Private facility
Dallas Mavericks	18.5	17.7	2.3	42.2	23.3	4.6	5.1	$125 million
Atlanta Hawks	12.3	17.7	5.8	41.3	24.1	-2.8	4.4	$62.5 million
Milwaukee Bucks	14.2	15.6	2.8	36.4	24.9	-3.5	2.2	$90 million
Los Angeles Clippers	10.1	19.1	2.5	35.5	22.6	-1.4	15.6	$5 million

Notes: (1) Teams pay rent that reduces a portion of the public subsidy. (2) Renovation cost of $110 million paid by city but supported by facility revenues.

Sources: *Financial World*; Much and Friedman, 1998.

markets (New York, Los Angeles, Chicago, Detroit) or played in facilities where the public sector paid for more than half of the cost of the arena (Phoenix, Cleveland). One team that amassed large revenues, the Portland Trail Blazers, is owned by one of the wealthiest people in the country, Paul Allen, cofounder of Microsoft. Allen also paid most of the construction costs for the Rose Garden, the new home of the Portland Trail Blazers. The eight teams that entered the second round of the playoffs in 1996 had average revenues of $66.3 million, $8.9 million above the league average. Revenue differentials of this magnitude produced very different team payrolls. For the 1997–98 season, nine teams had player payrolls in excess of $35 million while seventeen teams spent less than $30 million. Differences of this magnitude when a team may have as few as fifteen players can have a substantial impact on quality and winning percentages. NBA teams do not share any arena-related income, ticket revenues, or income generated through local media contracts. The league does share its national television contract, but that accounts for less than 30 percent of team revenues. The NBA's salary cap allowed teams to spend money based on league averages for income. If a particular team generated less income, the only way for it to pay the average salary was by seeking a subsidized arena that can match the revenue potential of teams in the largest markets.

By the end of the 1997–98 NBA season the revenue disparities had created a world of haves and have nots. Two teams had gross revenues that exceeded $100 million whereas eight earned less than $50 million. Seven teams had gross revenues in excess of $80 million, but twenty teams earned less than $60 million, creating a revenue mismatch that had effectively destroyed competitive balance (see Table 3-5).

After the 1998 NBA season, team owners invoked a clause in the existing contract with the NBA Players Association that enabled

TABLE 3-5
NBA Team Values, Revenues, and Operating Income in 1997
(all figures in millions of dollars)

Team	Market Value	Revenues	Operating Profit
Chicago Bulls	303	112.2	8.6
New York Knicks	296	109.7	18.3
Los Angeles Lakers	268	92.4	24.8
Portland Trail Blazers	245	94.1	34.2
Phoenix Suns	235	87.0	15.3
Washington Wizards	207	76.5	8.2
Detroit Pistons	206	85.9	30.0
Utah Jazz	200	80.1	20.7
Philadelphia 76ers	196	69.9	8.6
Boston Celtics	176	65.0	10.5
Seattle Supersonics	169	64.9	3.3
Houston Rockets	166	72.1	20.3
Cleveland Cavaliers	161	61.9	13.5
New Jersey Nets	157	65.5	8.4
Indiana Pacers	152	56.4	-4.8
Miami Heat	145	50.0	-7.5
Atlanta Hawks	140	46.6	-9.1
Orlando Magic	134	63.7	-1.9
Vancouver Grizzlies	133	51.1	1.3
Golden State Warriors	130	48.0	-2.5
Charlotte Hornets	124	56.4	9.2
San Antonio Spurs	122	55.3	0.7
Toronto Raptors	121	44.9	1.6
Dallas Mavericks	119	41.2	-6.8
Sacramento Kings	119	51.9	-5.2
Minnesota Timberwolves	119	51.8	5.8
Denver Nuggets	110	37.8	-6.8
Los Angeles Clippers	102	39.3	-4.9
Milwaukee Bucks	94	42.7	-3.2

Source: Ozanian, 1998.

them to terminate the agreement since the players' share of league revenues had exceeded the agreed-upon level. A "lockout" began that led to the cancellation of thirty-one games for each team as the season's start was postponed from November until February. The NBA's new agreement placed a hard cap on team salaries by limiting the amount of money that could be paid to any one player. Players with five or fewer years of experience could not earn more than $9 million. Those with between six and nine years of service could earn no more than $11 million, and the most any one player with more than nine years of service could earn was $14 million. The mega deals earned by Michael Jordan and Patrick Ewing were now but a distant memory. The union also accepted a total salary cap of $30 million per team in 1999. For the 1999–2000 season the cap will expand to $34 million, but thereafter the cap will grow by approximately $1.5 million a year. Exceptions to the cap cannot exceed $3.25 million for the initial three years of the new contract.

With team and player salaries capped it was hoped that smaller-market teams with new revenue-rich arenas would be able to have competitive teams and to retain their stars. This potential certainly exists; however, the NBA's achievement of a plan to balance competition and protect free markets ironically did not involve a sharing of revenues between teams. Rather, the costs of putting a team on the court were controlled by limiting the money players could earn. Larger-market teams could still earn as much profit as they wished, and the players' access to expanding revenues would only be possible if defined basketball revenues exceeded certain levels. In the past some owners had been particularly clever in defining basketball revenue, and these skills may well translate into larger profits for teams in the best markets.

National Football League. The NFL, by virtue of sharing revenues from the national broadcast contracts and from the sale of tickets, has a fiscal equalization plan that is far more robust than any of the other leagues. However, the revenues that are not shared lead to the existence of important revenue differences between clubs. In 1996, seventeen teams earned less than the league average of $77.7 million and seven teams earned more than $80 million (see Table 3-6). The Cowboys benefited from being the team with the most in-stadium revenues and earned a total of $121 million in 1996. In 1997, the Cowboys, Redskins, and Dolphins had income after expenses that dwarfed the potential profits of every other team in the league (see Table 3-7). One other team that was quite successful financially, the St. Louis Rams, plays their home games in a new stadium that was built by the public sector. Under the terms of their lease the Rams retain virtually all revenues. Revenue differences for teams in the smallest markets in the NFL were substantial. For example, the Indianapolis Colts, Arizona Cardinals, and Seattle Seahawks each earned at least $6 million less than the league average and more than $10 million less than the teams with the largest revenue bases. Differences of this magnitude inevitably will lead to a concentration of the best players on teams with the largest revenue bases. As a result, the Seahawks threatened to move to Los Angeles in an effort to secure more revenues, but then the voters approved a new subsidized stadium. The Colts, though never directly threatening to leave Indianapolis, publicly disclosed the hardship of their position and the options that other communities were willing to provide. As a result of these discussions, the city of Indianapolis agreed to a new lease for the team's use of the RCA Dome and a series of capital improvements designed to enhance the revenue potential of the team. Taxpayers in Indianapolis will have to pay more in taxes to assist the Colts. Indeed, the Colts only agreed to stay in Indianapolis when their lease was rewritten. The new subsidies created the opportunity for the team to earn as much as $9 million in revenues that they would not have to share with other teams. Indianapolis's taxpayers, of course, were left with the bill.

Table 3-6

Team Revenues and Expenditures and Selected Community Characteristics:
NFL Teams in 1996
(all figures in millions of dollars except population)

Team	Revenues				Player Salaries	Income	1996 Population (in millions)	Public Investment
	Gate	Media	Facility	Total				
Dallas Cowboys	23.3	47.0	41.5	121.3	61.1	30.2	5.1	New stadium discussed
Miami Dolphins	26.2	44.4	20.0	95.4	49.5	20.7	3.7	$12.5 million
San Francisco 49ers	25.9	46.7	9.3	85.9	58.8	3.6	6.5	$100 million
St. Louis Rams	24.6	44.7	12.0	85.8	51.9	16.4	3.0	$280 million
Kansas City Chiefs	23.9	44.1	10.0	82.0	50.1	10.9	3.3	$43 million/note 1
New York Giants	25.1	45.8	5.2	80.6	65.4	-0.6	19.8	$78 million/note 1
Philadelphia Eagles	23.6	44.9	8.3	80.3	51.6	6.7	7.7	$50 million/note 1
Chicago Bears	22.2	48.0	5.7	79.5	55.8	2.9	8.8	New stadium requested
Oakland Raiders	25.0	44.8	4.9	79.3	56.2	3.6	6.5	$197 million/note 1
Atlanta Falcons	23.8	44.9	6.5	79.2	54.3	5.4	4.4	$214 million/note 1
New England Patriots	20.8	46.4	7.0	79.1	57.0	0.1	7.3	$375+ million
New Orleans Saints	20.2	42.9	9.3	79.0	58.6	4.7	2.5	$134 million/note 1
Buffalo Bills	24.2	44.1	5.9	77.7	60.7	-2.5	2.6	$180 million/note 2
Baltimore Ravens	24.4	43.9	3.0	75.8	47.8	9.0	7.8	$220 million
San Diego Chargers	23.0	43.4	5.7	75.6	51.3	6.7	2.7	$105 million/note 1
New York Jets	20.4	45.2	5.2	75.4	62.2	-8.0	19.8	$78 million/note 1
Carolina Panthers	32.5	19.4	16.2	75.1	49.9	1.7	6.8	$50 million
Green Bay Packers	19.3	43.2	7.8	74.9	46.5	7.2	5.1	$960,000
Minnesota Vikings	20.6	43.5	6.6	74.2	46.4	8.9	3.9	$55 million/note 3

Denver Broncos	22.9	46.7	0.0	73.4	56.4	0.7	3.8	$260 million
Pittsburgh Steelers	22.7	43.6	2.7	72.5	49.6	4.9	2.9	$35 million/note 1
Cincinnati Bengals	20.2	43.0	1.4	72.1	44.0	10.1	6.9	$400 million/note 1
Tampa Bay Buccaneers	17.5	43.6	6.9	72.1	47.5	8.9	3.5	$300 million
Seattle Seahawks	20.0	45.0	2.6	71.2	49.4	3.3	4.0	$325 million
Arizona Cardinals	19.1	43.9	4.5	71.1	52.1	0.8	4.4	New stadium requested
Washington Redskins	20.2	45.7	1.2	70.7	41.1	7.5	7.8	$71 million infra.
Indianapolis Colts	20.2	42.8	3.2	69.7	52.4	3.0	3.2	Note 4
Detroit Lions	21.8	43.2	0.8	69.4	47.0	3.3	6.0	$240 million
Jacksonville Jaguars	30.8	20.0	11.6	67.3	53.1	-4.8	1.4	$121 million/note 1
Tennessee Oilers	14.6	44.4	3.2	65.7	43.5	5.2	4.6	$292 million

Notes: (1) Team pays a small rent reducing the public subsidy. (2) Original stadium cost was $85 million; a state aid package passed in June 1998 provided $63 million for stadium improvements, $18 million in capital to help the team, and $2.9 million to cover the team's rental payments to Rich County. (3) Team is requesting a new stadium. (4) In 1997 the city of Indianapolis changed the lease to give more revenue to the Colts—the public costs for the RCA Dome will be in excess of $80 million.

Sources: *Financial World*; Much and Friedman, 1998.

TABLE 3-7

NFL Team Values, Revenues, and Operating Income in 1997
(all figures in millions of dollars)

Team	Market Value	Revenues	Operating Profit
Dallas Cowboys	413	118.0	41.3
Washington Redskins	403	115.1	31.7
Carolina Panthers	365	83.0	0.7
Tampa Bay Buccaneers	346	76.8	2.6
Miami Dolphins	340	103.1	31.6
Baltimore Ravens	329	73.2	-1.0
Seattle Seahawks	324	77.1	-10.9
Tennessee Oilers	322	71.5	-0.4
St. Louis Rams	322	91.9	17.1
Denver Broncos	320	76.3	2.5
Detroit Lions	312	74.2	-20.9
Cincinnati Bengals	311	69.2	1.7
Pittsburgh Steelers	300	75.1	-1.6
Jacksonville Jaguars	294	66.8	-14.1
New York Giants	288	82.3	0.4
New York Jets	259	76.2	2.1
Kansas City Chiefs	257	85.6	3.7
San Francisco 49ers	254	84.7	0.6
New England Patriots	252	84.0	8.1
Buffalo Bills	252	78.7	6.6
Philadelphia Eagles	249	83.0	13.0
San Diego Chargers	248	82.5	6.1
Green Bay Packers	244	78.8	-1.2
New Orleans Saints	243	80.9	18.5
Chicago Bears	237	79.0	2.7
Oakland Raiders	235	78.3	2.5
Minnesota Vikings	233	77.7	6.7
Atlanta Falcons	233	77.6	-0.8
Arizona Cardinals	231	76.9	8.5
Indianapolis Colts	227	70.9	0.4

Source: Ozanian, 1998.

Compared to the taxpayers in New York and Connecticut, however, those in Indiana may have thought they received a bargain. The Bills threatened to leave the Buffalo region and only agreed to stay when the state and local governments provided more than $60 million in funds for stadium renovations and local businesses purchased $11 million in luxury seating tickets. The level of subsidies to already-wealthy football team owners was then escalated to the stratosphere when Connecticut agreed to build a new stadium for the New England Patriots (estimated cost, $350 million) and guarantee the team $14 million in annual nonshared revenues. If the private sector did not buy luxury seats, Connecticut's taxpayers would purchase the seats. Now a government was willing to subsidize the team and guarantee revenues; performance or winning is not necessary to secure profits.

The NFL also has one of the most aggressive salary cap programs, designed to regulate the highest amount each team can spend for players. The goal or objective of this program is to ensure that teams with larger revenues do not attract all or most of the league's best players. However, as Much and Friedman (1998: 161) observed, "One of the most common misconceptions about the salary cap is that it limits the total amount that teams can spend on players. The CBA [collective bargaining agreement] states that the league will spend at least 58 percent of DGR [direct gross revenues] on player costs in any capped year." As a result, any team with substantial cash from nonshared revenues (which include all stadium-related income, such as luxury seating, signage, advertising, and so forth) has a greater ability to attract and retain the best players. Much and Friedman (1998: 161) concluded, "The easiest way to raise the cash necessary . . . is through the creation of stadium-generated revenue sources, which are not shared under the league's current revenue-sharing plan. The lesson here is that stadium economics play an important role in determining the chances for on-field success of NFL franchises." As a result of these nonshared revenues, there is substantial variation in the amount of revenue available to each team and the money paid to players by teams. In 1996, ten teams spent more than $55 million on their players while twelve spent less than $50 million. Although spending more money never guarantees a championship or a winning team, in the long run those teams that spend more attract the best players and, as a result, tend to win more games.

Despite the extensive levels of revenue sharing in the NFL, differences between teams still exist. The Cowboys, Redskins, and Dolphins each earned more than $100 million in 1997, but eighteen teams earned less than $80 million. Several of these teams played in new facilities in 1998 or will play in new stadiums in 1999 and 2000, changing the flow of revenues. Yet the different abilities of teams to earn nonshared revenues, and the taxes forced on cities and states to cover these differences, also began to grow despite the NFL's staggering contract from the television networks.

National Hockey League. Revenue differences are very diverse in the National Hockey League (NHL). In 1996, six teams earned more than $50 million while thirteen had revenues below $40 million (see Table 3-8). Five teams earned less than $30 million. The NHL lacks a large national media contract, so there is no substantial pool of resources to be shared. The shared revenues in the NHL account for less than 30 percent of an average team's income. Teams are quite dependent on their own local revenues, and those franchises with subsidized facilities have a potential to earn far more money than those teams that do not. In 1997, while fifteen teams earned less than $50 million, three earned more than $70 million and two others, and the Rangers and Bruins will easily eclipse that plateau as soon as their performance improves (see Table 3-9).

TABLE 3-8

Team Revenues and Expenditures and Selected Community Characteristics: NHL Teams in 1996
(all figures in millions of dollars except population)

Team	Gate	Revenues Media	Revenues Facility	Total	Player Salaries	Income	1996 Population (in millions)	Public Investment
Chicago Black Hawks	38.7	6.0	24.5	73.1	23.8	26.9	8.8	Tax reduction only
New York Rangers	36.0	8.3	20.7	70.4	34.1	10.2	19.8	Private facility
Detroit Red Wings	37.5	8.3	15.0	65.2	30.6	9.1	6.0	$57 million/note 1
Boston Bruins	35.9	11.8	12.8	64.9	22.2	17.8	7.3	Private facility
St. Louis Blues	38.1	5.2	8.6	54.8	28.5	6.3	3.0	$34.5 million
Philadelphia Flyers	34.1	7.9	8.7	53.6	22.4	9.7	7.7	Infrastructure only
Pittsburgh Penguins	35.6	7.0	4.6	48.6	24.2	10.1	2.9	$22 million
Toronto Maple Leafs	24.7	8.4	8.8	46.2	23.4	3.4		Private facility
New Jersey Devils	27.1	7.2	8.5	43.6	23.4	4.3	19.8	$85 million/note 1
Vancouver Canucks	26.3	7.3	4.8	42.7	26.5	-0.3		Private facility
San Jose Sharks	25.5	4.2	10.5	42.4	18.9	8.1	6.5	$162.5 million/note 1
Los Angeles Kings	27.8	7.0	4.8	40.4	28.4	-2.0	15.6	New private facility
Montreal Canadiens	22.7	7.2	6.4	40.2	20.1	-0.4		Private facility
Anaheim Mighty Ducks	22.6	5.5	9.0	39.5	15.8	6.9	15.6	Note 2
Calgary Flames	22.3	5.0	8.4	38.6	17.1	7.8		Can$176 million/note 1
New York Islanders	19.8	10.9	5.0	37.1	18.0	3.9	19.8	$31 million
Colorado Avalanche	25.9	3.0	6.6	36.9	21.5	-0.6	3.8	Note 4
Washington Capitals	22.1	4.7	7.3	36.5	18.5	0.5	7.8	$60 million/note 5
Dallas Stars	26.9	4.3	1.9	33.9	21.4	-0.1	5.1	$125 million

(continues)

TABLE 3-8 (*continued*)

| Team | Revenues | | | | Player Salaries | Income | 1996 Population (in millions) | Public Investment |
	Gate	Media	Facility	Total				
Florida Panthers	23.2	5.4	2.7	32.6	17.8	-0.9	3.7	$185 million/note 1
Ottawa Senators	17.7	5.5	6.4	31.9	13.8	0.1		Can$200 million
Buffalo Sabres	19.3	5.1	4.1	29.3	19.9	-3.3	2.6	$122 million/note 5
Edmonton Oilers	13.7	5.0	6.1	27.6	11.7	-0.1		Can$14 million/note 6
Tampa Bay Lightning	12.9	5.5	5.7	25.0	15.4	-4.2	3.5	$139 million
Carolina Hurricane	16.6	4.1	2.2	23.8	22.4	-9.2	2.4	$130 million/note 7
Phoenix Coyotes	11.9	4.6	3.3	20.6	22.8	-11.7	4.4	New facility requested

Notes: (1) Teams pay a small rent reducing the public subsidy. (2) Private sector assumed debt for facility. (3) City provided $4.5 million for infrastructure, $2.25 million in sales tax rebates, and $2.1 million in annual property tax reductions. (4) The public sector investment is limited to infrastructure. (5) Ticket charge reduces public subsidy to approximately $32 million. (6) Team may move to U.S. city. (7) Team will share new facility with university—team pays $20 million and public sector pays $88 million.

Sources: *Financial World*; Much and Friedman, 1998.

TABLE 3-9
NHL Team Values, Revenues, and Operating Income in 1997
(all figures in millions of dollars)

Team	Market Value	Revenues	Operating Profit
New York Rangers	195	69.6	-3.9
Philadelphia Flyers	187	74.6	2.0
Boston Bruins	185	66.1	18.0
Detroit Red Wings	184	80.1	-1.9
Washington Capitals	178	74.2	14.1
Chicago Blackhawks	170	63.1	13.6
Montreal Canadiens	167	61.8	8.3
St. Louis Blues	154	70.0	13.6
Colorado Avalanche	138	53.2	-6.9
New Jersey Devils	125	54.4	4.4
Toronto Maple Leafs	119	47.5	6.8
Dallas Stars	118	45.6	-2.6
New York Islanders	111	46.2	12.9
Mighty Ducks of Anaheim	109	49.6	6.3
San Jose Sharks	108	49.2	-2.6
Florida Panthers	105	32.7	-9.3
Los Angeles Kings	104	38.5	1.0
Tampa Bay Lighting	101	41.9	-1.7
Vancouver Canucks	100	41.8	-10.4
Ottawa Senators	94	42.8	1.2
Buffalo Sabres	91	41.5	-1.3
Pittsburgh Penguins	89	52.6	8.7
Phoenix Coyotes	87	41.2	0.7
Carolina Hurricanes	80	25.1	-13.4
Calgary Flames	78	38.9	0.6
Edmonton Oilers	67	33.6	2.3

Source: Ozanian, 1998.

SHOULD SPORTS LEAGUES HAVE THE POWER TO LIMIT THE NUMBER OF TEAMS?

The answer to this question rests on your assessment of the profitability of team sports and the likelihood that the current economic state of professional sports is either stable or likely to improve. Those who argue that the leagues should have the power to limit the number of teams point to the instability and frequent failure of teams in the early years of each of the professional sports leagues. Yet the failure rate for professional sports teams is not substantially different from that in other sectors of the economy, and few other businesses have the protected status afforded the professional sports leagues. While the current levels of popularity and prosperity for the NBA, NFL, and NHL are a phenomenon of the past three decades, the review of the various ways in which teams earn money indicates that there are many sources of income, making teams more stable and lucrative business ventures than in the past. On balance, these sources of money have established a robust and profitable sports world.

Even if some teams are losing money, a point that is debatable, the average value of franchises indicates the industry as a whole, in each of the four major sports leagues, is extremely healthy. Twenty-six of twenty-eight baseball teams are valued at more than $100 million, as are twenty-eight of twenty-nine NBA teams, all thirty NFL teams, and nineteen of the twenty-six NHL teams (Miller and Friedman, 1998; Ozanian, 1998). According to *Forbes* magazine (December 14, 1998), at least eighteen professional sports teams are now worth at least $300 million. As a result of the NFL's new television contract, the Dallas Cowboys are now the most valuable franchise in professional sports, worth an estimated $413 million. The Yankees, playing in "antiquated" Yankee Stadium, are estimated to be worth $362 million. The Cowboys also lead the pack in terms of estimated operating profits, $41.3 million, and the Colorado Rockies are the most profitable baseball team, with $38.3 million in extra cash. To secure a franchise in the NFL, prospective owners submitted bids in excess of $500 million for the Cleveland Browns. Similar bids are anticipated for a new franchise to be awarded in 1999.

To be sure, some selected teams still encounter financial problems. The Seattle Pilots, for example, an MLB expansion team in 1969, were forced to move to Milwaukee (the Brewers) after going bankrupt at the conclusion of their first year of play. The Brewers continue to struggle financially, but a competitive team, a new assignment to the National League, and a new stadium may improve their financial future. However, without a fundamental change in revenue or talent sharing by MLB, the public and private investments in a new ballpark for the Brewers will never produce sufficient income for the franchise to build a championship team. The Seattle Mariners, created in partial response to the lawsuit by the city of Seattle against MLB as a result of the Pilots' move, also have had financial problems. However, a proposed new stadium to replace the aging King Dome, which has few of the revenue capabilities of newer facilities, combined with rekindled fan interests in a very competitive team (they attracted more than 3 million fans in 1997), have made this franchise quite profitable. The Pittsburgh Pirates also are having severe financial problems and "need" a new stadium to settle their debts.

Financial World and *Forbes* magazine have found that the several teams lost money in 1996 (see Table 3-10). It also must be noted that many sports finance experts have questioned some of the figures used in the data reported by the teams and relied upon for this assessment. Scully best summarized the caution with which these data must be viewed when he noted:

> It is difficult to separate fact from fancy about operational profits in professional team sports for several reasons. As privately owned entities, the clubs have no obligation to reveal their finances. Fearing political scrutiny of their business practices, the teams tend to overstate expenses and understate operating profits in public pronouncements. Stated losses from operations are often a figment of

TABLE 3-10
The Teams with Estimated Operating Income Losses in 1996 and 1997

1996

MLB Teams	NFL Teams	NBA Teams	NHL Teams
Atlanta Braves	New York Giants	Los Angeles Clippers	Dallas Stars
Chicago White Sox	**Buffalo Bills**	**Atlanta Hawks**	Edmonton Oilers
Anaheim Angels	New York Jets	Milwaukee Bucks	Vancouver Canucks
Seattle Mariners	**Jacksonville Jaguars**		**Montreal Canadiens**
Philadelphia Phillies			**Colorado Avalanche**
San Francisco Giants			**Florida Panthers**
Cincinnati Reds			Los Angeles Kings
Detroit Tigers			**Tampa Bay Lightning**
Minnesota Twins			Hartford Whalers
			Phoenix Coyotes

1997

MLB Teams	NFL Teams	NBA Teams	NHL Teams
Chicago White Sox	Baltimore Ravens	Indiana Pacers	**New York Rangers**
San Diego Padres	Seattle Seahawks	**Miami Heat**	**Detroit Red Wings**
Anaheim Angels	Detroit Lions	**Atlanta Hawks**	**Colorado Avalanche**
Toronto Blue Jays	**Pittsburgh Steelers**	**Orlando Magic**	**Dallas Stars**
Cincinnati Reds	**Jacksonville Jaguars**	Golden State Warrior	San Jose Sharks
Philadelphia Phillies	**Green Bay Packers**	Dallas Mavericks	**Florida Panthers**
Milwaukee Brewers	Atlanta Falcons	Sacramento Kings	Los Angeles Kings
Kansas City Royals		Denver Nuggets	Tampa Bay Lightning
Minnesota Twins		Los Angeles Clippers	Vancouver Canucks
Montreal Expos		Milwaukee Bucks	**Buffalo Sabres**
			Carolina Hurricanes

Note: Teams in bold type won more games than they lost.

Sources: *Financial World*; Ozanian, 1998.

creative accounting. It is not unusual for a club, even one with a losing record located in a small-market, to generate a positive cash flow while the books show red ink. This is due in part to the way clubs are purchased. A common method of purchasing a club is for investors to form a separate corporation that owns the club. The investors lend the money for the purchase and receive interest payments. These payments are a cost on the club's books, but are in fact a method of taking a cash flow from its operations. Further, an owner (managing partner) may take a large salary, a generous expense account, insurance, and other benefits. These are operational costs to a club, but may in part represent a profit withdrawal. . . . In my judgment considerable effort was made by *Financial World* to avoid some of these pitfalls . . . [but] one should be somewhat skeptical of their estimates for any particular club (1995: 116–117).

A total of twenty-six professional sports teams had operating losses in 1996, and in 1997 it was estimated that thirty-nine teams had operating losses. The teams identified in Table 3-10 in bold type are those teams that won more games than they lost. Of the twenty-six teams that lost money in 1996, just ten had winning records. With two of these teams part of a media corporation (Atlanta Braves and Atlanta Hawks), their reported losses may have been a result of the teams receiving far less revenue than they should have for the broadcast of their games. This would mean there were but twenty-four teams with operating losses in 1996, with just eight of these franchises having winning records. It might be expected that a losing team, just as any business that did poorly in a particular year, should lose money. Of the 113 major league teams reviewed by *Financial World*, 21.2 percent had operating losses. But when "won" and "loss" records are included as a small measure of success, just 8.8 percent of the successful teams lost money. This level of performance would be the envy of any industry, including all of those that do not have the protections afforded to professional sports teams. Indeed, if creative accounting were involved in the estimated losses of any of the teams, the number of teams that actually are in fiscal distress would hardly be worth listing. The overall picture of team sports is one of a very successful industry where special protection from market forces is not needed.

In 1997, *Forbes* magazine estimated that fourteen teams with winning records had operating losses. Three of these teams, the Atlanta Hawks, New York Rangers, and Anaheim Angels, are owned by media firms and it is not clear if fair value was received for televised games and other marketing issues. The finances of the Florida Marlins also raise some questions with the team's real profitability. If it is assumed that ten teams with winning records actually lost money, then but 8.8 percent of the successful teams continued to lose money.

WHO WINS AND WHO DOESN'T

The era of the small-market baseball champion may well be a poignant part of baseball's lore. Virtually all the serious contenders for pennants and World Series crowns have payrolls in excess of $60 million, making small-market and small-revenue champions a thing of the past.

Since 1980 in the NBA, only three teams from market areas with fewer than 3 million people have ever made the NBA finals. The Portland Trail Blazers and Utah Jazz have appeared twice in the NBA finals (market areas of 2.6 and 2.2 million people) and the Orlando Magic (2.7 million) have made an unsuccessful appearance in the finals. In comparison, from 1980 to 1997, the Los Angeles Lakers have been in the NBA finals nine times, the Boston Celtics and Chicago Bulls five times, the Houston Rockets four times, and the Detroit Pistons and Philadelphia 76ers three times each. Large-market teams clearly have been more successful in the NBA: None of these teams plays in a market area with fewer than 4.6 million residents. Teams in smaller markets, if they are to compete for a championship, will need publicly subsidized playing facilities with substantial potential for luxury suite and club seat revenues. It is unlikely that these teams can share these revenues with any public-sector partner if they are to be competitive with teams in much larger markets. And it must also be remembered that the mere existence of a subsidized stadium does not ensure on-the-field success. Smaller markets must also guarantee that the luxury suites and club seats are purchased, and this can become a real obstacle for the private sector in some smaller markets.

The NFL's champions, despite the impressive revenue-sharing program that exists, also have been from the league's largest cities. Prior to the victories by the Packers and Broncos in 1997, 1998, and 1999, the last time a team from a region with fewer than 3 million residents won the Super Bowl was in 1980 (Pittsburgh Steelers). Ironically, after the Packers and Broncos won their titles, both teams needed to raise more revenue. The Packers sold additional stock that has no value, and the Broncos renewed their demands for a publicly subsidized stadium. The Broncos' demand culminated in the public's approval of a tax subsidy to build a subsidized stadium. Prior to winning two Super Bowls, however, the Broncos—and, subsequently, the Buffalo Bills— were representative of a small-market team that repeatedly made losing trips to the Super Bowl. The Broncos' partner in futility, the Buffalo Bills, recently demanded $60 million from the public sector for improvements to their stadium. This demand was met, but the team did not agree to stay until the private sector purchased $11 million worth of new luxury seats.

TAXPAYERS' BURDENS AND REFORM

Congress has permitted the major sports leagues to operate as cartels, and the leagues have used this power to restrict the supply of teams. On selected occasions assurances have been made that one league or another would protect small markets and that teams would not move. These commitments have been ignored. Teams located in smaller markets are able to match the revenues of larger-market teams only when their host communities build subsidized stadiums and arenas, and permit teams to retain most, if not all, of the revenues generated at the facility. In this manner the burden or cost of the cartel structure of sports has been transferred to urban taxpayers. Since 1985 more than $7 billion in public debt has been negotiated to build new facilities (Noll and Zimbalist, 1997). Over the next several years it is anticipated that the total state and local debt for sports facilities will climb to $15 billion (Cagan and deMause, 1998; Zimmerman, 1998). As a result, taxpayers will be paying for these subsidized facilities for the next three decades. (Estimates of the public investments in the facilities used by each team are also provided in Tables 3-2, 3-4, 3-6, and 3-8.) The burden of this debt, though small in relative terms, is nevertheless quite substantial. For example, taxpayers in the Cleveland area are responsible for more than $600 million in sports-related debt. In the Seattle region the total is in excess of $700 million. Dallas's residents recently voted to accept $120 million in debt, while the city of Arlington's voters have agreed to provide $135 million.

The available evidence clearly indicates that too few teams exist relative to the number that the market for sports or the demand from fans would support. With the supply of teams artificially constrained, cities and fans are forced to pay higher prices to have a team or see a game. Before detailing any solutions to change the system, it must be demonstrated that cities do not enjoy a financial return on their expenditures for professional sports teams. In other words, the case has to be made that the use of tax dollars for constructing facilities for professional teams does not generate a meaningful financial return to taxpayers. If the subsidies exist because the leagues control the market for teams, then reforms are needed.

4

What Do Teams Really Mean for Cities?

A new ball park represents an investment in the future. It becomes a matter of good business practice. A state-of-the-art facility reflects a community's confidence in its potential. Cities want to be regarded as big league or first class. It is a matter of pride. Major league baseball remains a significant factor in the quality-of-life equation. No community today wants to lose a franchise. It would send the wrong message to business and industry that might have an interest in it.

Gene Budig, American League President

The ability of the four major sports leagues to control the supply and location of teams forces communities to provide subsidies. Although it may not be fair, communities from Quebec to Houston to Los Angeles have learned that if you do not offer what is demanded, you will lose a team. Further, once a community loses a franchise, the costs to the public and private sectors to secure another one will be far higher than the cost of meeting the demands from the original team. St. Louis learned this lesson, as did the Minneapolis/St. Paul area. The state of Missouri and the city and county of St. Louis paid far more to attract the Rams than they would have spent to keep the Cardinals from moving to Arizona. St. Paul's costs to attract the NHL back to Minnesota may well exceed what the North Stars wanted when they moved to Dallas. These costs, as well as those likely to be borne by Houston and Los Angeles to get back into the NFL, are vivid and painful reminders of the power of the four major sports leagues.

Are the dollars spent by taxpayers to attract or retain a team an investment or a subsidy? If the community receives an adequate return on its expenditure of tax dollars and if the benefits exceed the costs, then the power of the leagues to control teams may be unfortunate but relatively meaningless. If taxpayers, fans, players, and owners benefit from the existence of four stable but powerful sports leagues, then there may well be no real issue. However, if the monopoly status of the four leagues increases taxes and costs without generating offsetting benefits, then cities and taxpayers are *major league losers.*

SPORTS DOLLARS AND COMMUNITIES: ARE THE EMPEROR'S CLOTHES REAL?

A new ballpark means security for many working men and women. It provides needed jobs and has a direct impact on the local economy. Major league baseball means millions of dollars for its member communities. Figures vary, but most clubs place their economic impact at well over $200 million a year. This, in fact, is a conservative number.
Gene Budig, American League President

Professional sports have become an important part of the entertainment business and a significant factor in the nation's economy. Not only do millions of spectators pay anywhere from five dollars to more than five hundred dollars per head to see professional sports in person, the public appetite for athletic entertainment has opened the way to multi-million-dollar television contracts for promoters, lucrative personal endorsement agreements and enormous salaries for successful athletes, and the utilization of millions in tax revenues to provide new stadiums and services for owners and fans.

James Edward Miller, *The Baseball Business*

When league officials boast of annual economic impacts of $200 million and when facilities such as Cleveland's Jacobs Field and Gund Arena attract more than 5 million spectators, it is natural to expect that sports teams generate large economic returns for a community and that the teams themselves are "big businesses." Maryland's Department of Economic and Employment Development determined that "during the 1992 baseball season, fan expenditures on such items as tickets, concessions, souvenirs, gifts, parking, transportation, lodging and other travel-related incidentals, as well as visiting team expenditures, directly supported $117 million in gross sales, $44 million in employee income, and over 1,500 full-time equivalent jobs" (Ahmadi, 1992). The Target Center study for Minneapolis's Timberwolves noted "annual spending of approximately $57.5 million. This spending level supports an estimated 693 jobs in full-time equivalent terms" (Arthur Anderson, 1994). When the city of Arlington sought to convince its voters to support an increase in a local sales tax to fund the Ballpark in Arlington, an information sheet distributed by the city manager's office stated, "The Texas Rangers currently have an annual economic impact on Arlington's economy of approximately $98 million." The city of Jacksonville and its taxpayers were told that their new NFL team would generate $130 million and create three thousand jobs (Norton, 1993). If these claims of new wealth for a local economy from professional sports are true, the tax dollars spent by communities may be wise investments. If these gains are as fictitious as the emperor's new clothes, then chasing fool's gold with tax dollars leads to nothing more than subsidies for teams and their players.

Economic Impact and Substitution Effects

Much like a manager going to his bullpen for his "closer" and substituting one pitcher for another (leaving nine players on the field), most of the spending by fans at games is nothing more than the substitution of one form of entertainment (sports) for another (leaving the same number of dollars in the economy). When fans attend games, they buy tickets, frequently eat out, and usually purchase refreshments and souvenirs. All of this spending, when joined to the income received from television and radio broadcasts, does indeed produce as much as $200 million of economic impact.

However, suppose fans do not attend a game. What do people do when they don't attend sporting events? How much would they have spent on other activities? If people who do not attend sporting events still eat lunch or dinner at a favorite restaurant, then any spending on food and beverages at a sporting event is a mere substitution for spending that would have taken place if they had not attended the event. If the people decide to eat at home, those expenditures (food purchased, energy to prepare the food, and so forth) become part of the economy offsetting the dollars not spent at a restaurant. Similarly, if instead of purchasing a ticket to a game, people went to a show or did something else in their community, then the spending at a sporting event also is nothing more than a substitution of one form of entertainment for another. What about souvenirs? Those expenditures might be additional spending, but if a fan buys an Oriole jersey instead of a shirt at a mall later that week, then this purchase also is merely a substitution of one form of clothing for another. Simply put, the *positive* impact of the spending at many sports events is offset by the *negative* impact or lack of spending at the mall or at some other recreational venue. If a stadium or arena is built and creates five hundred new jobs in restaurants near the facility, but five hundred jobs are lost in other parts of the city because people now eat near the stadium or arena, there is no positive impact, just a reshuffling of economic activity, with many winners balanced by losers.

What, then, is positive economic impact or economic development? Positive economic impact is new spending or economic activity brought to a city or county in which the stadium or arena is located. This occurs in two ways: (1) People from outside the city or county attend a game and spend money they would not have spent in the city or county for some other type of entertainment, or (2) people in the city or county decide to spend money there instead of going outside the area for their recreation. In terms of this second point, we usually refer to this growth as deflection. It is *deflected impact or growth* in the sense that instead of going elsewhere for a game, people spend their recreation dollars at home. Arlington residents can attend events in Dallas or Fort Worth, but if they stay in Arlington, then there is deflected growth.

Measuring Impact or Development

To understand what a team means for a local economy it is necessary to focus on the positive impacts. The total economic impact is irrelevant and misleading, although it is far easier to calculate. Measuring positive economic development and subtracting the substitution effects for spending that would have taken place had people not attended games is a complex task.

Fort Wayne, Indiana, for example, was considering an investment to attract a minor league baseball team to the city. Fort Wayne is a medium-sized city and the recreational hub for a region of approximately 675,000 people. Within this region, most movie houses, theaters for live shows, and concert facilities are located in the city of Fort Wayne. As a result, the city is already the site of a substantial portion of the region's recreational trade. If a team existed, how much more recreational trade would it attract, or would the team simply take spending away from other venues? Similarly, Indianapolis has a population base of more than 2 million people. Many of the region's recreational venues are located in the consolidated city-county of Indianapolis, and all professional sports teams play their home games in the city. How much positive economic impact could the city expect when a new stadium or arena is built if a substantial portion of the recreational spending in the region already takes place within the city?

Several cities that have built new facilities have found that the teams attract record numbers of fans when their new facilities open. For example, the Baltimore Orioles drew one million more fans to Camden Yards than they had drawn to Memorial Stadium in their last year at the older facility. The Cleveland Indians also have drawn one million more fans to their games at Jacobs Field. However, how many of these fans would have attended games at the older stadium since the Indians won the pennant in 1995 and 1997? What proportion of the record attendance levels at "the Jake" or Camden Yards should be considered new economic development attributable to the stadium?

Two assessments of the spending habits of fans identified how much of the spending at sporting events is nothing more than a substitution of one form of recreation for another. In 1987 a random survey of 786 households in the Fort Wayne region found that 39.9 percent had made a trip to another city to attend a sporting event. These respondents then were asked if they would reduce the number of trips they made to other cities if a minor league team moved to the city. A total of forty respondents, 12.7 percent, indicated they would cancel some of their trips. These respondents also indicated that it was likely they would attend seven games in Fort Wayne. From the model developed to predict attendance, it could then be argued that these fans would account for 11.9 percent of the revenues generated by the new stadium in this community. This 11.9 percent of the revenues resulting from the stadium and team would be real growth for the Fort Wayne economy (Rosentraub and Swindell, 1993).

A similar survey was conducted in 1988 of those who attended Cincinnati's celebration of Tall Stacks and Cincinnati's 1990 Travel, Sports, and Boat Show. Tall Stacks is an annual celebration along the Ohio River commemorating Cincinnati's riverboat heritage. The travel, sports, and boat show is an annual event with approximately four hundred exhibitors for which an admission charge is paid. When asked if the Tall Stacks event had substituted for another trip to another location, 23 percent of the those surveyed said it had. For the travel and sports show, 19 percent of the people indicated that the existence of the show deflected their spending into the Cincinnati area (Cobb and Weinberg, 1993). These people, though less likely to rent hotel rooms, still would consume meals and purchase souvenirs, activities that would have taken place in another city's economy. As a result, their spending means real growth for a city or community.

A study of the costs and possible revenue sources for a new stadium for the Pittsburgh Pirates also estimated the effect of the team on the city's economy. Pittsburgh is an interesting city to study because the community has often feared that without a new stadium the team would leave, eliminating all of the recreational spending associated with baseball. All those dollars would not be lost to the local economy, of course; instead, fans would redirect their spending to other forms of recreation. However, there would be some loss. How much?

Pittsburgh collects an amusement tax on all recreational activities within the city. A University of Pittsburgh research team compared tax revenues in the year of the baseball strike, 1994, with revenues in previous years. Their analysis indicated that 41 percent of the fan attendance at Pirate games was real growth (positive impact) for the city because 59 percent of the tax revenue was still collected during the strike year. But this analysis did not include the entire Pittsburgh region, and it is likely that some people who live in suburban areas stayed there for their recreation rather than attend Pirate games in Pittsburgh. If that did indeed take place, more substitutions may have taken place than were recorded in the study. There are more than 2 million people in the Pittsburgh metropolitan region, but less than 20 percent live in the city of Pittsburgh. Therefore, although it is likely that the presence of Pirate games does substantially enhance revenues for the city of Pittsburgh, much of that spending comes from people who live in areas in the surrounding region. When the Pirates do not play, some recreational dollars spent on Pirate games stay in the Pittsburgh metropolitan region (Applebaum et al., 1995). At the minimum, then, 41 percent might be considered a very generous "upper limit" of the revenue lost if a team leaves a region. It must also be remembered, however, that the unit of analysis in the study of the Pirates was the city of Pittsburgh. Because many Pirate fans live in the suburbs, the loss to the city's economy was probably far less than 41 percent of the spending at Pirate games.

When calculating economic development, it is also prudent to subtract the spending that would have taken place had the team remained in the older facility. In 1993, with a vastly improved team, the Cleveland Indians drew more than 2 million fans to antiquated Cleveland Stadium, but attendance was more than 3.2 million at Jacobs Field in 1995 when the Indians won the pennant. If the increase in attendance is attributed totally to the new stadium, then the maximum new development created by the stadium would be equal to the spending by the extra 1.2 million fans attending games at "the Jake." However, the spending by these additional fans was comprised of substitution effects and deflection. Removing the likely substitution effects means the real economic gains could be limited to between 12 percent of the increase in attendance (12 percent of 1.2 million), or the spending from 144,000 new visitors. If the deflection was equal to 24 percent, the spending from 288,000 visitors would constitute new economic development.

What does all this mean for a community considering investments in sports? Projections of overall economic impact include a great deal of money that already is circulating in their economy. The team or arena will attract recreation spending from other local activities. A substantial portion of the restaurants developed in an arena or stadium or near the new facility will draw business away from existing outlets. *But there also will be positive economic impact or growth from recreational spending deflected back into a local economy and from visitors.* How much of the total economic impact will be development? The answer depends on the recreational patterns within the city and region. If the city or county already is the site of much of the recreation activity in the region, real growth may not exceed 24 percent. If the city has lost its role in entertainment and recreation, the growth may be closer to 40 percent, but some of that growth will come at the expense of other cities in the region. In short, the economic impact of a team will never come close to what many proponents claim. And when one traces who actually received the dollars spent, the impact on the local economy actually declines.

Multipliers and the Recirculation of Dollars

Estimates of the value of teams to a local economy often include a weighting of the spending that occurs at a stadium or arena.

These weights, or multipliers, are based on the observation that when someone spends a dollar, that dollar is respent by firms and workers. The increased economic value of the recirculation of money does generate real economic development. Total economic development from a sports facility or team is equal to the positive economic impact or economic development multiplied by the appropriate weight or multiplier.

Total Economic Development from a Sports Team or Facility =
Real Economic Growth (Total Spending – Substitution) x
Appropriate Multiplier

Real economic growth, as discussed above, is the total spending attributed to the team or facility, less the substitution effect or money that would have been spent for another recreation activity, food, or clothes. Once that factor is determined, then one needs to select the appropriate multiplier. That complicated process is made somewhat easier because of the production of multipliers for the national, state, and local economies by the U.S. Department of Commerce and many other reputable sources. Nonetheless, these multipliers need to be selected carefully.

Multipliers are derived by studying the interactions in a local economy. For example, I live in Indianapolis. Suppose I eat dinner at a restaurant before I attend an Indiana Pacers basketball game. After paying the dinner bill, the money is used to pay the workers, provide a return to the owner, and pay for the food and other costs involved in operating a restaurant. The vegetables for our salads may have come from farms in Illinois or Texas. The chickens we ate could have come from Arkansas. The beer or wine we drank could have come from Milwaukee, St. Louis, or Napa Valley. Although our expenditure may have taken place in Indianapolis, the dollars recirculate in Indianapolis to local workers and businesses and also "leak" into other economies that are not part of the local economy or the multiplier developed for Indianapolis. Some of the money from our dinner bill might be used to pay the businesses that supplied the food and other provisions, the interest charged on the loan for the restaurant, the restaurant's overhead (dinnerware, tables, equipment utilities), the salaries of employees, or the owners in the form of profits.

Economists long have used multipliers to record economic effects accurately and fairly. All dollars spent are respent. When you purchased this book, some of the money was respent by the publisher on salaries and for profit. I also get a share of the revenue, and I respend those dollars on my children's college tuition, a new car, or maybe a new computer. Each dollar that you spend, whether for a ticket to a baseball game or for dinner, is respent several times. Parts of the money you spent for a ticket to the ball game become parts of the salaries of players, managers, and others who work at the stadium or arena. They, in turn, spend their salaries, and so on and so forth. In this manner we refer to the recirculation of dollars spent as having a "multiplier effect," and by studying spending patterns, economists have developed numbers that indicate how many times a dollar recirculates. When recreation spending is analyzed in a large city, one could use a multiplier of 1.9 to 2.0. In smaller areas, a multiplier of 1.5 or 1.6 is appropriate. Obviously, if you want to inflate the total economic impact of an arena or team, you could use a higher multiplier, say 3.0, 4.0, or 5.0, making $100 million in direct spending become $500 million or more in the economic effects from the respending of fans' expenditures for tickets, souvenirs, etc. If you want to deflate the economic impact, use a low multiplier, say 1 or 1.1.

A multiplier is not a contrived number. If someone uses a multiplier in any analysis you review, ask the person where it came from and why it was considered appropriate and valid. Also remember that multipliers are valid only for specific geographic areas. If you buy something in New York City, a city with more than 12 million workers, it is more likely that a part of what you bought was manufactured or developed in New York City than if you bought the same item in a small town in southern Indiana. The multipliers for a small town will be much smaller than those in a larger city. For this reason the multiplier for any good or service will be larger if the region or state is the unit of analysis instead of the county, city, or a zip code area. If we calculated the multiplier effect of sports spending, the figure for Ohio should be larger than the figure for Cuyahoga County. But that figure would likely be larger than the figure for the city of Cleveland (whose population is less than two-fifths of its county, Cuyahoga). The multipliers for Cleveland might be larger than the figure for a suburb of Cleveland or for a neighborhood.

There is one more word of caution that must be considered when determining multipliers for professional sports. Multipliers are based on the spending patterns of average consumers and average businesses in an area. Players receive approximately half of all revenues earned by teams, and the respending of these dollars is far from typical or average. For example, players have far higher savings or investment rates than the average worker because they know their high incomes will last for only a very short time. As a result, as much as half of the money they receive may never be spent locally and will therefore have no impact at all on the local economy. In fact, the dollars spent by fans that go to players would have a far greater impact on the local economy if they were directed toward local workers. The dollars that players save is a net loss to the local economy. Players also may decide to build their permanent residence in another state or region, further reducing the impact of their salary on the local economy. The typical worker lives in the region in which he or she works. Players also have a greater tendency to buy certain luxury items that may not be part of the local economy, further reducing the positive impact of sports revenues.

Because of the great care that must be taken to measure real economic development, select appropriate multipliers, and iden tify the appropriate base of funds to be used in the equation related to total positive economic impact, there are many opportunities for misuse and exaggeration. In 1994, for example, a study to measure the economic value of tourism to the city of Arlington used a multiplier of 3.0 for its analysis. However, the *regional or statewide* multiplier for each of the components of the tourist industry is not 3.0. In terms of the hotel, restaurant, and amusement sector of the Texas economy, the highest multiplier effect for the entire State of Texas was 2.51. That would mean each dollar of output produced $2.51 in all of Texas, not in any one particular city within the state.

Indeed, as my example of a restaurant meal illustrates, the economy of the entire nation is entwined. For any metropolitan area the linkages are quite pronounced. People work in one city, live in another, and sometimes shop or pursue recreational opportunities elsewhere. People travel to other parts of the country and other countries, spending their dollars as they tour. With all these linkages, what dollars stay in a city? Most likely in a small geographic area such as a city it will be the dollars spent on salaries.

What multiplier should be used if one looks only at salaries? Again, multiplier figures are not subjective numbers but the product of extensive analyses of any economy. Professional sports fits into the category established for hotels, amusement services, and recreation by the U.S. Department of Commerce. As the information in Table 4-1 indicates, it would seem prudent to use a multiplier of 2.0 or less for spending related to tourism, sports, and amusements. Indianapolis, a city with a population of approximately eight hundred thousand, had an earnings multiplier of 1.95 for these kinds of businesses. Fort Wayne, at the center of a county of approximately three hundred thousand residents, had an earnings multiplier of 1.7 for these services. For the State of Texas as a whole, the earnings multiplier was 2.06, not the 3.0 indicated in the consultant's report. The forecasted economic impact, therefore, was overstated by at least one-third in that report. In addition, since the multiplier of 2.06 was for the State of Texas and not the city of Arlington, it is quite likely that an even smaller multiplier would have been appropriate.

Should you use a multiplier when you are trying to estimate the economic impact of a sports team or arena? Yes, but what multiplier? As a rule of thumb, for a region of more than one million people, don't use a multiplier of more than 2.0, and apply that to the wages earned or paid, not the total output or purchases. That was the strategy we followed when we estimated the growth that cities similar to Fort Wayne could expect if they attracted teams. So if an arena or team is going to generate about $100 million in annual salaries, recall that between 12 percent and 24 percent of that is real economic growth and multiply that figure by 2. If the economic impact in terms of salaries is $100 million, expect no more than $48 million in economic growth ($100 million times 24 percent times 2).

What does a team contribute to an economy? In 1996 the Baltimore Orioles had gross revenues of $105.3 million and a player payroll of $55.8 million (as reported by *Financial World* magazine). For this example, suppose that the team had moved from Baltimore, resulting in a loss of 41 percent of this revenue from

TABLE 4-1
Earnings Multipliers for Services in Selected Areas, 1996

Service	State or City			
	Texas	Indiana	Indianapolis	Ft. Wayne
Hotels, recreation	2.0635	1.8850	1.9487	1.7043
Personal services	1.7806	1.7039	1.7003	1.5147
Business services	1.7747	1.6186	1.6605	1.4904
Restaurants	2.2061	2.0304	1.9336	1.8198
Health services	1.6553	1.5727	1.5764	1.4457
Other services	2.0744	2.0591	2.0556	1.9143

Source: U.S. Department of Commerce, Economics and Statistics Administration, Bureau of Economic Analysis.

recreational spending in the city of Baltimore. In other words, had the team moved, the maximum loss might have been as high as $43.2 million. This figure can be used to identify the maximum gain to the local economy from the team's presence. The 41 percent figure is drawn from the analysis of the changes in spending in Pittsburgh when baseball was not played in the city.

Since the players receive 53 percent of the Orioles' total revenues, a portion of this incremental growth will not be spent locally. The players' share of the $43.2 million is $22.9 million. It is likely that only $11.4 million of the $22.9 million would have been spent in the region; the remainder would have been saved by the players or spent elsewhere. As a result, the maximum increment is $31.8 million. With a multiplier of 2.0, the total economic development from the team's presence is $63.6 million. This estimate assumes, however, that the team would leave the area and that nothing would replace it in terms of what people might utilize for recreation. As such, the $63.6 million is a high-end estimate of the team's value to the local economy.

What is the low-end estimate? Suppose that the actual deflection of total spending is in the range of 12 percent to 24 percent and not the 41 percent represented by the complete absence of the team. In that case, with total revenues of $105.3 million, as little as $12.6 million or as much as $25.2 million would be the total of new dollars for the economy. If 53 percent of these funds go to the players and they do not spend 50 percent of their salaries in the local economy, then the estimates of new dollars must be reduced by 26.5 percent (half of the 53 percent). This would mean that the new dollars could range from $9.4 million to $18.8 million. With a multiplier of 2.0, the development would range from $18.8 million to $37.6 million. And all of these estimates assume that if the team left, people would not find other activities in the local economy on which to spend their money.

So what is a team like the Baltimore Orioles worth to a local economy? At the low end, the gain may be as small as $18.8 million; at the high end it may be as much as $63.6 million. Teams with smaller payrolls obviously will have smaller impacts. As a result, whether one accepts the high or low estimate, the impact of the team on the local economy is considerably less than the $200 million figure frequently touted. The emperor does indeed have new clothes, but they are worth far less, even when the multiplier effect is considered, than most touts would have you believe. In addition, if a community "invests" in sports, other opportunities may be lost. The "gains" reported have to be considered against lost investment opportunities and the returns that would have been realized from alternative expenditures.

Professional Sports and a Local Economy

Economic gains of $18.8 million or $37.6 million or $63.6 million certainly are important for any community. But how big are these numbers in a city's economy? Does this spending represent 10 percent or 20 percent of the total spending in a community? Believe it or not, this spending represents less than 0.5 percent of the economy of most cities.

Sports and teams are nothing more than relatively small businesses and "small potatoes" in an economy. Prior to the NFL's new contract with its television partners, the New York Yankees, Baltimore Orioles, Cleveland Indians, Colorado Rockies, New York Knicks, Dallas Cowboys, and Miami Dolphins were the only franchises that had annual revenues of more than $100 million. With annual television revenues of $73.3 million per club in 1998–99, each of the NFL's thirty teams became $100 million businesses. It is probable that the Atlanta Braves and Chicago Cubs (owned by media corporations) could have had $100 million in revenues if they had received adequate income from the telecast of games by their media parents. In total, perhaps one-third of MLB's thirty teams have gross revenues in excess of $100 million.

Firms with annual budgets of $100 million certainly are vital, vibrant, and valued in terms of the development of any region's economy. But businesses of this size are quite small when compared to other organizations in urban areas. For example, few would consider urban campuses of state universities to be engines that drive a city's economy. Yet in budget terms they are quite a bit larger than even the most successful sports teams. The budget for Indiana University–Purdue University Indianapolis, with its enrollment of more than twenty-five thousand students and excluding its health center, is in excess of $300 million. Columbia University in New York has a budget that is more than three times the size of the budget of the New York Yankees.

In 1992, in no county with approximately three hundred thousand residents did sports account for more than 0.06 percent of all private-sector jobs. In terms of total payroll dollars, these jobs accounted for 0.1 percent of the $1.5 trillion in income reported

TABLE 4-2
Private-Sector Employment and Payroll Levels in
All United States Counties with 300,000 Residents, 1992

Standard Industrial Code Classification	Employment as a Percentage of Total	Payroll as a Percentage of Total
Eating and drinking places	6.56	2.16
Hotels and other lodging places	1.55	0.82
Amusement and recreation services	1.26	0.94
Commercial sports	0.12	0.18
Professional sports, managers	**0.06**	**0.10**
Remaining retail trade	13.05	8.21
Remaining services	32.76	31.49
Manufacturing	16.66	21.42
Wholesale trade	7.33	9.35
Transportation	6.34	7.90
Finance, insurance, and real estate	8.88	11.59
Agriculture	0.59	0.39
Mining	0.32	0.55
Construction	4.64	5.12
Unclassified	0.05	0.07
Total jobs/payroll	55,662,194	$1,502,221,516,000

for these 161 counties (see Table 4-2). However, this tiny percentage still amounted to more than $1.5 billion.

The information in Table 4-3 describes employment patterns within counties of different sizes; interestingly enough, there is little difference by population size. Professional sports *never* accounted for more than 0.08 percent of the jobs in any group of counties. Professional sports payrolls are the greatest in the largest counties; even there, though, this grouping accounted for just 0.52 percent of the private sector's total payroll.

Sports teams represent a small portion of the economy of suburban communities as well. Arlington, Texas, with approximately three hundred thousand residents, is located between the cities of Dallas and Fort Worth, and to the south of the Dallas/Fort Worth International Airport. Since the early 1979s

TABLE 4-3

The Percentage of Employment and Private-Sector Payrolls
by County Populations, 1992

Industry	Population of County			
	300,000 to 500,000 (n=66)	500,001 to 1,000,000 (n=65)	1,000,001 to 2,000,000 (n=22)	More than 2,000,000 (n=8)
Professional sports employment as a percentage of total employment	0.03	0.06	0.08	0.06
Professional sports payrolls as a percentage of private-sector payrolls	0.14	0.13	0.24	0.52

the city has tried to develop its identity through sports and recreation services. In 1973 the city's leadership was able to attract the Washington Senators, which then became the Texas Rangers. The Rangers played in Arlington Stadium, a former minor league stadium that was substantially improved in 1977 and then razed in 1994 when the city and team built "The Ballpark in Arlington." Arlington is also home to the Six Flags over Texas amusement park, the largest theme park in the southwestern United States, and to the Wet n' Wild water amusement park.

The success of these three ventures in Arlington convinced Dallas's leadership to consider building an arena for the NBA's Dallas Mavericks and the NHL's Dallas Stars. Both teams play their home games at Dallas's Reunion Arena, located approximately fifteen miles east of Arlington, but fear that the teams would leave Dallas for Arlington helped convince the Dallas voters to approve a $120 million subsidy for a new arena that will open just after the turn of the century. Arlington's existing tourist attractions, together with its convention center, have clearly established the city as a recreational center. But is the sports industry or even the entire recreation industry the engine that drives Arlington's economy?

In 1992 the private-sector payroll for the city of Arlington was estimated at $1,885,222,215 (see Table 4-4). Twenty-six percent of this income originated in businesses classified as services. The second largest industry group, accounting for 19.3 percent of Arlington's private-sector payroll, was manufacturing, and retail trade was the third largest at 12.8 percent. The combined payrolls (citywide) for *all* entertainment, including sports-related businesses, amusement parks, recreation, hotels, and restaurants, amounted to 11.4 percent of the private-sector payroll. This made the *citywide* entertainment grouping the fourth largest industry in the city. Wholesale trade was almost as large as entertainment, accounting for 10.9 percent of all private payroll dollars.

Without questioning the potential value of the image created for Arlington (or any city) through sports and entertainment, these data underscore that sports and entertainment are very small components of any region's economy, and even in small- and medium-sized cities (similar to Arlington), the sports industry is not the economic engine some would like to believe it is. The sports industry is, simply put, too small to drive an economy.

Sports and Related Spending

Possibly the true value of sports lies in their ability to induce high levels of related spending on food, souvenirs, and hotel accommodations. To get a fair or balanced picture of the economic importance of sports, those impacts must be calculated to avoid biasing the picture. But how big is the spending on these items associated with sports?

If you read some of the justifications of public support for teams or playing facilities, the expected growth in spending at ho-

TABLE 4-4
Industry Size As Measured by Private-Sector Payrolls in Arlington, Texas, 1992
Total Estimated Private-Sector Payroll: $1,885,222,215

Industry Grouping	Estimated Percentage of Private-Sector Payroll Dollars
Services	26.0
Manufacturing	19.3
Retail trade	12.8
Citywide entertainment[1]	11.4
Wholesale trade	10.9
Other (combined)	7.6
F.I.R.E	6.0
Transportation	6.0

[1]Includes all restaurant, recreation, and hotel spending throughout the city.

Sources: Center for Urban Policy and the Environment, Indiana University; County Business Patterns, U.S. Department of Commerce, 1992.

tels and restaurants is enormous. Indeed, many justifications for tax support for stadiums or arenas frequently include the expectation of increased restaurant and hotel activity. For example, an economic impact assessment of the Target Center in Minneapolis reported that "22 new eating and restaurant places have opened resulting in new construction in excess of $10 million" (Arthur Andersen, 1994). A study of the impact of Oriole Park at Camden Yards concluded that fans spent $38 million at downtown restaurants, hotels, and souvenir stores (Ahmadi, 1992). In the city of Arlington, hotel and restaurant activity produced an annual private-sector payroll of $214.9 million. The development of Jacobs Field and Gund Arena in Cleveland also led to the opening of more than ten new restaurants and a new hotel near these projects. But just how big is this benefit to an economy?

First, back to the issue of the relative size of this portion of any county's economy. For example, Maricopa County in Phoenix, Arizona, is home to the NBA's Suns, the NFL's Cardinals, the

NHL's Coyotes, and MLB's Diamondbacks. The region is also the spring training home for several baseball teams. All restaurant and hotel payrolls in 1992 amounted to just 3.9 percent of that county's private-sector payroll. This proportion included *all* hotel and restaurant payrolls, including those produced by the convention and winter tourist trade (unrelated to sports) in Phoenix, Scottsdale, and Mesa. In 1992, Los Angeles County was home to several sports teams: the Dodgers, the Lakers, the Clippers, the Kings, and the Raiders (the Rams played in Orange County). That county also hosts a large convention center and several important tourist and shopping facilities. Payrolls at hotels and restaurants in this area amounted to 2.7 percent of the private-sector payroll. In Fulton County (Atlanta), home to the Braves, Falcons, and Hawks, hotels and restaurants accounted for 3.2 percent of the private-sector payroll. From coast to coast, and in counties of various sizes, even if we include all hotel and restaurant payrolls, not just the portion that could or should be attributed to sports, this segment of the economy is too small to drive any local economy.

SPORTS, IMAGE, AND ECONOMIC DEVELOPMENT: DO TEAMS ATTRACT BUSINESSES?

Five "hard determinants" are, in our experience and analysis, related to successful entrepreneurship. They are: (1) universities, (2) interstate highways, (3) airports, (4) advanced telecommunications, and (5) a nice place to live.

David Birch et al., *Entrepreneurial Hot Spots*

At bottom, the practice of selling places entails the various ways in which public and private agencies, local authorities, and local entrepreneurs, often working collaboratively, strive to sell the image of a particular geographically-defined placed, usually a town or city, so as to make it attractive to economic enterprises, to tourists, and even to inhabitants of that place. The chief ambitions are to encourage economic enterprises (and notably footloose high-technology industries) to locate themselves in this place and to entice tourists to visit the place in large numbers, and both of these ambitions obviously tie in with the attempts that all sorts of localities in Britain, North America, and elsewhere are making to secure inward capital investment a degree of local job creation and hence local economic (re)generation.

Gerry Kearns and Chris Philo, *Selling Places*

Many community leaders support actions to attract and retain teams because of the belief that the presence of professional sports franchises persuades other firms to locate in a community. Although a team clearly adds to the cultural and recreational amenities of a city, do businesses actually decide to locate in a particular area because of the presence of a team? It certainly is true that corporations carefully evaluate the quality of life in a community when making decisions about their location; it is also true that professional team sports make an important contribution to that quality and can contribute to or help define a city or region's image and its attractiveness. But economic factors still are the most critical factors in dictating business location.

PHH Fantus is a consulting and management firm that assists more than one hundred corporate clients annually to find new locations for their business activities. Robert Ady, president of PHH Fantus Consulting, summarized the importance of sports for business location when speaking to a group of Kansas City's community leaders at Arrowhead Stadium in 1993:

In fact, the single most important location criterion today is grouped under operating conditions. No, I must tell you now that it is not the presence of a professional sports team; it is, in fact, the availability of a qualified workforce. In today's competitive and ever-changing environment, companies are locating where they feel assured of securing such a workforce—not only the availability of managerial talent but, more importantly, the availability of skilled and technical talent. Other typical operating criteria might include proximity to an international airport, tranquil labor-management relations, sophisticated telecommunications availability, and dual-feed utility systems.

Ady also noted that sporting events are a great opportunity to bring prospective companies to a city and to highlight the city's accomplishments in the private sector. Since bringing a prospect to town is essential to any relocation process, sports can be a tool when making the deal, but corporate locations are dictated by economic factors that enhance profits.

Business location decisions seem to involve a two-stage process. At the first level or tier, firms seek to maximize their profits or market shares. As a result, businesses select locations where their costs for producing a good or service—such as those for transportation, energy, taxes, and labor—are minimized. (The quality and level of public services also enter the decision process at this stage since taxes are payments for services received from the government.) Generally, more than one area may permit a company to maximize its profitability (Bartik, 1991). The second tier involves choosing the specific location from this group of cities and may also involve an assessment of the quality of life. Sports teams contribute to the quality of life, but so do cultural events, museums, universities, libraries, public schools, public safety, parks, and civic pride.

Sports Teams and Government Revenues

Another benefit produced by teams relates to the tax revenues collected as a result of a team's presence in a community. Players and others whose jobs are dependent on the team's existence may pay property, sales, and income taxes. The team itself may also pay taxes. Some communities administer an amusement tax, and the consumption related to spending at a facility or a result of the team's presence can increase public revenues. In all instances, however, the only tax revenues that should be counted are those related to new spending in the area. Spending at a stadium or arena that would have taken place on another form of recreation if the team were not present should not be considered new taxes for a community.

The Pirates have asked the city of Pittsburgh for help in building a new stadium, believing they could earn more money and thus be able to attract and retain the best players, and this would generate substantial tax revenues for the city. When the 1998 season began, the Pirates' payroll was the second lowest in MLB. While Gary Sheffield and Albert Belle each earned $10 million for 1998, the Pirates' entire twenty-five-man roster was paid $13,752,000. How much tax revenue could Pittsburgh anticipate earning if the team had a new facility? How much indirect tax revenue would be created through the team's impact on the economy? A study by Carnegie Mellon University helped that community answer those questions (Applebaum et al., 1995).

Pittsburgh receives revenues from an amusement tax, a business privilege tax, a mercantile tax of an occupation tax, a parking tax, and a wage tax. There also is a countywide sales tax of 1 percent for the support of regional assets, and there is a state sales tax and a state income tax. If the city built a new stadium, increased attendance would affect each of these revenue sources. Attendance levels at the new stadium were projected based on the patterns for all new baseball facilities built since 1960 and the base of fans usually attending Pirates' games. If the Pirates were able to sell 95 percent of their tickets at the new stadium, their annual attendance would be 2,885,625. This fiscal analysis was based on a plan for a facility with 37,500 seats.

The total fiscal impact analysis is presented in Table 4-5. Direct tax revenues will increase by approximately $2.1 million each year. Indirect taxes from the income earned as a result of the team's presence would generate an additional $1.9 million in taxes each year. The tax revenue earned by the city of Pittsburgh would be approximately $4 million. To finance and maintain a new stadium, as much as $13.4 million will be needed. If the team made no contributions to the cost of building and maintaining the stadium, the investment for taxpayers in Pittsburgh would be approximately $9.4 million each year. The tax revenues generated by the team cannot offset the investment required by the public sector. Since much of the consumption that would take place at the stadium would occur in the absence of the team, the city's gains in terms of new tax revenues is really quite small.

Relatively small tax gains are obtained from minor league teams as well. In 1989, Fort Wayne, Indiana, a medium-sized city, considered a small investment, approximately $2 million, in a stadium for a Class A minor league team. Fort Wayne had had a long and impressive history as a "sports city" prior to the 1950s. Its Zollner Pistons (the Zollner company actually does manufacture pistons) was one of the charter members of the NBA, but it moved to Detroit in 1957 despite receiving a new arena that the team had demanded from Allen County (Fort Wayne). The movement of the Zollner Pistons, one of the first moves by a team from a city with a history of supporting its franchise, to a larger community, Detroit, was made in anticipation of greater financial success.

Fort Wayne also was home to one of the most successful women's baseball teams, the Fort Wayne Daisies. The success and history of the Daisies was part of the inspiration for the movie *A*

TABLE 4-5
New Tax Revenues Anticipated from the Pittsburgh Pirates

| Year | Tickets Sold | New Taxes Collected | | | | |
		Amusement	Mercantile	Business	Parking	Total
2000	2,805,400	624,992	37,992	4,065	440,710	1,107,759
2001	2,672,700	563,581	34,259	3,665	397,406	998,911
2002	2,659,269	576,001	35,014	3,746	406,164	1,020,925
2003	2,885,625	703,074	42,739	4,572	495,769	1,246,154
2004	2,885,625	731,197	44,448	4,755	515,599	1,295,999
2005	2,885,625	760,445	46,226	4,946	536,223	1,347,840
2006	2,885,625	790,862	48,075	5,143	557,672	1,401,752
2007	2,885,625	822,497	49,998	5,349	579,979	1,457,823
2008	2,842,188	872,234	53,021	5,673	615,051	1,545,979
2009	2,885,625	889,613	54,078	5,786	627,306	1,576,783
2010	2,687,243	800,726	48,674	5,208	564,627	1,419,235
2011	2,510,561	666,713	40,528	4,336	470,129	1,181,706
2012	2,801,604	972,989	59,146	6,328	686,098	1,724,561
2013	2,791,480	999,720	60,771	6,502	704,947	1,771,940
2014	2,582,531	820,283	49,863	5,335	578,418	1,453,899
2015	2,582,531	851,371	51,753	5,537	600,340	1,509,001
2016	2,582,531	883,638	53,714	5,747	623,093	1,566,192
2017	2,582,531	917,128	55,750	5,965	646,708	1,625,551
2018	2,582,531	951,887	57,863	6,191	671,218	1,687,159
2019	2,582,531	987,964	60,056	6,425	696,657	1,751,102
2020	2,582,531	1,025,408	62,332	6,669	723,061	1,817,470
2021	2,582,531	1,064,271	64,694	6,922	750,465	1,886,352
2022	2,582,531	1,104,606	67,146	7,184	778,907	1,957,843
2023	2,582,531	1,146,471	69,691	7,456	808,428	2,032,046
2024	2,582,531	1,189,922	72,332	7,739	839,067	2,109,060
2025	2,582,531	1,235,020	75,074	8,032	870,868	2,188,994
2026	2,582,531	1,281,828	77,919	8,337	903,874	2,271,958
2027	2,582,531	1,330,409	80,872	8,652	938,130	2,358,063
2028	2,582,531	1,380,831	83,937	8,980	973,686	2,447,434
2029	2,582,531	1,433,165	87,119	9,321	1,010,588	2,540,193
2030	2,582,531	1,487,482	90,420	9,674	1,048,890	2,636,466
2031	2,582,531	1,543,857	93,847	10,041	1,088,642	2,736,387
2032	2,582,531	1,602,369	97,404	10,421	1,129,902	2,840,096
2033	2,582,531	1,663,099	101,096	10,816	1,172,725	2,947,736
2034	2,582,531	1,726,131	104,927	11,226	1,217,172	3,059,456
2035	2,582,531	1,791,551	108,904	11,652	1,263,302	3,175,409
2036	2,582,531	1,859,451	113,031	12,093	1,311,182	3,295,757
2037	2,582,531	1,929,924	117,315	12,552	1,360,875	3,420,666
2038	2,582,531	2,003,068	121,762	13,027	1,412,453	3,550,310
2039	2,582,531	2,078,984	126,376	13,521	1,465,984	3,684,865
2040	2,582,531	2,157,778	131,166	14,033	1,521,545	3,824,522
Total		48,222,539	2,931,331	313,622	34,003,861	85,471,353
Average		1,176,159	71,496	7,649	829,362	2,084,667

League of Their Own. However, after the collapse of the women's baseball league and the movement of the Pistons, Fort Wayne's stake in the world of sports was limited to a minor league hockey team. (An indoor soccer team began play in 1986 but went bankrupt in 1990.) As a result, the possibility of attracting a minor league baseball team to the city was quite appealing to several different groups (investors, city officials, chamber of commerce, and sports fans). In 1988 the ownership of the Wausau Timbers came calling on Fort Wayne; with a population of 675,000, Fort Wayne is a much larger market area than Wausau, Wisconsin.

The existing facility in which the Timbers were playing would have required approximately $2 million in modifications. The city offered the team's owners a fifteen-year loan for $1.25 million (the interest rate on the loan was to be 6.48 percent). The team would be responsible for repaying the loan, and the renovations would require an additional $750,000. Although the team also would be responsible for these additional funds, the city's leadership would join with the team owners to raise the funds from fans, the private sector, and the nonprofit sector. If the team was unable to make the payments on the loan, the city would accept responsibility for the loan. When the funds from the private and nonprofit sectors could not be found for the $750,000 cash investment, the owners ended their discussions with the city, and Fort Wayne lost the opportunity to have minor league baseball.

Should the city of Fort Wayne have provided more incentives to encourage the relocation of the team? Fort Wayne and Allen County's main source of tax revenues is a property tax. There is a small local option income tax, and the majority of these revenues accrue to Fort Wayne. In 1989 this tax was just 0.2 percent. A 1 percent food and beverage tax is collected in the county for all consumption at restaurants and bars. These revenues are dedicated to the Allen County Coliseum Commission, which operates the facilities in which the hockey team plays its home games. There is also a 5 percent innkeepers tax on all hotel room charges. Although some of these revenues accrue to Allen County and not the city of Fort Wayne, all local taxes were combined in the fiscal analysis. Initially, only the city of Fort Wayne was involved with the effort to recruit a team, but when the region was finally successful in attracting a team, both units of government worked together to bring professional baseball to northeast Indiana.

To measure the fiscal gains to local governments, the anticipated positive economic impact was projected at 27.3 percent of total expenditures (best case). The worst-case estimate was that 11.9 percent of the economic impact would be new activity in the city of Fort Wayne. These estimates were developed through household surveys that asked people about their interest in both attending games and changing their recreational patterns (staying in Fort Wayne as opposed to going elsewhere if a team were in the city). An estimate of the expected influx of people from other counties was also included based on a survey of attendees at other Fort Wayne recreational sites (Swindell and Rosentraub, 1992).

Based on attendance levels for other Class A teams, and adjusting those market penetration rates for the size of the Fort Wayne region, it was anticipated that a team would attract 235,000 fans in 1989. A "honeymoon" or first-year effect of an additional 23,500 fans was included, raising the anticipated attendance level to 258,500 fans. (In 1994, during the MLB strike and their second season in Indiana, the Fort Wayne Wizards drew 254,503 fans.) The league average for ticket prices, adjusted to include the cost of promotions, was 81 cents per fan (Peck, 1985). In the Fort Wayne fiscal impact analysis, an average ticket price of $1.00 to $1.25 was used. Estimated ticket revenue was between $235,000 and $293,750; the midpoint of this range, $265,000, was used to estimate local tax dollars.

The city's consultant and team owners estimated spending at the stadium by fans for food and souvenirs to be $1.58 per fan. If 235,000 fans attended games, approximately $371,300 would be spent inside the stadium. Peck (1985) performed a survey of fans to estimate spending outside the stadium and found the average to be approximately $8.00 per fan. This figure was then adjusted for inflation to 1989 levels, meaning that the city could anticipate $1.9 million of spending by fans outside the stadium (including parking fees).

An estimate of players' salaries was made based on league averages, and I anticipated that some portions of salaries, at least half of the $316,000 payroll, would be spent outside Fort Wayne since few of the players made their permanent homes in northeast Indiana. Estimates of spending by visiting teams were drawn from analyses done by several minor league teams (Swindell and Rosentraub, 1992); these suggested that $178,500 in spending would occur. It was anticipated that the presence of the team would create a few seasonal jobs with total salaries of $200,000, and the team's office staff would have annual salaries of about $100,000 (based on estimates produced by surveying all other Class A teams in the same league).

The average number of jobs created was then multiplied by the expected salary level, based on salaries paid in Fort Wayne for similar tasks. Local governments would collect all parking fees, estimated to be $100,000 per year. Applying all the relevant taxes possible, and using a multiplier of 2.0, local governments would receive $135,532 in new revenues per year. This was the high-end estimate; the low-end estimate was $121,036 per year. The information in Table 4-6 includes estimates of growth in the local economy and in the local taxes, assuming an increase of either

TABLE 4-6
A Fiscal Impact Summary for Fort Wayne and Allen County
(all figures in dollars)

Revenue	Total Impact	Economic Activity New Economic Growth Estimate		Local Tax Revenues New Economic Growth Estimate	
		11.9 Percent	*27.3 Percent*	*11.9 Percent*	*27.3 Percent*
Fan Spending					
Ticket sales	265,000	31,535	72,345	315	726
In stadium[1]	371,300	44,185	101,365	442	1,017
Outside[2]	1,880,000	223,720	513,240	4,027[3]	9,273
First year	241,450	28,733	65,916	591	1,514
Subtotal	2,519,250	328,173	752,866	5,375	12,530
Team Spending					
Salaries	316,000[4]	158,000[5]	158,000[5]	316	316
Jobs created	200,000	200,000	200,000	400	400
Operations	100,000	11,900	27,300	71	164
Subtotal	616,000	369,900	385,300	787	880
Visiting teams	178,500	178,500	178,500	4,356[6]	4,356[6]
Parking				100,000	100,000
SUBTOTAL	3,313,750	876,573	1,316,666	110,518	117,766
Multiplier	2.0	2.0	2.0	2.0	2.0
TOTAL	6,627,500	1,753,146	2,633,332	121,036[7]	135,532[7]

[1]Includes advertising revenues.

[2]Includes parking fees.

[3]Assumes 20 percent of expenses subject to 5 percent hotel tax; 80 percent of expenditures subject to 1 percent food and beverage tax.

[4]Players salaries, though paid by the Major League affiliate, do have a direct impact on the Fort Wayne economy and local government tax revenues.

[5]Although all of the players' salaries are new economic gains, a portion of their income will be spent at their permanent homes. A portion, however, will be spent in Fort Wayne.

[6]Assumes half of the expenditures subject to 5 percent hotel tax; half of the expenditures subject to 1 percent food and beverage tax.

[7]The multiplier was not applied to the direct expense of $100,000 for parking but was applied to all other figures.

11.9 percent or 27.3 percent in economic activity. Since these are the low-end and high-end estimates, the real outcomes are probably somewhere between these levels.

If the city had decided to assume all the costs for renovating the stadium, to recoup its investment of approximately $2 million would have taken at least fourteen years. And that would not have included the costs associated with any other renovations or maintenance at the stadium. The economic gain or growth in the private sector would have been in excess of $7 million *per year*, but no one was willing to provide the team with even $750,000 to help support the renovations to the stadium. With the city unwilling to improve their efforts, the Timbers eventually were sold to another group and never moved to Fort Wayne.

In 1992 another Class A team, the Kenosha Twins, indicated that they were prepared to move to Fort Wayne. However, under the Professional Baseball Agreement passed by MLB in December 1990, certain new guidelines had to be followed for all minor league baseball parks (Johnson, 1992). The effect of these new guidelines raised the cost of the renovations at Fort Wayne's facility from slightly less than $2 million to more than $5 million (Swindell and Rosentraub, 1992). Based on the continued success of the minor league hockey team and the success of a new minor league basketball team (Continental Basketball League), Fort Wayne and Allen County decided to jointly fund the entire cost of the renovation, subject to a lease that protects the exposure of the city and county.

The Kenosha Twins, now the Fort Wayne Wizards, agreed to pay rent of $222,000 per year, but they receive all advertising revenues. All parking revenues and concession profits are placed in a pool for stadium operations, and if all costs are met, any profits belong to the Wizards. If all costs are not met, the team is responsible for any shortfalls. Additionally, the maintenance of the physical plant is the responsibility of the city and county. How has this arrangement worked? So far, no tax dollars have been used to pay for any of the costs of renovations or operations. The team is a financial success; both partners in this arrangement are satisfied.

The Intangible Benefits from Professional Sports Teams

Although many assessments of the value of teams still focus on the direct and indirect economic returns, the true value of a franchise to a community may lie in its intangible benefits. As has already been discussed, sports are a critical component of life and have been for thousands of year. There can be little debate that today's professional teams are the focal point of much of the modern year's sports mania.

In the early spring of 1995, Michael Jordan "unretired" from professional basketball. The first game he appeared in after his "I'm Back" announcement was against the Indiana Pacers in Indianapolis. NBC seized the game for its Game of the Week and broadcast the return of "His Airness" to numerous countries. During various breaks in the action, NBC displayed aerial and ground-level shots of Indianapolis's skyline, civic fountains and monuments, and downtown parks. On a glorious spring afternoon, Indianapolis received worldwide attention and publicity. That night each of the network news programs highlighted Michael Jordan's return, as did the following morning's breakfast shows. In each of these newscasts Indianapolis was mentioned and was sometimes even highlighted. Did anyone move to Indianapolis because of that coverage? No, but what would Indianapolis have had to pay to get that kind of attention to help identify and market itself? Indianapolis received that attention because it is part of the cultural icon known as sports, as a result of the presence of the Indiana Pacers basketball team. Knowing that, the city also has made an investment to keep and retain the Pacers.

The intangible benefits from sports can be seen if one stands on the concourse between Jacobs Field and Gund Arena in downtown Cleveland. A short decade or so ago this section of

Cleveland's downtown was a high crime area. Today, more than 5 million visits are made by fans who root for the Indians and Cavaliers. Concerts and shows are also held at the facilities, and virtually every evening one is likely to find people, dressed in the colors of the Indians or Cavs, visiting the teams' homes and the restaurants in the area. Although much of this economic activity is undeniably a substitution of one form of recreation for another, there is an electricity in the air when the teams play that only the most cynical do not enjoy.

The reputation and image of many cities is frequently defined by high-profile teams and sporting events. The celebratory atmosphere that is created in a city when a team wins is another "intangible" benefit. Even people who do not attend games enjoy the holiday atmosphere that is created in the wake of a team's victories. In a society where sports are a dominant cultural icon, teams create a level of recognition that can generate pride for residents of a community (Kotler, Haider, and Rein, 1993; Baade, 1996; Rosentraub, 1996; Danielson, 1997).

Increasingly, a city's image has become a critical component of economic development efforts. As the world has been shrunk by jet planes, fax machines, and the Internet, and when products manufactured in one part of the world can be easily sold anywhere within days, cities and regions have become locked in a competitive struggle for identity and economic development. It is through these identities that cities differentiate themselves and seek to become places that attract businesses, jobs, and economic activity. Sports teams have become a very visible component of the competition to establish an identity for economic development.

> Professional sports leagues are a unique form of business. On one
> level they sell entertainment, but they also sell civic identity, emo-

tion, and community involvement. The name Kansas City Chiefs says it all. The Chiefs belong to the fans and the community of Kansas City. We support the team. We share the glory of their victories. We share the bitterness of their defeats. It is because we, the citizens of Kansas City, share so much with our team that we have been willing and we will continue to be willing to make the public investments in stadia and other projects to provide the teams with the facilities which are necessary to their operation.

Richard Berkeley, Mayor of Kansas City

There is no statistical data indicating that the presence or absence of a team influences the location decisions of firms or households, but it is apparent that teams do generate a substantial level of "identity" benefits. These benefits may do little more than enhance civic pride, but that does not make them any less real or valuable. In an era when shopping malls and restaurants in one city, state, or nation are strikingly similar to those in other locations, sports teams provide a unique dimension for a community's identity.

Large cities or supercities such as New York, Chicago, and Los Angeles need the identity of a sports team far less than smaller communities. In these communities there are myriad cultural, historical, and economic organizations that provide an identity and a level of civic pride. For cities that are smaller than the supercities and for communities that lack the cultural amenities of Broadway or Hollywood, professional sports teams have become a critical asset that help establish a community's national and international identity. As an example, without the Packers it is unlikely that many people outside of Wisconsin would be as familiar with the small town of Green Bay as they are today. Many smaller regional centers and some second-tier cities frequently want to be considered "major league" or "big-time places" to live and work. As such, these areas try to emulate the supercities and their amenities. But with smaller populations and fewer concentrations of wealth this is sometimes difficult. As a result, included in the frequent justifications used to defend the public sector's support for professional sports is the explanation that a team is needed to:

1. establish and maintain an identity for a city or region's economic development;
2. compete with larger supercities as a desirable location with the same amenities but lower costs; and
3. stimulate economic development.

Although some cynics may disdain the identity bestowed on communities by sports, many residents of cities do not. In 1996 the city of Indianapolis asked me to measure the intangible benefits of the Indiana Pacers and Indianapolis Colts. The Pacers wanted a new facility to replace their aging home, and the Colts wanted a change in their lease to permit them to retain more of the revenues produced from luxury seating, advertising, and the sale of food and beverages. If the economic benefits and taxes produced by the teams were too small to warrant any public subsidies, were there intangible benefits that would justify the use of tax dollars to save the teams? Of course neither team indicated that it would leave the city if its needs were not met, but the veiled threat was never far from the surface. If a new facility was not built for the Pacers, the team might have to look elsewhere for a friendly government. The Colts were quick to point out that their financial plight did not permit them to attract the best players and build a competitive team.

More than fifteen hundred randomly selected respondents in the Indianapolis metropolitan area were asked to describe the importance of several of the area's cultural amenities, including the

Indiana Pacers, the Indianapolis Colts, auto racing (the Indianapolis 500 and the Brickyard 400), and local museums. A telephone survey was conducted in May 1996 after the conclusion of the Pacers' season. In order to determine the value placed on sports vis-à-vis other cultural amenities, metropolitan respondents were asked how important the various sports teams, sports events, other events, museums, performing arts, and cultural amenities were in "making you feel proud" to be a resident of the Indianapolis region. Responses were coded from a high of 5 for an asset that was described as "very important" to a 1 if a respondent believed the regional asset was "very unimportant." Respondents were also permitted to indicate if they were "unsure" of the value of an asset, event, or amenity. Unsure ratings were coded with a value of 3, indicating a neutral position within the 5-point scale. The results of this civic pride measure are presented in the first column of Table 4-7.

Sports teams clearly are critical in establishing the sense of pride respondents had in living in Indianapolis. Although museums generated the most pride, professional sports teams ranked second and third. Indeed, the Pacers virtually tied the museums as a source of pride for community residents. "Other sports" (such as the RCA tennis tournament and golf tournaments) ranked in the middle of the list (sixth) whereas the minor league Indians (baseball) and Ice (hockey) were eighth and ninth, respectively, suggesting that they are considered relatively less important.

Respondents also were asked to describe the importance of these assets and events in defining Indianapolis's national reputation, using the scale from the civic pride question. There are interesting differences here. For instance, auto racing (the Indianapolis 500) ranked highest even though it ranked only seventh in terms of generating civic pride. This is the result of

TABLE 4-7
The Importance of Sports Teams and Other Amenities
to Residents of Metropolitan Indianapolis, 1996

Asset or Event	Civic Price	National Reputation	Others Mention (%)	Visitors See (%)	Loss Hurts Reputation (%)
Auto racing	3.94	4.49	31.7	14.5	85.1
Black expo	3.17	3.55	0.8	2.1	36.8
Colts (NFL)	4.07	4.33	10.5	4.3	74.9
Ice (IHL)	3.22	—	0.2	0.4	—
Indians (AAA)	3.65	—	0.5	1.1	—
Museums	4.27	4.29	2.3	6.6	68.3
Music	4.02	4.03	0.4	3.2	59.4
Other sports	3.98	4.17	1.1	2.4	59.5
Pacers (NBA)	4.26	4.47	15.5	5.0	81.1
Shopping	4.00	3.87	1.5	3.5	58.8

different dimensions of pride and identity. The greater importance of an amenity in the everyday life of individuals and families can account for a higher ranking on a question focusing on
pride associated with living in an area. The length of the Indiana
Pacers' season also might explain the relatively higher profile it
has on the issue of pride relative to auto racing or the Indianapolis Colts. Auto racing clearly is believed to be very important for
the region's reputation, but the Pacers scored nearly as high. Even
though respondents hold museums in high esteem in creating local pride, they do not think museums play as important a role in
establishing the region's reputation.

Respondents also considered the question, "When you tell people who do not live in the Indianapolis region that you live here,
what organization or event do you hear them mention when you
say Indianapolis?" Each respondent could list up to four events or
organizations. The results show that the patterns that emerged
were almost identical to the national reputation question. Auto
racing, the Pacers, the Colts, and museums, in that order, were the
most frequently noted assets. This may indicate that respondents'

ideas of what determines a city's national identity are reflected or mirrored by those outside the area.

Similarly, all respondents were asked what activities, events, or amenities in Indianapolis brought friends and family members to the region. In this manner, respondents were not asked where they took visitors but what amenities brought their out-of-town family and friends to Indianapolis. Again, the pattern generally was consistent with the previous indicators. Visitors asked most often to visit the Indianapolis 500 racetrack; however, the Pacers and Colts fell to third and fourth places, behind museums. This indicates that auto racing is a major draw for out-of-town guests, while museums and professional sports teams are not as valuable but are still ahead of the other assets and events on the list.

The final indicator used to measure civic pride and identity was whether or not respondents thought the loss of a given asset or event would hurt the reputation of the community. The results are given in the final column of the table. Again, auto racing, professional sports, and museums ranked highest. In fact, the ranking pattern was identical to the national reputation question (column 2). Given that these two questions were not asked consecutively during the survey, the consistency of the rankings adds a degree of reliability to the findings.

These results add support to the argument that residents enjoy substantial social spillover benefits related to the presence of the Pacers and the Colts. However, just as important as the individual scores are for understanding the feelings of pride generated by each asset, so are the values placed on each asset by different groups of respondents. In other words, who enjoys the benefits the most, or is enjoyment evenly distributed across the population? The data indicate that there are very distinct patterns in the pride respondents derive from different assets.

The most consistent differences related to attendance or "direct consumption" of an asset. This issue is particularly important when considering civic pride since sports proponents have argued that people receive a sense of pride or enjoyment from teams, events, or the presence of cultural assets even if they do not attend games or events. For example, respondents who lived in households where at least one member had attended a Pacers game within the last year gave the team a rating of 4.65 in terms of its importance in making them feel proud to be a resident of the area (see Table 4-8). If no one in the household had been to a game, the team's rating declined to 4.01. Similarly, if someone in the household had been to a Colts game, the importance of the team rose from an average of 4.07 to 4.54. In households where people did not attend a game, the importance of the team to a person's pride in living in Indianapolis declined to 3.86. The relationship between frequent contact with an asset and a respondent's sense of its importance is probably best underscored by the different ratings accorded auto racing. If people had attended the Brickyard 400 or the Indianapolis 500, the importance of auto racing in establishing their pride as a resident increased from an average rating of 3.94 to 4.40.

The overall pattern of more favorable impressions if the respondent or a household member had attended an event is consistent across each of the assets (for which specific attendance questions were asked). The differences are statistically significant. If respondents or members of their households visited the asset or attended a game (event), that asset was far more important to the respondent's pride in living in Indianapolis than if no household member had attended a game (event) or visited the asset.

PUBLIC EXPENDITURES FOR PROFESSIONAL SPORTS: INVESTMENTS OR SUBSIDIES?

When taxpayers are asked to pay for sports facilities, the economic returns received are far too small for the expenditures to

TABLE 4-8
The Importance of Different Assets in Establishing Pride in Living in
Indianapolis by Attendance (5=Very Important, 1=Very Unimportant), 1996

Asset or Event	Mean Score	Attended	Did Not Attend	t-test[1]
Museums	4.27	4.42	3.97	7.3
Indiana Pacers	4.26	4.65	4.01	12.3
Indianapolis Colts	4.07	4.54	3.86	12.6
Music	4.02	4.30	3.71	10.2
Auto racing	3.94	4.40	3.62	12.4
Indianapolis Indians	3.65	4.19	3.46	12.3
Indianapolis Ice	3.22	3.95	3.08	11.3

[1]All statistical tests exhibit significance (p< 0.0001).

be considered wise investments. The forecasts of hundreds of millions of dollars in new expenditures fail to note that most of these dollars already are in a region's economy. And even if a team relocated, new recreational opportunities might take up most of the slack resulting from a team's absence. Consultants who specialize in corporate locations do not believe that a team's presence or absence affects business locations. Economists have never found any statistical relationship between economic development and the presence of a team (Baade, 1996). Even the intangible benefits generated by teams, though substantial, mean more to fans than nonfans. As such, charging fans more for their seats or charging advertisers more for reaching those fans is a far more equitable way to finance a sports facility.

All this does not mean that sports do not make a contribution to the economy of an area or to the quality of life. Sports are an important part of life. However, all the available data clearly indicate that those who consume sports (the fans) and those who benefit from the business operations of sports (players, owners, and those who sell products related to sports) should bear all the costs. The tangible and intangible benefits to the community at large are too small to justify or warrant the public's investment. A general sales tax to help build a stadium or arena is a subsidy, not an investment. Placing taxes on food consumption throughout a city or county, on hotel usage, and on the renting of cars in order to fund the building of a facility is subsidizing that facility. Subsequent chapters will discuss the best ways to finance a sports facility, but it should be clear from this chapter that there are insufficient returns to any community to warrant the use of broad-based taxes to pay for a stadium or arena.

5

Indianapolis's and Cleveland's Efforts to Change Their Images and Downtown Areas

It is sometimes easier to understand the effects of sports on communities through a retrospective analysis of projects and facilities. Lost in the reams of data used to evaluate impacts is the context in which public leaders attempted to use sports to recast their communities identities and invigorate economies. To learn from the experiences of different cities and to understand what sports can and cannot accomplish, it is necessary to review the outcomes of specific stadium and arena projects. Leadership in Indianapolis and Cleveland wanted new identities for their communities and to revive deteriorating downtown centers. Both communities turned to sports to change their images and enhance their economies.

Why choose sports to rebuild a city? For the past three decades cities have focused on entertainment, recreation, and retail activity as a strategy for urban renewal. Frustrated by the rush of families and businesses to the suburbs in the post–World War II era, mayors across America hoped to rekindle the magic of "trips downtown" with the building of new and different retail centers. In the 1970s, "festival marketplaces" began to fill abandoned train stations, warehouses, and other aging relics in cities from Boston to Dallas. Several cities with waterfront areas focused their attention on these natural assets and placed their new restaurants and retail complexes adjacent to underutilized or abandoned marine facilities. Baltimore's Inner Harbor, Cleveland's Flats, Miami's Bayside Complex, and San Antonio's RiverWalk were among the most ambitious programs implemented. In later years New York City joined these cities by creating new shopping and entertainment vistas along waterfront areas previously used for shipping and passenger traffic. Adding sports facilities and convention centers to this "entertainment" and retail strategy seemed like the next logical step in rebuilding the reputation of cities.

Indianapolis and Cleveland both were attracted to and seduced by this scenario. In the 1960s and 1970s, Indianapolis was a city without a national identity and a region where urban sprawl precipitated moves by both homeowners and businesses to more suburban locations. Cleveland was a city known for racial riots, a burning downtown river, intense political battles between its elected officials and the business community, and a cavernous stadium called the "Mistake by the Lake." In many late-night monologues Cleveland itself was sometimes described as a mistake by the lake. Likewise, Indianapolis was the much maligned "Hoosier" capital. Cleveland and Indianapolis became the tale of two cities with strongly segregated communities divided by race and income. Neither city was a destination: They were areas from which people moved and rarely returned; and the downtown areas in both cities had become places to avoid. These harsh realities convinced Indianapolis's leadership to turn to an "amateur" sports strategy to rebuild the city, complemented by the presence of the Indiana Pacers, the Indianapolis Colts, and professional tennis. Cleveland's approach involved saving one team and convincing another to move home. Cleveland replaced the Mistake by the Lake with an architectural masterpiece, Jacobs Field. A new arena for the NBA's Cavaliers was added to form the "Gateway Complex." How much did both cities pay for their sports strategies? What did they get for their money and effort? What lessons can we learn from their policies?

SPORTS AND THE DOWNTOWN DEVELOPMENT STRATEGY IN INDIANAPOLIS

The city of Indianapolis found itself considering economic development policies and programs at the same time that many cities in North America were dealing with the "rustbelt's" decline and deep recession. Indianapolis was a city with a declining job base, a deteriorating downtown core, and a very limited image in the national and international economic landscape. It also was shrinking in size; between 1970 and 1980 the consolidated city of Indianapolis lost residents while the metropolitan area enjoyed a 17.6 percent growth rate (see Table 5-1). When Indianapolis and its county consolidated in the early 1970s to form "UniGov" (unified government), a considerable amount of suburban land was joined with Indianapolis's older neighborhoods and downtown area. This new structure for the city did not stop the flight to the suburbs. By 1980 the consolidated city accounted for just 53.7 percent of the region's population. Indianapolis's leadership realized that different programs were needed to bring people back to the Hoosier capital.

Most believe that part of Indianapolis's problem was its bland to negative image. Favorite son Kurt Vonnegut underscored the problem when he described the city as a cemetery with lights that came to life one day a year for the Indianapolis 500. A survey

TABLE 5-1
Population Growth in Indianapolis, 1970 Through 1992

Area	Year				Percentage Change 1970 to 1992
	1970	1980	1990	1992	
Consolidated Indianapolis	737,000	701,000	731,000	747,000	1.4
Percentage change		−4.9	4.3	2.2	
As a percent of the region	66.3	53.7	53.0	52.5	
Metropolitan Indianapolis	1,111,000	1,306,000	1,380,000	1,424,000	28.2
Percentage change		17.6	5.7	3.2	

commissioned by the Greater Indianapolis Progress Committee in the mid-1970s found the city to have a "non-image"—neither positive nor favorable—in the national media and among convention planners. A finding of no image was actually a substantial improvement over early assessments of Indiana's capital city. Indianapolis had been called "Naptown" by some and IndianaNOplace by others. John Gunther, in 1947, almost ended the city's future when he described Indianapolis as "an unkempt city, unswept, raw, a terrific place for basketball and auto racing, a former pivot of the Ku-Kluxers" (Hudnut, 1995). For a city with aspirations for regional and national leadership, a very different image was needed.

The downtown redevelopment strategy that Indianapolis launched involved numerous projects and the creation of several organizations to recast the city's image and encourage businesses to locate in the downtown area. An economic development corporation was created to assist companies considering a move to Indianapolis and help local corporations that wanted to expand their operations. Another group was created to market the city as a venue for sports events and as the headquarters location for amateur sports organizations. A third organization focused on the image of Indianapolis in the national media and on increasing the positive exposure of the city in national and international publications.

At first glance a focus on sports as a tool for economic development might seem to have been a poor choice. As already discussed, sports is a very small component of any economy, and the direct (and indirect) spending associated with restaurants and hotels always proves too small to change economic patterns. However, Indianapolis targeted amateur sports as an industry, and a collection of individual sporting events (NCAA Final Four, NCAA championships, and others) became the focal point of its development efforts. The economic effect of international and national amateur sports is very different from that of a professional sports team because they attract large numbers of visitors from other cities and countries. The sports and downtown development strategy, implemented in the 1970s, was sustained for more than twenty years. Its plan emphasized and supported an amateur sports development strategy unlike that of any other community. In addition, a large number of non-sports-related facilities were built to create an image of an entirely new downtown area. Was this combination of activities capitalizing on sports able to rebuild the Hoosier capital?

Rebuilding Downtown Indianapolis

In 1974, Market Square Arena opened as the new 16,950-seat home for the Indiana Pacers; this facility was designed to be the eastern end of the downtown redevelopment effort. For events that did not attract more than twenty thousand spectators, Market Square Arena was a viable facility. Its lack of luxury seating and broad concourses for the sale of refreshments and its poor access (the playing surface and stage for events is three stories above street level) led to the call for the building of a new arena. In 1999, Market Square Arena will be closed, and the Conseco Fieldhouse will open in another part of the downtown area.

From 1974 through 1990 more than thirty major development projects for the downtown area were initiated. The State of Indiana developed its new Government Center at a cost of $264 million, and Indiana University's investment in its Indianapolis campus totaled more than $230 million. Seven projects were completely related to the sports identity that Indianapolis hoped to establish. In 1984, Indianapolis opened the sixty-one-thousand-seat Hoosier Dome (RCA purchased the naming rights in 1994); that became the home for the Indianapolis Colts. The dome has hosted the NCAA Men's Basketball Final Four twice, and this event will return to Indianapolis for the fourth time in 2000. (Market Square Arena was the site of the tournament before the dome opened.) Other new sports facilities include a tennis stadium for the annual hard-court championships, the Indiana University Natatorium, the Indiana University Track and Field Stadium, the Velodrome (bicycle racing), and the National Institute for Fitness and Sports. By 1989 a total of seven national organizations (Athletics Congress of the USA, U.S. Canoe and Kayak Team, U.S. Diving, Inc., U.S. Gymnastics Federation, U.S. Rowing, U.S. Synchronized Swimming, and U.S. Water Polo) and two international organizations (International Baseball Association and International Hockey League) had moved their governing offices to Indianapolis.

The projects identified in Table 5-2 do not include all development that took place in the downtown area. Some developments (such as the city's monuments, a large park area, the state's refurbishing of the Capitol, new fire stations, and so forth) were not appropriate for consideration here given that they would have taken place even if a sports strategy had not been specified. To be

TABLE 5-2

Sources of Funds for Economic Development Projects (in millions of dollars)

Project	Year	Source of Funds Federal	State	City	Private	Philanthropic	Total
Market Square Arena	1974	0	0	16	0	0	16
Children's Museum	1976	0	0	0	0	25	25
Hyatt Hotel/Bank	1977	0	0	0	55	0	55
Sports Center	1979	0	0	4	1.5	1.5	7
Indiana Theater	1980	1.5	0	0	4.5	0	6
Capitol Tunnel	1982	1.4	0	0	0	0	1.4
IU Track and Field Stadium	1982	0	1.9	0	0	4	5.9
IU Natatorium	1982	1.5	7	0	0	13	21.5
Velodrome	1982	0.48	0	1.1	0	1.1	2.68
2 W. Washington Offices	1982	1.2	0	0	11.8	0	13
1 N. Capitol Offices	1982	3.2	0	0	10.41	0	13.61
Hoosier Dome	1984	0	0	48	0	30	78
Lower Canal Apartments	1985	7.9	0	10.3	0	2	20.2
Heliport	1985	2.5	0.12	0.6	2.36	0	5.58
Walker Building	1985	2	0	0	0	1.4	3.4
Embassy Suite Hotel	1985	6.45	0	0	25.05	0	31.5
Lockerbie Market	1986	1.8	0	0	14	0	15.8
Union Station	1986	16.3	0	1	36.01	0	53.31
City Market	1986	0	0	0	0	4.7	4.7
Pan Am Plaza	1987	0	0	5.7	25	4.5	35.2
Lockfield Apartments	1987	0	0	0.62	24.6	0	25.22
Canal Overlook Apartments	1988	0	0	0	11	0	11
Zoo	1988	0	0	0	0	37.5	37.5
Nat'l Institute of Sports	1988	0	3	3	0	3	9
Eiteljorg Museum	1989	0	0	0	0	60	60
Westin Hotel	1989	0.5	0	0	65	0	65.5
Indiana University	1990	0	231	0	0	0	231
Farm Bureau	1992	0	0	0	0	36	36
State Office Center	1992	0	264	0	0	0	264
Lilly Corporate Expansion	1992	0	0	0	242	0	242
Circle Centre Mall	1995	0	0	290	0	10	300
Other Projects	1974–1992	0	0	0	1,008.53	0	1,008.53
Property Tax Abatements	1974–1992	0	0	55.8	0	0	55.8
TOTAL		46.7	507.0	436.1	1,536.8	233.7	2,760.33
PERCENT		1.7	18.4	15.8	55.7	8.5	100

Source: Department of Metropolitan Development, City of Indianapolis.

sure, there is a subjective element to this classification process, but we did try to ascertain via interviews which projects were specifically intended to be part of the strategy.

Several important points emerge from a review of Table 5-2. First, a total of $2.76 billion for capital development was invested in downtown Indianapolis. This clearly represents a substantial commitment of funds targeted to a specific area and in support of a tightly designed policy program. Second, there was an extensive commitment of private funds to the strategy. Indeed, more than half of the funds invested, 55.7 percent, were from the private sector. Third, the nonprofit sector was an active participant, although it was responsible for slightly less than $1 of every $10 invested, or 8.5 percent. Taken together, then, the private and nonprofit sectors were responsible for approximately two-thirds of the funds invested in the amateur sports and downtown redevelopment strategies. Fourth, the city of Indianapolis's investment amounted to less than one-fifth of the total investment, or 15.8 percent. Fifth, the investment by the State of Indiana and Indiana University was more than the expenditure made by the city of Indianapolis.

In spite of the criticisms made regarding certain sports development, the city of Indianapolis was quite successful in leveraging funds for its sports strategy. Basically, a $2.76 billion investment for an economic development program required $436.1 million from the city of Indianapolis. For every dollar invested by the city, it was able to leverage $6.33.

The Economic Impact of Indianapolis's Investments

It would be unfair to simply ask the question, *Did the sports and downtown strategy succeed?* and then provide a simple yes or no.

Important changes did take place as a result of the program, but there also were disappointments. A balanced review of Indianapolis's efforts requires several different perspectives to determine if they worked.

The Growth in Sports-Related Employment

There was a very large increase in the number of sports-related jobs in the region, and this increase was a direct result of the sports strategy.

The number of people employed in the sports sector increased by almost 60 percent, ranking the city second among all communities in the United States relative to job growth in this sector (see Figure 5-1). In terms of the growth in sports payrolls, Indianapolis had the largest increase of any city in the United States (see Figure 5-2).

Sports-related employment and payrolls remained a relatively inconsequential component of the Indianapolis economy, however. In 1989 all sports-related jobs accounted for 0.32 percent of all jobs in the Indianapolis economy, and the sports-related payroll accounted for less than 0.5 percent of the total payrolls of all Indianapolis businesses.

Overall Economic Growth in Indianapolis

City officials had hoped that the sports strategy would attract firms to Indianapolis. The city's major competitors, as identified by economic development and municipal leaders, are Columbus (Ohio), Minneapolis, St. Paul, St. Louis, Dayton, Cincinnati, Louisville, Milwaukee, and Fort Wayne (Indiana). During the sports strategy period, Indianapolis had the third highest growth rate among these communities, and the number of jobs in

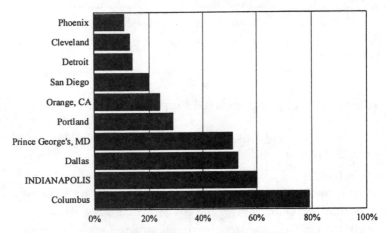

FIGURE 5-1   Growth in Sports-Related Employment, 1983–1989

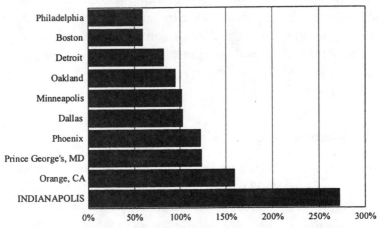

FIGURE 5-2   Growth in Sports-Related Payrolls, 1983–1989

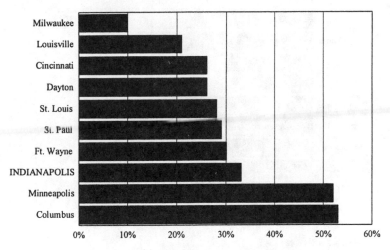

FIGURE 5-3   Total Employment Growth, in Central Courtries 1977–1989

Indianapolis increased by 32.9 percent, exceeded only by Columbus and Minneapolis. As illustrated in Figure 5-3, the increase in the number of jobs in Indianapolis was similar to the rates of increase for Fort Wayne (29.8 percent), St. Paul (28.9 percent), and St. Louis (28.8 percent).

In 1977, 10.1 percent of all the jobs in the ten counties studied were located in Indianapolis; in 1989 this share had increased by just 0.2 percent (see Figure 5-4). In contrast, Columbus's share of jobs increased by 1.6 percent, and Minneapolis's share increased by 2.2 percent. Fort Wayne's share of the job market was unchanged, while the proportion of jobs declined for Cincinnati, Dayton, Milwaukee, St. Paul, St. Louis, and Louisville. The sports strategy did not attract a large number of jobs to Indianapolis.

In 1977, for the ten counties studied, Indianapolis had the second highest average salary, exceeded only by Dayton. In 1989,

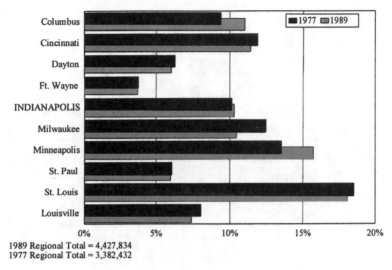

1989 Regional Total = 4,427,834
1977 Regional Total = 3,382,432

FIGURE 5-4   Regional Shares of Total Employees, 1977–1989

Indianapolis's average salary of $22,794 (see Table 5-3) was ranked fifth behind Minneapolis, St. Louis, St. Paul, and Cincinnati. Dayton was the only area that had a higher average salary than Indianapolis in 1977, but by 1989, Minneapolis, St. Louis, St. Paul, and Cincinnati all had higher average salaries than Indianapolis at the county level. At the metropolitan area level, the Indianapolis region fared somewhat better; ranked second in 1977, the region was fourth in 1989 with the seventh largest percentage increase . However, regardless of whether one looks at the county or region, the sports strategy did not bring higher-wage jobs to Indianapolis.

Reviving the Centrality of Downtown Indianapolis

The sports strategy was unable to change the concentration of jobs in the metropolitan area. In 1970, the 95,562 people working

TABLE 5-3
Average Salary Levels in Indianapolis and Comparison Areas

Area	Avg. Salary 1977	Rank	Avg. Salary 1989	Rank	% Increase 1977 to 1989	Rank
			COUNTY			
Minneapolis	12,233	6	24,617	1	101	1
St. Louis	12,401	5	23,949	2	93	2
St. Paul	12,471	4	23,318	3	87	3
Cincinnati	12,546	3	22,959	4	83	5
Indianapolis	**12,593**	**2**	**22,794**	**5**	**81**	**6**
Dayton	13,445	1	22,711	6	69	10
Milwaukee	12,226	7	21,958	7	80	8
Columbus	11,661	9	21,351	8	83	4
Ft. Wayne	11,836	8	21,292	9	80	7
Louisville	11,645	10	20,580	10	77	9
			MSA			
Minn/St. Paul	12,081	6	23,506	1	95	1
St. Louis	12,088	5	22,651	2	87	2
Cincinnati	12,098	4	21,870	3	81	4
Indianapolis	**12,152**	**2**	**21,849**	**4**	**80**	**7**
Milwaukee	12,131	3	21,843	5	80	6
Dayton	12,633	1	21,539	6	71	9
Columbus	11,530	8	21,088	7	83	3
Ft. Wayne	11,650	7	20,992	8	80	5
Louisville	11,344	9	19,845	9	75	8

downtown represented 30 percent of all workers in the county and 22.8 percent of workers in the region (see Figure 5-5). In 1980, the 111,400 downtown workers accounted for 26.8 percent of the county's jobs and 20.9 percent of the region's employees. By 1990, the percentage of downtown jobs continued to decline from 1980 levels, and the 105,500 downtown workers represented 21.2 percent of the county's jobs and 15.8 percent of those in the region. By 1990, then, downtown employment opportunities, while fewer in number when compared to 1980, were still greater in number than in 1970. Indianapolis's strategies for economic

Number of Employees (thousands)

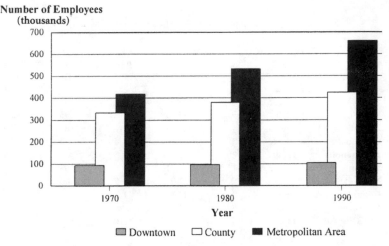

FIGURE 5-5   Job Locations in the Indianapolis Region

development were unable to stop the trend toward job development in areas outside the downtown center, but progress has been made in at least stabilizing the downtown job situation somewhat.

WHAT DID INDIANAPOLIS'S SPORTS STRATEGY ACCOMPLISH?

More so than any other city, Indianapolis developed an articulated economic development strategy for its downtown that emphasized amateur and professional sports. This policy was designed to rebuild the core area and avoid a "doughnut" pattern of prospering areas along an outer beltway surrounding a deteriorating center.

Although there were important achievements that should be attributed to Indianapolis's sports strategy, on balance it seems fair to conclude that there were no significant or substantial shifts in economic development. Simply put, the sports strategy did not achieve its economic objectives. In 1992, as described in Table 5-4, sports accounted for approximately 1.1 percent of the private-sector payroll in downtown Indianapolis and about 3.1 percent of all jobs. In addition, even if all hotel and restaurant jobs are assumed to be a direct result of sports, just 4.3 percent of the private-sector payroll was produced by these parts of the private-sector economy. As such, other communities' leaders should be quite cautious with regard to the possible benefits from a sports development program.

Economically, the best that can be said for Indianapolis's sports strategy is that it was marginally successful in creating a number of service-sector jobs. This growth did create, on an annual basis, more than 100 million new payroll dollars. This important outcome must be contrasted with other stark realities. The Indianapolis metropolitan area grew faster than the city in terms of new jobs created and total payroll growth. Overall, average salaries in Indianapolis declined in comparison to salaries with many of those cities with which Indianapolis's leadership believes they compete. Indianapolis slipped from having the second highest average salaries among these ten communities in the 1970s, to fourth or fifth depending on whether the basis of comparison is the city or the metropolitan region. In addition, the entire impact of sports, under the best of circumstances, would amount to only 1.1 percent of the Indianapolis economy.

In terms of overall development, including the benefits from an image as a major league city (the Colts and the Pacers) and a capital city for amateur sports, Indianapolis's experience indicates that sports will not generate the growth or overall impact that its boosters and supporters frequently claim. A sports strategy involving large numbers of attendees at events who do not

TABLE 5-4
Employment in the Indianapolis City Center, 1992

Industry	Employment as a Percentage of Total for Indianapolis Central Business District	Annual Payroll as a Percentage of Total for Indianapolis Central Business District
Sports-related industries combined	10.3	4.3
Eating & drinking places total	5.5	2.9
Hotels & other lodging places	1.7	0.3
Sports, amusement & recreation	3.1	1.1
Remaining retail trade	4.7	3.5
Remaining services	35.2	33.2
Manufacturing	10.4	28.9
Wholesale trade	6.9	6.7
Transportation	11.0	9.7
Finance, insurance, & real estate	17.3	10.9
Agriculture	0.1	0.0
Mining	0.2	0.3
Construction	3.9	2.6
Unclassified	0.1	0.0
Total jobs / payroll	84,750	$1,792,971,687

Source: U.S. Department of Commerce,

live in the region can be successful only if it is evaluated solely in terms of the growth in sports-related or service-sector employment. Given how small sports is as an industry and the low pay associated with the numerous service-sector jobs created by teams and the hosting of national and international events, sports is not a prudent vehicle for raising salaries or bringing a large number of high-paying jobs to a region. A sports strategy—even one as pronounced as Indianapolis's and connected to a downtown development emphasis—has little potential to be an economic stimulus for a community or region.

CLEVELAND: A SHRINKING GIANT

The factors that persuaded Cleveland's leadership to create a "new Cleveland" were strikingly similar to conditions in Indi-

TABLE 5-5
Population Changes in Metropolitan Cleveland, 1970 to 1990

Census Area	City/County	1970 Population	1980 Population	% Chg. '70 to '80	1990 Population	% Chg. '70 to '90
	Cleveland	750,897	573,822	−23.6	505,616	−32.7
Akron PMSA	Portage	125,868	135,856	+7.9	142,585	+13.3
	Summit	553,371	524,472	−5.2	514,990	−6.9
Cleveland PMSA	Cuyahoga	1,720,835	1,498,400	−12.9	1,412,140	−17.9
	Geauga	62,977	74,474	+18.3	81,129	+28.8
	Lake	197,200	212,801	+7.6	215,499	+9.3
	Medina	82,717	113,150	+36.8	122,354	+47.9
Lorian-Elyria PMSA	Lorian	256,843	274,909	+7.0	271,126	+5.6
Region		3,000,276	2,834,062	−5.5	2,768,823	−7.7
Percentage Cleveland		25.0	20.3	−4.7	18.3	−6.7

Source: U.S. Bureau of the Census.

anapolis. Cleveland had become another shrinking city. In 1970 the city's 750,897 residents comprised 57 percent of Cuyahoga County and 25 percent of the region's population (see Table 5-5). By 1990, Cleveland's 505,616 residents made up 51 percent of Cuyahoga County and 18 percent of the region. In 1970, 7 percent of Ohio's residents lived in Cleveland. By 1990 the city accounted for 4.6 percent of the state of Ohio's population.

Not only had the population of Cleveland declined, but so had the population of Cuyahoga County and of the Greater Cleveland Metropolitan Region. In 1970 the region had 3,000,276 residents; by 1990 the population had shrunk to 2,768,823 (a decline of 7.7 percent). Across the same two decades, Cuyahoga County's population declined from 1,720,835 to 1,421,140 (17.9 percent), and the population of the city of Cleveland dropped by almost one-third from 1970 to 1990.

The shrinking of Cleveland involved more than just a loss of population. Cleveland's residents also had far less money than they once had. The Cleveland region had become segregated by a growing concentration of low-income households in a decaying

TABLE 5-6
Median Household Income of Cleveland Residents as a Percentage
of the Median Household Income of Suburban Residents, 1970 to 1990

Census Area	City/County	1970	1980	1990	Percent Change 1970 to 1990
Akron PMSA	Portage	82.8	65.3	58.9	−23.9
	Summit	82.3	66.8	61.5	−20.8
Cleveland PMSA	Cuyahoga	80.4	68.2	62.3	−18.1
	Geauga	73.3	50.4	43.3	−30.0
Lorian-Elyria PMSA	Lake	76.0	54.9	50.1	−25.9
	Medina	81.4	53.8	46.8	−34.6
	Lorian	84.4	60.3	57.3	−27.1

Source: U.S. Bureau of the Census.

center city surrounded by far wealthier suburban communities. In 1970 most households in Cleveland had incomes that were between three-fourths and four-fifths of the income of residents of suburban communities. By 1990 most Cleveland households had incomes that were about one-half that of their suburban counterparts (see Table 5-6). In just twenty short years, Cleveland had become two worlds—one of wealth and one of poverty (see Table 5-7).

Income was not the only factor dividing the residents of the area; metropolitan Cleveland also was divided by race. The region's African American community is concentrated in the city while the suburbs are home to an ethnic white population. African American migration to Cleveland began when there was a substantial need for workers in the growing smokestack economy of the late nineteenth and early twentieth centuries. As Cleveland's economy expanded, migration from the southern states brought large numbers of African Americans to the city. Although this community was devastated by the depression, more African Americans were attracted to the city as the economy recovered, and by 1940 the African American population had increased to

TABLE 5-7
Median Household Income of
Cleveland Region Residents, 1970 to 1990

Census Area	City/County	1970	1980	1990	Percent Change 1970 to 1990
	Cleveland	9,098	12,277	17,822	
Akron PMSA	Portage	10,989	18,788	30,253	−23.9
	Summit	11,057	18,381	28,996	−20.8
Cleveland PMSA	Cuyahoga	11,309	18,009	28,595	−18.1
	Geauga	12,411	24,351	41,113	−30.0
Lorian-Elyria PMSA	Lake	11,964	22,369	35,605	−25.9
	Medina	11,178	22,804	38,083	−34.6
	Lorian	10,786	20,371	31,098	−27.1

84,000, from 8,400 in 1910 (Grabowski, 1992). Propelled by the postwar expansion, the African American population increased to more than 147,000, accounting for approximately 16 percent of the city's population. As factories moved to the Sunbelt and smokestack jobs were lost, unemployment soared. Cleveland began to be defined by joblessness, failing schools, deteriorating neighborhoods, and high levels of racial and economic segregation.

TARNISHING THE IMAGE

The seeds for a social explosion involving race and income issues in Cleveland had been sown for more than half a century. Separation and isolation of a largely minority underclass created an explosive situation not unlike those found in many American cities. A riot began on July 18, 1966, during a summer of nationwide racial conflicts, and the Cleveland disturbance lasted for almost one week.

If there were any positive outcomes from this destruction, it was the election in 1967 of Carl Stokes as the first African

American mayor of a large U.S. city. The clear hope was that Stokes would bring peace among the city's racial groups (Swanstrom, 1985) and that an absence of violence would lead to a period of economic expansion. Political leaders understood that if the city's existing economic and social situation was left unchanged, the charged and destructive atmosphere of 1966 would do nothing but accelerate the cascading decline of Cleveland's economy and population base and lead to further violence. Cleveland needed leadership and economic development to generate excitement and hope for the future. Unfortunately, neither leadership nor sustained economic development took place during the Stokes years.

Stokes, with the financial support of Cleveland's business establishment, did launch the "Cleveland: Now!!" campaign. This effort was unable to offset the long-standing problems, however, and in 1968 the city was again the site of severe racial riots. In 1971, Stokes decided not to seek reelection, and a division within the Democratic Party enabled Republican Ralph Perk to become mayor. Perk attempted to stabilize the city's deteriorating finances by eliminating city jobs and reducing the salaries of retained employees. These efforts were not successful, and the city's debt actually increased. Mayor Perk also was a supporter of several proposals for downtown redevelopment and subsidies to businesses that stayed in downtown Cleveland. This perspective eventually cost him electoral support as neighborhood leaders began to question whether or not their communities would benefit from a redesigned and redeveloped downtown. There was the fear that the proposed downtown redevelopment effort would create more jobs for suburbanites and fail to address the problems plaguing the city.

As Cleveland continued to decline, various groups proposed several large-scale projects, including a new airport, a downtown people-mover, and a pedestrian mall, but these proposals did little to dispel the fear that downtown development would be at the expense of neighborhoods. Proposals to build a downtown of corporate headquarters and shopping facilities at a time when numerous inner-city neighborhoods needed redevelopment of their own deteriorating infrastructure, better schools, and increased police protection reinforced schisms in the community. With substantial conflict over the path for a new Cleveland, an advocate for neighborhood development, Dennis Kucinich, was elected mayor in 1977. This did not mean that the turbulent nature and character of Cleveland politics dissipated during the Kucinich years; the turbulence escalated because the region's business interests and the new mayor were in perpetual conflict.

High levels of racial segregation, job loss, identity problems, and bitter local politics became critical to the entire sports and downtown development effort in Cleveland. Dennis Kucinich's successor, strongly supported by Cleveland's business community, was committed to the identification of a redevelopment program that would minimize, if not avoid, the kind of tensions that had dominated Cleveland's local politics for more than two decades. George Voinovich, a Republican, was able to defeat Mayor Kucinich, a Democrat, in a city with a disproportionately Democratic voting base based on the sentiment that someone was needed who could bridge schisms and rebuild Cleveland.

With the support of the business community, George Voinovich was able to reverse some of Cleveland's fortunes. The financial community of Cleveland that was so opposed to Mayor Kucinich now helped design a plan to reverse the city's bankruptcy. Such a plan could have been developed with the Kucinich administration, but there was no common ground between the financial community and the mayor from which to develop such a plan. With the city's finances stabilized, Mayor Voinovich turned his attention to the "Flats." This former site of numerous factories located on the banks of the Cuyahoga River had become a decaying portion of Cleveland. During the Voinovich years the Flats became an upscale restaurant and entertainment area.

Redeveloping the Flats did not stem the tide of unemployment or population losses; the city lost 262,000 jobs between 1978 and 1982, and Mayor Voinovich conceded that in 1983 the downtown area alone had lost 15,000 jobs (Swanstrom, 1985: 248). Declines of this magnitude, similar to the loses that plagued Indianapolis even after its unified government merger, clearly indicated that "something else" was needed to reverse Cleveland's fortunes. The "Central Market Gateway Development" project became that something else, and the city embarked on a plan to keep the Indians in Cleveland and bring the Cavaliers back from the suburbs.

CLEVELAND AND PROFESSIONAL SPORTS: THE MISTAKE BY THE LAKE AND ADVENTURES IN SUBURBIA

Municipal Stadium was built in 1931 as part of Cleveland's efforts to attract the 1932 Olympics. The idea was to build a stadium that could be a home for professional sports teams, be the site for the opening and closing ceremonies for an Olympiad, and be the venue for the Olympic track and field events. The facility was a giant circle or oval, and it was also very large in order to impress the International Olympic Committee and to serve as a distinctive architectural statement for Cleveland. When completed, Municipal Stadium's seating capacity was 71,189, and in 1932 "it possessed the largest seating capacity of any outdoor arena in the world" (Grabowski, 1992: 48). A facility this large certainly was an asset for any community's bid to host the Olympics, but as a venue for baseball or football, it left many fans distant from the action on the field. Further, the facility was adjacent to Lake Erie and susceptible to cold north winds. Although this would not be much of a problem for the summer Olympic Games, the winds from the lake created a damp and drafty atmosphere for baseball and football games played at other times of the year. Because of these deficiencies, it was the public's sentiment that the building was a mistake. Built to satisfy many users, Municipal Stadium satisfied none.

The Cleveland Indians were not particularly impressed with Municipal Stadium. The team did play its 1932, 1933, and 1934 seasons in the vast new stadium, but in 1935 the Indians returned to League Park, a nineteenth-century venue, and played only selected games at cavernous Municipal Stadium. An interesting footnote to the Indians' "two-home" status was that Joe DiMaggio's fifty-six-game hitting streak reached its zenith on a Friday night at League Park. On the following Saturday night the streak ended at Municipal Stadium; even Joltin' Joe was stopped by the Mistake by the Lake.

The Cleveland Indians became full-time residents of Municipal Stadium in 1947 when Bill Veeck took over ownership of the team. Veeck was able to attract larger crowds to the game through the initiation of several promotions (including the first ever Ladies' Day) and, more important, the recruitment of star players from the Negro Leagues. Veeck recruited Minnie Minoso, Larry Doby, and Satchel Paige, and these three stars helped fill the seats of Municipal Stadium and give the Indians a World Series championship in 1948.

When the Indians moved to Municipal Stadium, the Cleveland Browns joined them. By the 1980s, however, there were frequent requests from the Indians for a new stadium. Cleveland politics and the Indians' lackluster performance kept the idea of a new stadium on the "back burner." When the NBA's Cleveland

Cavaliers moved to the suburbs, interest was renewed in a new home for the Cleveland Indians, but it would be another ten years before a new stadium proposal was developed and funded.

Cleveland's NBA franchise began play in 1970 in the Cleveland Arena, an aging downtown facility. The team soon elected to build its own arena in the suburbs, and in 1974 the Cavs moved to Richfield Coliseum, an entertainment venue that also hosted concerts and the circus. Richfield Coliseum placed the Cavs in the middle of the Cleveland/Akron markets, and it was hoped that better access to the large market would improve the team's fortunes.

The move of the Cavs to the suburbs, as well as the relocation of one of the region's prime sites for hosting entertainment and regional recreation events, did little to dispel the view that Cleveland was becoming two cities, one black and one white. The move to the largely white suburbs underscored the feeling that the region's future was not in the city of Cleveland but in the suburbs and intensified the isolation of the two racial groups from each other.

SPORTS FOR IMAGE AND
REDEVELOPMENT IN CLEVELAND

Against this backdrop of a declining image, political conflict, and a shrinking economic and population base, the planning for a new stadium for the Cleveland Indians began. The first proposal was to build a domed stadium in downtown Cleveland, but voters rejected a countywide property tax for a domed stadium in 1984. The unpopular choice of a property tax to finance the new stadium was not the only factor that led to this proposal's defeat. The scope and placement of the facility was not specified, and the cost of the stadium was unknown. In addition, several community leaders did not believe that a domed stadium was needed.

When the domed stadium was presented to voters, there was no viable threat that the team might move to another city if a new facility were not developed. Although the threat may not have been made in 1984, the possibility that the team might leave Cleveland clearly became an issue after David and Richard Jacobs bought the team in 1986 from the estate of Steve O'Neill. Ironically, a condition of the sale was that the team remain in Cleveland. The Jacobses, with their substantial investments in the redevelopment of downtown Cleveland, seemed to be the ideal owners to respect this commitment. Richard Jacobs, one of the nation's richest people, had committed his company to developing a downtown shopping center, office buildings, and a hotel in Cleveland (Keating, 1995). Although there may have not been a direct link between the purchase of the team and these other developments—the Jacobs brothers did receive property tax abatements worth $225 million for their proposed developments—Richard Jacobs was adding the Cleveland Indians to his portfolio (Keating, Krumholz, and Metzger, 1989). It was also clear, though, that the Jacobs family wanted a new stadium for the Indians in downtown Cleveland to complement their other investments.

THE GATEWAY PROJECT

Michael White was elected mayor in 1989, succeeding George Voinovich, who decided (in the spring of 1989) to seek the governorship of Ohio (he was elected in 1990). Mayor White joined several other elected officials and Richard Jacobs in supporting the building of two facilities, one for the Indians and an indoor arena that would lure the Cavaliers back from the suburbs.

On March 21, 1990, the Cuyahoga County Commissioners

approved a public/private partnership to develop the Central Market Gateway Project, an economic development zone that includes a new publicly owned stadium and arena. The 50/50 partnership includes a $174 million commitment of private sector finds for the

Gateway Project. To finance the public portion of the $344 million development, the Commissioners today placed an initiative on the May 8 ballot seeking voter approval of a small excise tax on the purchase of alcoholic beverages and cigarettes.

The $174 million in private funds was to come from several sources (see Table 5-8). The press announcement from the Cuyahoga County Commissioners indicated that the majority of the private funds, 56.9 percent, or $99 million, would come from the teams or the sale of luxury boxes (loges) or club seats. Cleveland Tomorrow, a nonprofit organization supported by the city's leading businesses, was prepared to commit from $18 million to $20 million, and $38.5 million in property loans was expected from banks. The loans would be repaid from facility leases and other activities. The commissioners also declared that the facility for the Indians would cost $128 million to build and a facility for the Cavs would cost $75 million. A total of $22 million was budgeted to secure the land for the sports facilities, and another $36 million to $51 million was set aside to acquire other lands for continued development. A budget line of $67.5 million for financing and working capital was included in the public announcement, and the material circulated by the committee was designed to secure the public's approval of a "sin tax" referendum, a tax on alcoholic beverages, cigarettes, and other tobacco products.

It did not take long for it to become apparent that potential problems existed with the plan. On April 15, 1990, three weeks after the county commissioners issued their press release, it was reported that a lease with each of the teams was unlikely before the referendum (Kissling, 1990). As a result, it became widely known that the expected commitment of $99 million from the teams or the facilities (sale of luxury seating) was not something that either team had accepted. It also was clear that no one knew how

TABLE 5-8
The Original Financial Plan for the Gateway Project:
A Proposed Baseball Stadium and Arena for Basketball

Anticipated Costs

Stadium construction	$128 million
Arena construction	$75 million
Land acquisition	$22 million
Land for future development	$36–$51 million
Financing and working capital	$67.5 million
Total cost	$343.5 million

Anticipated Revenues

Income from luxury seats	$99 million
Cleveland Tomorrow	$18–$20 million
Property loans[1]	$38.5 million
Interest earnings	$16.5 million
Total private investment	$174 million
"Sin tax commitment"[2]	$169.5 million
Total anticipated revenue	$343.5 million

[1]Property loans were to be repaid by income earned by the Gateway Corporation.

[2]The "sin tax" revenues would be used to pay for the bonds sold to generate $169.5 million.

Source: Gateway to the Future Committee.

much the two facilities would cost. Not only were there no architectural plans, but neither team had been asked what it wanted in a facility. Prior to the election, then, it appeared that no one knew what would be built, how much it would cost, or how much the teams had agreed to contribute to the total cost. The last piece of uncertainty involved the failure to produce a redevelopment plan for the area. The city of Cleveland's planners had not even begun to propose a plan for the redevelopment of the land adjacent to the sports facilities. Predictions and projections of anticipated economic activity were being presented without anyone's knowing what the redevelopment was to be.

The uncertainty in what the public's investment would be did not deter the owners of the Indians from threatening to leave the city if the public did not support the plan and the sin tax. Richard Jacobs claimed his fate was no longer in his hands but in the hands of voters (Larkin, 1990). If the voters rejected the proposal, the team would leave Cleveland. Larkin, a columnist for the *Cleveland Plain Dealer,* noted after his interview with team owner Richard Jacobs, "Anyone who thinks the Indians will still be playing in the [Cleveland] Stadium at the end of the century is nuts. They'll either be in a new stadium here or a new stadium elsewhere. Period." No plans existed for the stadium and no leases specified the private sector's obligations, but threats by the Indians to leave Cleveland were being made and widely reported. The sin tax vote had become a tool in a classic sports war battle. If the public did not agree to build a facility based on terms acceptable to the owner, the team would leave. It did not matter that no one knew what was to be built, how much it would cost, or what amount the teams would contribute. Vote yes or lose the Indians was the clear and distinct message.

The ownership of the Cleveland Cavaliers also entered the fray, copying the hardball sports war tactics of the Indians. The Cavs' owners did not agree to play at the proposed arena until May 2, less than a week before the referendum. Polls showed that the vote was going to be very close, and without a commitment from the Cavs, it is likely the vote would have failed. Using these political currents, the Cavs' ownership negotiated a very favorable deal. The announcement that the Cavs would play in the new arena also said the Cavs would provide $43.6 million "up front" for the project (DeLater, 1990a). This was to be their share of the proposed $99 million from the teams and the sale of luxury seating. However, the money was not to be paid up front but over a period of thirty years, and, as was learned later, it was contingent on numerous factors.

To increase the pressure on the voters, on the same day it was reported that the Cavs would leave their suburban home for a downtown arena, MLB's commissioner, Fay Vincent, declared, "Should this facility [for the Indians] not be available in Cleveland, should the vote be a negative one, we may be finding ourselves confronting a subject that we want to avoid" (Becker and Mio, 1990). Further, in comments before Cleveland's city council, Vincent made it clear that the Indians satisfied three of the criteria MLB used when reviewing requests to move: (1) the team was losing money, (2) the team played in a poor facility, and (3) the Indians would have lost the community's support if the tax referendum had been defeated. Ironically, the team's poor performance on the field for more than a decade was not one of the factors MLB considered when reviewing attendance levels and financial support for a team. The Cavs, the Indians, and MLB were playing with Cleveland and winning.

A total of $1 million was raised to convince the public to support the tax for a new stadium, a new arena, and the redevelopment of land adjacent to the facilities (Keating, 1995). The Indians contributed almost $200,000 to the campaign, and the Cavs' donation was reported to be $100,000. Approximately 383,000 votes were cast, and the measure supporting the sin tax passed with 51.7 percent of the vote. Ironically, within the city of Cleveland, the measure actually failed: 56 percent of the voters cast their ballots against the tax.

Defining "The Deal": The Indians Get a Showplace

The Indians and Gateway agreed to lease terms on December 8, 1990, six months after the sin tax vote. At a press conference to describe the agreement, it was reported that Gateway would receive $12.5 million from the sale of premium seats for the development of the stadium (Stainer, 1990). However, when the lease was signed, the team agreed that $20 million would be provided for the development of the baseball stadium (Gateway Economic Development Corporation, 1991). Although this was a substantial improvement over the figure originally suggested in December 1990, the stadium would cost $193.6 million, not the $128 million initially forecast. In addition to the $20 million from the luxury seating, the team also agreed to underwrite $2.9 million of the annual debt service. (This annual payment has a present value of $31 million because that was the specific bond the Indians agreed to repay. However, the up-front payment required from the Indians was $2.9 million.) An initial agreement with the Cavs stipulated an investment of $43 million spread over thirty years. These totals combined amounted to about two-thirds of what was initially anticipated and publicized.

The Indians also agreed to pay rent for use of the facility based on the number of fans who attended games. In addition, the team would pay no rental payments until 1.85 million tickets had been sold; however, because the team has consistently drawn more than 3 million fans to its games, Gateway has received additional revenues from the team. Gateway receives 75 cents for each ticket sold in excess of 1.85 million; $1 dollar for each ticket in excess of 2.25 million; and $1.25 for each ticket in excess of 2.5 million. When the Indians sold all their tickets for the 1996, 1997, and 1998 seasons, Gateway was guaranteed a payment of $1,718,000. The amounts paid to Gateway were to be adjusted in the eleventh and sixteenth years of the twenty-year lease, with the fee paid to increase by 40 percent of the average increase in ticket prices from year one to year eleven and by a similar percentage for the eleventh to sixteenth years.

The team was given the right to use the facility for non-base-ball events (concerts, meetings, and so forth) and to retain a substantial portion of the profits from these events. The owner also was given use of two private stadium suites and two complex offices for the team; no rent or fee was to be paid for either of these facilities. In addition, Gateway built, as part of the stadium, a restaurant for the team's owner and agreed to completely furnish the restaurant, all offices, and the suites given to the owners. Although the Indians' owner was not charged any rental fees for the restaurant and did not pay for any of the furnishings of the restaurant, he received all the income from the operation of the restaurant through his stadium management company. For all these assets, then, the team paid $22.9 million and agreed to pay rent for the use of the facility if more than 1.85 million tickets were sold. The team's owners retain all revenues from advertising and the sale of food and beverages. Gateway receives one-third of any new scoreboard advertising revenue in excess of $1.5 million (adjusted in later years relative to the consumer price index) and one-fourth of all net non-baseball-event revenue. Belonging to the team's owners is revenue from (1) all regular season games, (2) all playoff games that are part of the American League's championship series, (3) any other postseason games, (4) all World Series games, and (5) any All-Star games played at the stadium.

The Cost of Bringing the Cavs Back to Cleveland

In many ways the owners of the Cavs were in the best possible position to negotiate a very favorable lease with Gateway. The team owned its own arena in a suburban area that provided access to basketball fans from Cleveland, Cuyahoga County, and

Akron. The team controlled all revenue sources at their arena, including parking. Since there was no mass transportation to the facility, fans had to have private transportation to reach it. During the last three years that the team played at the arena, the fee to park a car for all events was $6. A substantial incentive package would be needed to entice the Cavs back to downtown Cleveland.

This is what the Cavs got in their lease: The team's owners received a restaurant to match one of the incentives provided to the Indians' owner. The Cavs were given the right to collect parking fees of $1.5 million before sharing any revenues with Gateway. After collecting $1.5 million in revenues, the Cavs would pay Gateway 67 percent of the excess subject to a set of conditions that would reduce the share given to Gateway. The ability to earn $1.5 million from parking was necessary to offset the parking revenues that the owners were receiving at the Richfield Coliseum.

The Cavs also agreed to pay "the sum of twenty-seven and one-half percent (27.5 percent) of the Executive Suite Revenue, and forty-eight percent (48 percent) of the Club Seat Revenue" (Gateway Economic Development Corporation, 1991a: 52). This money was not paid up front but in each of the thirty years of the lease. The Cavaliers did make an "up-front" payment of $4 million against their future obligations. Since the Cavs' owners only committed funds from their anticipated sale of suites and club seats, there was little, if any, investment of their own money in the new arena. The Cavs were investing the money they were going to charge their fans. The Cavs also agreed to a rental schedule somewhat similar to the one used for the Cleveland Indians. Since it was highly unlikely, however, that the attendance levels would ever reach the 1.85 million threshold, the effective rental liability for the team consisted of the payments received from the leasing of luxury seating.

Although it was originally believed that the arena would cost $75 million, the actual cost was substantially higher. In May 1994 the estimated cost of the arena was placed at $130 million; this was an update on an estimate of $118 million. In reporting the increase in cost to $130 million, Thomas Chema, executive director of the Gateway Economic Development Corporation, noted that the final cost would be "somewhat north of $130 million" (Kissling, 1994: 1). On December 15, 1994, the *Cleveland Plain Dealer* reported that the total cost of the arena would be $148 million (Koff, 1994). This price represented a cost overrun of 97.3 percent over the original figure presented to the voters by the Cuyahoga commissioners. Documents released and published in 1998 put the cost of the arena at $154 million; the cost overrun was therefore 105.3 percent. The total cost of the Gateway Complex was in excess of $473 million.

How Much Did the Teams Pay for Gateway?

One of the advertisements used by the Gateway to the Future Committee to secure passage of the sin tax featured a sports fan with the caption: "I said: Let the team owners and big shots pay. Then I found out they are paying. Big time. $174 million up front and all the costs to run it once it's done. If they finally got the big boys to put up their millions here's my two cents. I'm voting YES on Issue 2 [sin tax]."

The advertisement went on to note: "Big Corporations and sports teams will pay $174 million for Gateway. That's half of the cost, but the public will own and control the whole project. The tenants, not the public, will pay ALL the operating costs." The ad also said,

"What will the public pay?

No property tax
No sales tax
No tax abatement
Just a few pennies on alcohol and cigarettes"

To calculate what the teams paid, I performed an analysis of their commitments in terms of the leases that were eventually signed. The baseball team made two up-front commitments: $20 million from the sale of luxury suites and the assumption of $31 million in debt. There was then an up-front investment from the Indians of $22.9 million for the project and a commitment to invest $51 million in the facility. In the Indians' first year at Jacobs Field they drew 1,995,174 fans in the strike-shortened season. For the 1996, 1997, and 1998 seasons, every ticket was sold. This meant 3,434,000 fans in attendance at Indians games. (Gateway receives the payment even if the fans do not attend the game; its revenues are based on tickets sold, not the actual attendance.) I have assumed that the team will attract at least 3 million fans in the remaining seasons of their twenty-year lease.

With these attendance levels, the Indians would pay $12,501,586 to Gateway in rental fees. (This is the present value of the annual rental payments using a discount rate of 8.75 percent for all years after 1995. An adjustment was made in the eleventh and sixteenth years to reflect the potential for higher rents due Gateway as specified in the lease. The discount rate selected was based on the prime rate in effect in 1995.) The total commitment of the Cleveland Indians to Gateway, then, could be as high as $63.3 million (rental charges, bond payments, and up-front payments), but this total is dependent on an annual attendance of 3 million fans. If attendance declined in any year, the rental fees collected by Gateway would be less. Documents released in 1998 indicated, however, that the Indians never made the payments that were anticipated. For example, in 1997, instead of paying $2.1 million based on attendance, the Indians remitted only $1.12 million.

I also performed a similar present-value analysis of the payments made by the Cleveland Cavaliers to Gateway. The rental income that Gateway will receive from the Cavs will be related to the sale of luxury suites and club seats. For the team's inaugural season, 88 suites were sold, generating $10.5 million in revenue. Gateway was to receive $2,887,500 from this sale, less any of the agreed deductions. A total of 1,930 full-season club seat packages were sold for the inaugural season, as well as 30 partial-season seats. It is estimated that these sales produced $6,079,500 for the team, and the share due Gateway was $2,918,160, less any agreed deductions. In the first year, according to documents filed with Gateway by the Cavs and agreed to by both parties, the deductions permitted were equal to the payments due in the team's first season. As a result, Gateway received *no rental income* from the Cavs in the team's first year at Gund Arena. An official conceded to me that Gateway did not expect to receive any revenues from the Cavs "in the first few years" that the team played in Gund Arena. Some documents published in 1997 indicate that the Gunds have yet to make a rental payment to the public sector.

If the Cavs received the same level of income in each year of their lease as they did in the first year from the sale of suites and club seats, their maximum obligation to Gateway would be $66,329,733 (in present-value terms). As already noted, no payment was required for the 1994–95 season and new documents indicate no rent was paid through the 1997 season, so the "high-end" estimate of rental payments by the Cavs is $50,276,535. If Gateway does not receive any income for additional years, a low-end estimate of the revenue or rental income that Gateway should receive would be $41.6 million.

If the "best-case" figure is added to the high-end estimate of the payments to be received from the Indians, both teams would pay $113,603,784 for the facilities (in present-value terms). This figure is above the initial estimate of $99 million publicized during the sin tax election. If the worst-case scenario is used, the total payments by the teams to Gateway would still exceed $95 million.

Whether one uses the best-case or worst-case scenario to arrive at these projections, it should be remembered that several assumptions are built into these numbers: The Indians must continue to attract 3 million fans each season, and the popularity of the Cavs and NBA basketball must be sufficient to sell the number of suites and club seats sold in the initial year of the operation of Gund Arena. The Gateway concept was presented to the voters as a public/private partnership, with as much as $174 million coming from the private sector.

There were also other sources of private-sector funds for the Gateway Project. Gateway sold the naming rights for both the baseball stadium and the arena. Many cities have renamed facilities in exchange for an advertising fee. Both families that own the teams purchased the right to name the facilities for $400,000 for the years 1994 through 2003. From 2004 through 2013 the fee increases to $986,930. It should be noted that these fees are well below those that other cities have been able to negotiate with firms that want to advertise their name as part of a sports venue. Nevertheless, when combined (the payment for Gund Arena and the payment for Jacobs Field), Gateway will receive $800,000 each year from 1994 through 2003 and $1,973,860 each year from 2004 through 2013. The present value of these payments is $11,665,700 (see Table 5-9).

The Cuyahoga County auditor's office also expected Gateway to earn $1.2 million per year in parking revenues; the present value of these payments from 1994 through 2013 is $12,128,055. The Cleveland Tomorrow nonprofit foundation and another foundation contributed a total of $30 million to the Gateway Project, and interest earned by Gateway was estimated by the county auditor's office to be $9.3 million. When added together, the private sector's investment rises by $63,093,755. This $63.1 million has to be added to the investments by the teams themselves to arrive at the total private-sector share. The investment by the teams can range from $104.9 million to $113.6 million. This brings the entire private-sector investment to between $168 million and $176.7 million. The original campaign material prepared for the sin tax election indicated that the "big boys" were going to pay $174 million in up-front money. Although that did not occur, the *present value* of the twenty-year investment by the private sector will, at a minimum, reach $168 million and could exceed the anticipated $174 million in up-front dollars.

To estimate each sector's share of the total cost of Gateway, I used the total cost figure of $488.6 million for the project, the latest figure available when this chapter was revised. Using that figure, the public sector will be responsible for at least 64.8 percent of the cost of the project and perhaps as much as 66.7 percent if all future rental payments are made. If, as some fear, the Cavs will never pay any rent, the public's share of the cost of Gateway will increase. This level of the public sector's responsibility also *assumes* attendance levels for the Indians will remain at 3 million tickets sold per year and that the popularity of the NBA and the Cavs will not wane.

Table 5-9
Other Private-Sector Contributions to Gateway
(all figures in dollars)

Year	Naming Rights Annual Fees	Naming Rights Present Value	Parking Fees Annual Fees	Parking Fees Present Value
1994	800,000	800,000	1,200,000	1,200,000
1995	800,000	735,632	1,200,000	1,103,448
1996	800,000	676,443	1,200,000	1,014,665
1997	800,000	622,017	1,200,000	933,025
1998	800,000	571,970	1,200,000	857,954
1999	800,000	525,949	1,200,000	788,924
2000	800,000	483,631	1,200,000	725,447
2001	800,000	444,718	1,200,000	667,078
2002	800,000	408,936	1,200,000	613,405
2003	800,000	376,034	1,200,000	564,050
2004	1,973,860	853,147	1,200,000	518,667
2005	1,973,860	784,503	1,200,000	476,935
2006	1,973,860	721,382	1,200,000	438,561
2007	1,973,860	663,340	1,200,000	403,275
2008	1,973,860	609,967	1,200,000	370,827
2009	1,973,860	560,890	1,200,000	340,990
2010	1,973,860	515,761	1,200,000	313,554
2011	1,973,860	474,263	1,200,000	288,326
2012	1,973,860	436,103	1,200,000	265,127
2013	1,973,860	401,015	1,200,000	243,795
TOTAL		11,665,700		12,128,055

Other Private-Sector Contributions

Source	Amount
Cleveland Tomorrow	28,000,000
Interest income	9,300,000
Foundation	2,000,000
TOTAL	39,300,000

WHAT DID CLEVELAND GET FROM THE GATEWAY COMPLEX?

Cleveland's gains from Jacobs Field and Gund Arena are strikingly similar to those earned by Indianapolis. The direct economic gains have been small. An assessment of employment changes through 1995 indicated that fewer than eighteen hundred jobs had been created. Many of these are in the service sector. However, there have been several other investments made in the downtown area, including the Great Lakes Science Center, the Rock and Roll Hall of Fame and Museum, and two new hotels. Other development continues, and advocates point to the Gateway Complex as the catalyst for this new level of activity (Austrian and Rosentraub, 1997).

This level of development, though impressive, is still quite small. Indeed, growth in Cuyahoga County and the Cleveland metropolitan region was more robust (Austrian and Rosentraub, 1997). Nevertheless, the intangible benefits from the facilities have been substantial. Downtown Cleveland is a source of pride and has become the destination for millions of people who avoided the city in years past.

Cleveland's adventures with professional sports did not end with the Gateway saga. After watching the public sector lead efforts to build a new stadium and arena, Art Modell, owner of the Browns, threatened to leave Cleveland unless a similar effort to enhance the revenue potential of his NFL franchise was made. The community responded with a $175 million proposal, but that was not sufficient to convince Modell to stay in Cleveland. Three days before the election to approve the final piece of the $175 million package, stories circulated that he was actively discussing the relocation of the Browns to Baltimore. Modell himself did nothing to dispel these stories; indeed, he encouraged them.

> Citing a source close to Modell, the *Baltimore Sun* reported in today's editions that Modell intends to announce Monday in Baltimore that he is moving his franchise there. Details were still sketchy Friday, but *The Sun* reported that Modell is expected to be accompanied at the 12:30 P. M. news conference by Maryland Governor Parris

N. Glendening, Baltimore Mayor Kurt Schmoke, and Maryland Stadium Authority Chairman John Moag.

"I've got to do what I have to protect my family, my franchise, and my employees," Modell said in a lengthy telephone interview with several of the reporters who cover the team regularly. "We'll see what develops in the next few days, and I wouldn't jump to any conclusions. At the same time I don't want to hold out any false hopes either" (Associated Press, 1995).

The Browns had played in Cleveland for fifty years, and throughout the 1990s average home attendance for Browns games exceeded seventy thousand. This gave the team one of the largest average home attendance figures in the NFL and clearly demonstrated that the fans supported the franchise through winning and losing years (*New York Times,* 1995a). The Browns last won a league championship in 1964 and last appeared in a league championship game in 1967. They are one of the teams that have never appeared in a Super Bowl despite winning several division titles in the 1980s. Even with this mixed record of success on the field, the Browns were steadfastly supported by their rabid "dawg pound" fans for decades.

This support from loyal fans during the thirty years that the team did not win a championship did not stop Modell from playing one city against another in a game of "sports wars." Indeed, one day before the public referendum to provide more than $175 million to address the team's needs, he accepted a far more lucrative offer from Baltimore and the State of Maryland. That offer included $75 million in incentives and rent-free use of a new publicly financed stadium that had a final price tag in excess of $200 million. After fifty years in Cleveland, the Browns would become the Baltimore Ravens. As Art Modell summarized it himself, "I leave my heart and part of my soul in Cleveland. But frankly, it came down to a simple proposition: I had no choice. . . . What is required is beyond the capacity of Cleveland. I didn't want to be known as a shakedown artist" (Ginsburg, 1995). Modell continued to stress that he was losing money and could not earn a profit in Cleveland. Yet *Financial World* reported in May 1995 that the Browns had earned a profit of $6 million in 1994.

Even after the announcement of the Browns' move, the voters still approved the extension of the "sin tax" to complete the financing for the $175 million package. Subsequent efforts led by Cleveland's Mayor Michael White concluded with the award of an expansion franchise that will begin play as the Cleveland Browns in 1999. The NFL also agreed to lend the new ownership group up to $48 million to fund their portion of the costs of building the new stadium. The State of Ohio expanded the public sector's largesse by agreeing to pay 15 percent of the estimated $220 million construction cost. This investment brought the public sector's investment in sports to $700 million.

INDIANAPOLIS AND CLEVELAND: THE LESSONS LEARNED

Sports will bring visitors to downtown areas; and these excursions enhance the vitality and excitement of urban life and increase the contact between racial groups. Although these benefits should not be considered trivial and inconsequential, it should be remembered that a sports strategy will not substantially increase the supply of high-paying jobs. Gateway did create a number of service-sector jobs, and several hundred other jobs were added to the area by other firms. But the total impact of this employment is not enough to meet the needs of inner-city Cleveland and address the unemployment and infrastructure issues that plague these areas. A sports strategy did not herald a period of rising wage in Indianapolis. Average wage levels did not increase as much as the salaries paid to workers in other cities. Indianapolis's and Cleveland's images have been substantially changed. Both cities are now seen as destinations for tourism, recreation, and, in Indianapolis's case, conventions. In addition, both cities have picturesque downtown skylines. However, these substantial benefits have contributed precious little to the redevelopment of neighborhoods, the quality of urban education, or a reduction of crime and other urban ills.

Several other lessons can be learned from the experiences of both cities. From Cleveland we learn that voting on a proposed complex should not take place until what is to be built is defined, along with its cost and what the team(s) will pay. In addition, it should be specified which facility revenues will be retained by the team and which will be given to the public sector. In this manner voters will have an opportunity to evaluate a proposed plan. The Gateway plan did not exist before the election to vote on the sin tax, and there were no firm agreements concerning who would pay for what. A firm cap also needs to be set on what the public sector will pay for the facility.

If a sports facility is to be part of a redevelopment effort, a complete plan, as in the case of Indianapolis, should exist. Indianapolis's plan, initiated in 1974, was completed in 1995, and voters, the public sector, and the private sector can see what was accomplished and determine if the benefits were worth the commitments. It does not appear that any such plan existed when Cuyahoga County's voters were asked to vote for the sin tax, even though some groups persist in thinking that a plan did or does exist.

The Gateway saga also begs a third question or lesson for cities engaging in a sports war with professional teams. Could a better deal have been negotiated? Hindsight is more accurate, of course.

It is also a luxury to be able to second-guess decisionmakers who may not be able to analyze options when teams are threatening to move and elected officials are demanding signed contracts so that teams do not leave town during their administration. Even with these caveats there are still some things that can be learned from the Gateway experience.

The Richfield Coliseum was built in 1974 and lacked many of the revenue-generating amenities of more modern arenas. The Gund family eventually would have needed those amenities to survive and to keep the team competitive, given the changes in basketball economics. Those amenities might have consisted of extensive luxury suites and club seating. Who buys most of these suites and club seats? Business firms. And the Gateway Complex could have offered something to the Gunds that they could not get in suburban Ohio: a downtown location near those firms and business executives who buy premium seats, and this location would have access to mass transportation to the suburbs. These advantages, along with the need of all NBA owners to earn as much revenue as they can from facility operations, would eventually have forced the Gunds to downtown Cleveland. The Gunds needed a downtown location as much as Cleveland needed the Gunds downtown.

Would Cleveland have risked losing the Cavs to another market as some feared? If Cleveland did not give the Cavs everything they wanted, would the team have moved to Nashville or some other city willing to build an arena? Here again Cleveland's leadership may have underestimated the value of their market. Cleveland has more Fortune 500 firms and other large businesses that can afford to buy luxury suites and club seats than any other area without an NBA team. As such, a move to another city might have reduced the financial opportunities available to the Cavs.

It is also hard not to criticize aspects of the negotiations with the Indians. The potential existed for substantial gains for the Jacobs family from the continued successful redevelopment of downtown Cleveland. The Jacobs family is one of the largest landowners in downtown Cleveland. If the Gateway Complex was successful, the value of those assets would increase. Put another way, what was it worth to the Jacobs family to have the Gateway Complex developed? Before Gateway and the city of Cleveland initiated or completed its negotiations with Richard Jacobs, it would have been valuable to forecast the gains in real estate values that he would realize from the presence of the new stadium. The individuals who supported the Gateway concept were eager to point out the anticipated economic benefits for the region. A similar analysis was needed to determine how much other landowners and developers would gain from the anticipated renaissance in downtown Cleveland.

Rebuilding a downtown core area or reestablishing a city's image and reputation requires the cooperation of a number of people and firms. Coalitions have to be built and maintained. Indianapolis's partnership for sports and downtown redevelopment lasted for almost two decades. The excitement created by the attraction of numerous sporting events (the Pan American Games, the Men's Final Four Basketball Championships, and others) and the retention of the Indianapolis Colts and Indiana Pacers clearly helped maintain the coalition and attract new members. TA was able to attract events and teams creating an impression of economic success and vitality. These images certainly contributed to and helped maintain a focus on downtown development. Although there were few direct economic benefits, these political and social values should not be discounted. Sports may help maintain a coalition of groups, however they cannot bring economic development to a region creating a typical downtown and city center.

6

Cities, Sports, and Imagery

Sports teams long have been identified with a community's image; indeed, when cities pursue teams, taxpayers are reminded that without a major league franchise their region may be seen as "minor league" or second-rate. Former U.S. senator Thomas Eagleton summarized best the views of many when he said in June 1995, "Why do the deal for the Rams? Because some people around the nation think St. Louis's best days are behind us. We needed to do something dramatic." Few would disagree with the proposition that teams both help define a community and enhance the quality of life. However, what price should a community pay for "image," and how much is too much? St. Louis built a dome to attract the Rams from Anaheim, and the deal set new standards for public subsidies while making the Rams one of the NFL's most profitable teams. Montreal attempted to build a world-class architectural statement to enhance its economic and cultural links to the United States and ended up with one of professional sports' most subsidized and embarrassing situations: the dome that would not work. Determined to show their domination of Canada's economic scene, Toronto outdid Montreal and built the most expensive and subsidized stadium in North America.

REVIVING THE GLORY OF DAYS PAST:
ST. LOUIS'S IMAGE, IDENTITY, AND TEAMS

St. Louis's leaders, like those in Cleveland and Indianapolis, were struggling to maintain the vitality of an aging midwestern city with a declining population and economy. The bankruptcy of a highly visible employer, Trans World Airlines, seemed to intensify concerns that St. Louis's best days were behind it. In 1960 the residents of the city accounted for 51.6 percent of the population of St. Louis County and more than one-third of the residents of the metropolitan area. By 1970 the city's residents accounted for one-fourth of the metropolitan area, and by 1990 the city's residents were just 16.2 percent of the region's population. Table 6-1 illustrates the shrinking proportion of the city of St. Louis's population as a component of the region and the number of people who had left. In 1960 the city had three-quarters of a million residents; by 1996 the city had lost more than half of its 1960 population base.

But St. Louis was losing more than just population. In 1968 the NBA's Hawks left for Atlanta; twenty years later the NFL's Cardinals moved to Phoenix. In the 1980s the city's leaders worried that the NHL's Blues might also leave, and then in the 1990s the city's beloved baseball team, the Cardinals, were sold. Many leaders agreed with Senator Eagleton that a set of dramatic actions were needed to enhance St. Louis's image.

WHAT COULD CHANGE ST. LOUIS'S IMAGE?
SPORTS, OF COURSE!

St. Louis's attempt at "doing something dramatic" emphasized sports. There were certainly efforts to rebuild neighborhoods, improve schools, and make the city safe. St. Louis turned to sports to achieve a favorable national image and make people believe it was

TABLE 6-1

The City of St. Louis's Population and Its Percentage of All Residents of Missouri, St. Louis County, and the St. Louis Metropolitan Area
(percentages refer to the city of St. Louis's population as a proportion of the state, county, and metropolitan area)

Area	1960		1970		1980		1990		1996	
Missouri	4,319,813	17.4%	4,676,501	13.3%	4,916,766	9.2%	5,190,719	7.6%	5,306,000	6.9%
City	750,026		622,236		453,085		396,685		366,000	
County	703,532	51.6%	951,353	39.5%	973,896	31.8%	993,529	28.5%	1,005,200	26.7%
Metro Area	2,161,228	34.7%	2,429,246	25.6%	2,377,043	19.1%	2,444,099	16.2%	2,552,400	14.3%

Sources: U.S. Bureau of the Census; U.S. Department of Commerce.

a "can-do city" and not a "has-been place." The splash made when the Rams announced they would leave Anaheim certainly indicated that St. Louis was back in the NFL. However, St. Louis also increased the costs of professional sports for virtually every city that hosts an NFL team, and this change added millions of dollars to the tax burdens of families everywhere.

With nostalgia a growth industry for urban revival, it is not hard to imagine why the leadership of St. Louis focused on sports to recast St. Louis's reputation. The city has a long and storied history with professional sports. For more than fifty years St. Louis was home to two baseball teams: the American League Browns and the National League Cardinals. The apex of St. Louis's love affair with baseball was the 1944 World Series when the Cardinals defeated the Browns in the "streetcar" World Series. However, the first dent in St. Louis's sports armor took place in 1953 when the Browns, plagued by declining performance and attendance, left for Baltimore and a new life as the Orioles.

The Cardinals have always been the city's darlings. Founded in 1892, the Cardinals' total attendance ranks second in baseball to the New York Yankees, a remarkable achievement given the much smaller size of the St. Louis market. The Cardinals are an icon similar to the Brooklyn Dodgers and the Chicago Cubs. In 1996 the Cardinals welcomed the one-hundred-millionth fan to see one of their games. The Cardinals also have one of MLB's most successful on-the-field records; the team has appeared in fifteen World Series, winning nine. The Cardinals have also given baseball some of its greatest memories and stars including Roger Hornsby, Joe Medwick, Johnny Mize, Stan Musial, Enos Slaughter, the Dean brothers, the legendary Gas House Gang, Red Schoendienst, Bob Gibson, Lou Brock, and Vince Coleman. The Cardinals and their owner for forty years, Gussie Busch, also gave something more lasting to baseball. "Gussie" did not like paying high salaries to players, and many point to the confrontation be-tween Curt Flood and the Cardinals as the beginning of the changes in MLB's structure that have led to the current salary levels.

In March 1969, before sportswriters and the board of An-heuser-Busch, Gussie lectured his players on their excessive de-mands for additional pension funds. This lecture, on the heels of a "testy" salary fight with Curt Flood, soured both men on each other. At the end of the season Flood was traded to Philadelphia, and his subsequent lawsuit challenging the reserve clause un-leashed a series of changes that permanently altered the financing of sports. It is a bit ironic somehow that two strains of the real world of sports economics—escalating player salaries and exces-sive public-sector subsidies of sports—are both to be found in St. Louis.

THE COST OF REJOINING THE NFL: A FIVE-ACT MELODRAMA WITH AN EPILOGUE

Act I: St. Louis Builds a Stadium and Sets a New Standard for Corporate Welfare

Immediately after the flight of the football Cardinals, St. Louis's leadership recruited NFL legend Walter Payton to be part of a group with one objective: to bring an NFL team to St. Louis. The NFL Partnership (NFLP) adopted a two-part game plan for win-ning an expansion franchise. First, the NFLP would accept re-sponsibility for securing the funds to pay the steep franchise fee expected to be demanded by the NFL. Second, the NFLP would ask the public sector to build the stadium the NFL wanted as a condition for a new franchise. St. Louis and the NFLP joined to-gether to build political support for a domed stadium that would also enhance the attractiveness of the city's convention center. Inspired by Indianapolis's Hoosier Dome, which became an integral part of the Indiana Convention Center, St. Louis hoped to emulate that city's success in attracting a team and numerous conventions.

Ground was broken for the new domed stadium on July 13, 1992, and Mayor Vincent Schoemehl Jr. labeled the project "an economic engine for the entire St. Louis region." At one point during the planning process it was claimed that the expansion of the convention center and the attraction of an NFL team would add an estimated $580 million per year to the region's economy. Although clearly an overstated claim, during this maelstrom of football frenzy no one really questioned the report. All attention and zeal were focused on getting a new team—at some cost, at any cost—and since a stadium was required, the project moved forward.

The NFLP signed a thirty-year lease with the St. Louis Convention and Visitors Commission (CVC) for use of the new stadium and was granted an impressive array of income flows and other concessions if it could bring a team to St. Louis. The NFLP's team would receive all income from food, beverages, and concessions, all income from the sale or rental of luxury suites and club seats, and most income from advertising. And the CVC even agreed to manage, operate, and maintain the stadium on game days. The team's only expense would be an annual lease cost of $250,000. At the time, this represented one of the most subsidized deals ever given to a team, because the new franchise would have no responsibilities for the cost of constructing the facility. The city's leadership wanted to convince the NFL that they would do whatever was required to get a team back to St. Louis.

The stadium project and its funding was a political milestone in St. Louis's history. It represented the first time that the city was able to join with the county and the state to build a project for St. Louis's regional development. This outcome assumes even greater significance in this area in which regional cooperation is scarce and state involvement in such a clearly regional and urban endeavor is practically unknown. However, after the Rams arrived and taxpayers understood the full extent of the subsidy, several bills were introduced in the 1996 session of the Missouri legislature to eliminate any future state support for convention or sports projects.

Act II: Who's on First? No, Who's on Second! Who Is St. Louis's Ownership Group?!

When wooing the NFL in an expansion derby, two things are needed: a unified public sector with a plan for building a stadium and an ownership group with the cash to pay a franchise fee and operate the team. Ironically, the St. Louis public sector had their act together; it was the divided private sector and its infighting that cost St. Louis an expansion franchise.

The events that led to the demise of St. Louis's hopes for a franchise are summarized in Table 6-2. Disputes within the NFLP, exacerbated by the strains created to secure the financing needed to meet the NFL's steep franchise fee, led to disunity and the formation of a second partnership, the Gateway Football Partnership. With two ownership groups competing with each other, confusion reigned. The new ownership group believed they would receive the very favorable lease that the NFLP had been granted for use of the dome. The Gateway group had more substantial financial resources, which gave it an edge in meeting the NFL's requirements to be an owner, but the NFLP controlled the stadium lease and would not assign it to the other group. What would happen if the

TABLE 6-2

Losing an NFL Expansion Franchise: The Collapse of Private-Sector Unity

Date	Event
Spring, 1988	After twenty-eight seasons, the Cardinals move to Phoenix.
5/12/89	The Missouri legislature passes a bill for the state-city-county financing of a new stadium in St. Louis.
5/23/91	The NFL announces it will add two expansion teams in time for the 1995 season.
9/27/91	Jerry Clinton and Fran Murray bring James Orthwein into the NFLP as Chair and CEO; he owns a share of the New England Patriots, which is perceived to be a "backup" to getting an expansion team.
5/19/92	Five finalists are chosen for the two NFL expansion teams: St. Louis, Baltimore, Charlotte, Jacksonville, and Memphis. Many believe St. Louis is destined to receive a team.
7/13/92	Ground is broken for a new stadium to be completed.
11/5/92	Mr. Orthwein becomes the sole owner of the Patriots, which reinforces the view it is a backup team. If St. Louis loses its expansion team bid, Mr. Orthwein's hopes to move the Patriots to St. Louis.
9/9/93	Mr. Clinton and Mr. Orthwein part ways and Mr. Clinton assumes control of the NFLP. However, he lacks adequate resources to finance a new team.
10/26/93	Lacking cash, Mr. Clinton steps aside for wealthy Missouri businessman Stan Kroenke, who then becomes the financial support for Gateway.
10/26/93	The NFL awards the first franchise to Charlotte but the second franchise award is put off to allow St. Louis to "get its financial act together." Control over the stadium lease looms as the major deterrent to approval.
11/30/93	The second franchise is awarded to Jacksonville, and St. Louis's expansion team, the Stallions, "drops dead in the gate"

NFL wanted the Gateway group? With peace negotiations between the two groups under way, one member of the NFLP group was willing to "bow out" but another was not. Although there was some confidence within the Gateway group that if they were awarded an NFL franchise, they would be successful in a legal challenge to the existing lease arrangement, the NFL was clearly unimpressed with the fractious situation. Why expand in a community where legal action might await the NFL?

Act III: The NFL Really Wants to Come to St. Louis, but No One Can Agree on Who and Where

The NFL delayed its final decision to award the second of two expansion teams until November 30, 1993. The NFL wanted to place a team in St. Louis, and additional time was needed to resolve the conflict between the two ownership groups. The price for an expansion franchise was set at $140 million, with $70 million up front and $16 million in interest charges on the balance. In addition, potential ownership groups were informed that they would receive only 50 percent of the shares other teams would receive from the national television package. The NFLP formally named their anticipated team the St. Louis Stallions. The NFL, committed to adding two teams, awarded one franchise to Charlotte in October 1993 and then agreed to wait to see if St. Louis could resolve its lease problems. When that could not be done to the league's satisfaction, Jacksonville received the second franchise.

Act IV: The Emergence of a New Knight

A new leader was needed to end the feud between the warring partnerships and head the efforts to attract an existing team to St. Louis because the NFL had no immediate plans to add more teams. The milestones in Act IV, St. Louis's successful grab of the Los Angeles Rams, are summarized in Table 6-3. After the failure of the expansion team bid, a third group was formed, FANS Inc. FANS was prepared to pay $3.5 million to one NFLP partner for his share of the lease for the new stadium. The other partner in the NFLP eventually agreed to relinquish his 65 percent share of the stadium lease. FANS now had a facility for a team to use.

TABLE 6-3
A Chronology of Events in The Rams' Odyssey

Date	Event
1/6/94	The Rams warn Anaheim that they want out of their stadium lease.
1/21/94	Mr. Orthwein sells the Patriots to a Massachusetts buyer and St. Louis loses its fallback team.
5/3/94	The Rams give Anaheim a lease termination notice.
8/7/94	The Rams give FANS Inc. a "wish" list for their move to St. Louis.
8/10/94	The Rams await the solving of St. Louis's lease problems.
8/11/94	FANS recruits Senator Thomas Eagleton, who masterminds a settlement of the maze of legal, financial, and political issues surrounding the stadium lease.
9/15/94	FANS purchases Mr. Clinton's control of the lease and secures its right to award the lease arrangements to the Rams.
1/17/95	Rams owner Georgia Frontiere announces the Rams' move to St. Louis for the 1995 season. The team will play at Busch Stadium until the new stadium is completed.
3/15/95	The NFL owners vote overwhelmingly to block the Rams' move. Eyeing the millions of dollars in St. Louis's personal seat license money, they want a multi-million-dollar payment before approving a relocation.
4/12/95	After rumblings of litigation from the Rams and Missouri attorney general Jay Nixon, the NFL owners settle for a lower sum and vote 23-6-1 to approve the Rams' move to St. Louis; the Raiders abstain and the Cardinals' owner, Bill Bidwell, votes no. Ironically, the Rams' owner, Ms. Frontiere, casts the deciding vote since 23 were required for approval

FANS began to think about teams that could be attracted to St. Louis and focused their attention on the Los Angeles Rams. The Rams were dissatisfied with their existing stadium. Having left the Los Angeles Coliseum for suburban Anaheim, the team still desired a stadium with more of the revenue sources available in newer facilities. When Los Angeles, Anaheim, and Orange County seemed unwilling to build a new facility, the Rams cast a roving eye toward their original midwestern roots (the team had been founded in Cleveland). FANS was only too eager to respond.

With a stadium built and an incredible lease already available as a "lure," Senator Eagleton initiated negotiations with the team.

The Rams, however, had other demands or needs in addition to access to the dome and its very favorable lease. The team wanted additional revenues to "buy out" their lease with the city of Anaheim and cover the cost of their move to St. Louis. The Rams also wanted St. Louis to build a new practice facility. Although the team would not have to pay a franchise fee and could have used some of their newfound wealth to cover these costs, the Rams knew they were in a very strong position to have all their demands met. Indeed, St. Louis and the Rams knew there were no plans for the NFL to expand. To satisfy each of these additional demands, FANS sold personal seat licenses (PSLs)—fees paid for the permanent right to buy season tickets and transfer this right to someone else—and used the majority of these revenues to meet the additional stipulations made by the Rams. With all the incentives in place, the Rams moved to St. Louis for the 1995 season.

St. Louis's football fans did not balk at the thought of paying for the right to buy season tickets through PSLs or to provide the funds to the team to help with their move from Los Angeles. FANS received seventy thousand requests for PSLs, far exceeding the supply. In the end, more than fifty-two thousand PSLs were sold, and fifty-three hundred club seats and ninety luxury boxes were leased to local fans and businesses. Suites were leased for five, ten, or fifteen years and ranged in price from $47,500 to $75,000, with a seating capacity of ten to sixteen. Club seat leases ranged in price from $700 to $2,200. The $74 million received through the sale of PSLs provided the funds needed to pay the costs associated with the termination of the Rams' lease ($26 million), relocation costs ($13 million), fees to the NFL ($10 million), and a new practice facility ($5 million). A total of $8 million was used to fulfill various claims between the partnership groups, and $6.5 million was used for legal and advertising fees (see Table 6-4).

TABLE 6-4

The Final Tally for the Rams: Who Receives and Who Pays

Amount	Purpose	Revenue Source(s)
The Rams Receive		
$26 million	To meet financial obligations in Anaheim	PSL income
$13 million	Relocation fee, moving expenses	PSL income
$15 million	Practice facility, NFL fee	Fans Inc., city, county
$5–$10 million	Stadium improvements	PSL income
Other Expenses		
$8 million	For Mr. Clinton's lease rights	PSL income
$6.5 million	Legal and marketing expenses	PSL income
Rams' Expenses		
$29 million	NFL relocation fee	$2 million PSL income, Rams
$17 million	NFL share of PSL income	PSL income
$13 million	Share of future NFL expansion fees	Foregone income
$0–$12.5 million	Potential fee to Fox Television	Foregone income

Act V: The Dangling Threads

When the Dome was completed, a new controversy emerged involving its external advertising. Some believed that the advertising was "tacky" for a public facility, but both the team and the convention center were planning on this revenue for their own use. Advertising raised approximately $6 million during the first year; the convention center received 25 percent of the first $6 million and 10 percent of all remaining funds. The Rams received the rest of the money. In addition, Trans World Airlines (TWA) will pay $1.3 million per year, increased by an inflation factor of 3.5 percent per year, for twenty years to paint its logo on the top of the dome. The CVC receives $325,000 from the TWA deal; $975,000 goes to the Rams.

Epilogue: An Escape Hatch for the Rams

The lease given the Rams permits the team to move as early as 2005 if the Trans World Dome is not considered one of the best facilities (top 25 percent) for professional football. If the stadium or any of its components are not "first tier" on March 1, 2005, or March 1, 2015, the thirty-year lease becomes a one-year lease. This provision of the lease strongly implies that more public funds, in addition to the original cost, will need to be spent on the stadium on a "regular" basis to keep up its status as a first-tier facility.

BATTLES FOR IDENTITY
NORTH OF THE BORDER

Enormous subsidies have been provided for sports in Montreal and Toronto for image, economic development, and to integrate Canadian cities into American life. The two most expensive single-site sports projects are to be found in Canada. Montreal's Olympic Stadium cost more than Can$1 billion, and the Sky-Dome in Toronto had a final price tag in excess of Can$625 million. In reviewing the costs associated with Toronto's edifice, or what one columnist referred to as Ontario's "St. Peter's Basilica" (Stein, 1994), Paul Godfrey, a former chair of Toronto's Metropolitan Government Council, reviewed the public sector's failure to control expenditures and noted wryly: "They could have asked for business plans. I don't think they really did their jobs" (Van Alphen, 1992).

The anticipated or hoped-for return from these investments involved the typical expectations of an enhanced image, expanded downtown development through related private-sector investments, and greater economic growth. And some people, including those who benefit from the existence of teams, have proclaimed the public's investment worthwhile. In 1994, Dave Perkins, a columnist with the *Toronto Star,* wrote:

> The province [Ontario] has written off the loss and the general public doubtless has better things to get excited about now.

Besides, it's here [SkyDome] and the roof works and everybody goes to it and many even profess to love it. Plus, it allowed the Blue Jays to make enough money to buy the players to win two World Series and how much was that worth to everyone?

It might seem a bit ironic that Canada's largest investments in sports did not focus on hockey facilities. But while sports fans in Canada have very deep passions for hockey, both Montreal and Toronto have extensive histories with baseball. The city of Montreal has an illustrious baseball history as home to one of the most successful AAA franchises in North America, the Royals. An affiliate of the old Brooklyn Dodgers, the Royals were not only league champions in seven seasons from 1941 through 1958, but they also won three Junior World Series championships during this era and were the team for which Jackie Robinson made his initial inroads into "white" professional sports. Roy Campanella and Don Newcombe were among other African American stars who gained early experience with the MLB system as members of the Royals.

Toronto also was home to a minor league baseball team from 1912 to 1967. Toronto's AAA team won ten league pennants and one Junior World Series. The Yankees' first African American star, Elston Howard, was a member of the 1954 pennant-winning team, and Babe Ruth hit his only minor league home run against Toronto. Both Montreal and Toronto have also been quite supportive of their MLB teams when these teams won. The Toronto Blue Jays were the first MLB team to attract more than 4 million fans in a single year, and at the height of their success, the Montreal Expos drew more than 2 million fans (1979, 1980, 1983, and 1984). The Expos might have been able to repeat this success in 1994, but the MLB strike destroyed the team's chance for a divisional title and an appearance in the playoffs.

The public sector has been a lavish and overly indulgent supporter of professional baseball in Canada. Some of this public support for professional sports is a result of the willingness of Canadian voters to accept higher levels of taxation and greater public-sector responsibility for public services and quality of life. Why would Canadian governments be interested in investing in professional baseball? There are several reasons, most of which are shared with governments in the United States. In addition, as economic and political ties to the United States increased and became more crucial, some community leaders in Canada believed there was a need to make baseball part of Canadian life.

BATTING GIANTS

For more than forty years Canada's two eastern giants, Montreal and Toronto, and their respective provinces, Quebec and Ontario, have battled for economic and demographic supremacy. Where once both provinces were about the same size, today Ontario is substantially larger than Quebec. Montreal, Canada's largest metropolitan region through the early 1970s, lost that distinction and is now three-quarters the size of Toronto. While Quebec Province had an 80 percent increase in population from 1951 to 1995, Ontario's population increased 139 percent (see Table 6-5). Metropolitan Montreal's population increased by 126 percent from 1951 to 1994, but Metropolitan Toronto grew by 254 percent. Metropolitan Toronto's population is now 29 percent larger than Metropolitan Montreal's, and Ontario's population is 51 percent larger than Quebec's.

While Indianapolis coupled sports and downtown development into one set of policies and programs, Montreal sought to redefine its image through redevelopment and then joined sports to its efforts. Redevelopment began in Montreal in the 1950s with

TABLE 6-5
Population Growth in Metropolitan Montreal and Toronto
and Quebec and Ontario Provinces, 1951–1995

Year	Metropolitan Montreal	Metropolitan Toronto	Quebec Province	Ontario Province
1951	1,471,851	1,210,353	4,055,681	4,597,542
1956	1,745,001	1,502,253	N. A.	N. A.
1961	2,109,509	1,824,481	5,259,211	6,236,092
1966	2,570,982	2,289,900	5,780,845	6,960,870
1971	2,743,208	2,628,043	6,027,764	7,703,106
1976	2,802,547	2,803,101	6,234,445	8,264,465
1981	2,828,349	2,998,947	6,438,403	8,625,107
1991	3,127,242	3,893,046	6,895,963	10,084,885
1994	3,322,400	4,281,900	N. A.	N. A.
1995	N. A.	N. A.	7,300,000	11,004,800

the widening of major streets to improve east-west traffic flow. René Lévesque Boulevard was designed to be a center for corporate headquarters, and Place Ville-Marie became "without question, the single most important development in the history of Montreal's downtown" (Nader, 1976). Between 1962 and 1967 a number of other large multifunctional office complexes were built in the central business district: Place Victoria, Place Bonaventure, and Place du Canada. Each of these complexes has an extensive underground pedestrian system and set of shopping arcades, but the erosion of Montreal's economic status continued.

Just as in several U.S. cities, Montreal joined sports and other festivals to its effort to redevelop its downtown area and change its image. Jean Drapeau, Montreal's mayor from 1960 through 1986, initiated several other grand projects including the 1967 World Exposition, the establishment of the Montreal Expos, the 1976 Olympics, a subway, new highways, and new boulevards. In the latter years of the Drapeau administration and in the progressive administration of Mayor Jean Doré (1986 through 1994), attempts were made to revitalize Montreal with a number of different policy efforts even though for numerous years through 1996 the area had an unemployment rate exceeding 10 percent. To stem the flight of manufacturing to the suburbs, ten industrial parks were created after 1980. Neighborhood commercial arteries had extensive street and sidewalk renovations. Operation 20,000 Houses was a successful subsidized housing effort for middle-income citizens.

When Montreal was awarded a new franchise in 1968, the National League wanted a new, modern facility. In developing their plans for the Olympic Games, the city's leaders had a vague idea of combining the facility for the Expos with an Olympic stadium, but the city had also promised MLB a domed stadium for the expansion team. Prior to building any new facility, Jarry Park, a small stadium, was used. Jarry Park was improved and expanded, but for the Expos' first few years the stadium's capacity was only thirty thousand. This small stadium was not a liability in these early years, however, because the team's play could probably have been considered representative of AAA teams. In their first year in Montreal, the Expos lost 110 games, and these losing ways became a tradition and part of the team's legacy. From 1970 through 1978 the Expos never won as many games as they lost, and in 1976 their futility almost matched their pitiful first year (107 losses to 110). Despite their poor performance, Montreal's fans provided substantial support for the team. From 1969 through 1974 more than 1 million fans attended games. Attendance dropped in the Olympic year, 1976, but in 1977 and 1978 more than 1.4 million fans attended games.

When the Expos moved to Olympic Stadium, their fortunes on the field changed. Building on their improved performance in 1977 and 1978, the Expos compiled the best overall record in the

National League during the 1979, 1980, 1981, and 1982 seasons. Unfortunately, in no year did they win a pennant. When the Expos became a team that was a potential pennant winner, fan support increased, and attendance surpassed 2 million in four different seasons. The frustration over not winning a title that developed during these years seemed to usher in a period of gradual decline for the Expos, both in their performance and in their presence in the sports life of Montreal and Canada. Ironically, however, their declining popularity may have been as much a result of external forces as it was related to their inability to win a pennant.

Off the field, the team had substantial problems with the image created by its players. Two players in the early 1980s admitted to drug use. A third player was released from his contract when it was suspected that he, too, was using drugs (Carter with Abraham, 1993; Williams and Plaschke, 1990). The stories that circulated concerning the use of drugs contributed to the impression that the Expos of the late 1970s and early 1980s were indulgent underachievers.

When drugs were not undermining the image of the team, the failure of some of the players to embrace the local culture also hurt marketing efforts. Establishing or integrating MLB into the Quebecois culture is a challenge and an obligation some players were not willing to embrace. While Rusty Staub became proficient enough in French to make public speeches, others did not make the effort. One player's wife was reported to have told many people that she needed to shop in Plattsburgh, New York, because "there are important staples we have to go there for, like Doritos" (Richler, 1992: 6). In 1995 an Expos player complained because the flight attendants spoke French on a team flight. Former Expos manager Dick Williams, an admirer of Montreal as a city, claimed "modern-day baseball players don't like Montreal, not because of your city but because they are baseball players. . . . For the mod-

TABLE 6-6
The Former Expos and Their New Teams

Player	New Team	Position	Year
Gary Carter	Mets	Catcher	1985
Andres Galarraga	Rockies	First Base	1992
Delino DeShields	Dodgers	Second Base	1992
Tim Wallach	Dodgers	Third Base	1994
Hubie Brooks	Dodgers	Shortstop	1993
Andre Dawson	Cubs	Outfield	1987
Marquis Grissom	Braves	Outfield	1995
Larry Walker	Rockies	Outfield	1995
Ken Hill	Cardinals	Pitcher	1995
Mark Langston	Angles	Pitcher	1990
Randy Johnson	Mariners	Pitcher	1989
John Wetteland	Yankees	Pitcher	1995

ern-day player, differences are not to be tolerated. The modern-day player doesn't hate Montreal so much as he's afraid of it" (Williams and Plaschke, 1990: 205).

With declining attendance and support, management began to trade players to other teams. The number of players who left the Montreal Expos since 1985 could form a National League All-Star team (Farber, 1995).

The team's fortunes were reversed temporarily in 1994 when it appeared the Expos would likely win their first outright divisional title. Baseball seemed ready to succeed in Montreal, but the season-ending strike ended visions of a World Series for Montreal. Frustrations grew for both team owners and players, and the Expos' management continued its policy of dealing away their most expensive talent. Under instructions from the team's owners, General Manager Kevin Malone tried to reduce the team's payroll from the $18.6 million spent in 1994 to $15 million for 1995. In this environment, Larry Walker, Marquis Grissom, Ken Hill, and John Wetteland all left for other teams, and the Expos were able to meet their payroll target.

OLYMPIC STADIUM

The final cost for Olympic Stadium was in excess of $1 billion. The substantial public investment in Olympic Stadium might have been worth the tangible and intangible benefits if it had not become a symbol of failure. When the project was initiated, there was great hope that Olympic Stadium would become a signature architectural statement for the city, and when the Olympics began in 1976, the stadium received critical acclaim. Jean Claude Marsan, a leading authority on Montreal's architecture, observed, "If Montreal has any building that merits the title of monument, it certainly is the Olympic Stadium. It has all the attributes of Beaux Arts architecture: beauty, clarity of style and function, harmony of the ensemble, which itself is well balanced and rhythmic. Its design is dynamic and vibrant, enclosing spaces by ample movements. The majesty of this structure, particularly from the infield, is impressive" (Marsan, 1981: 392). It seemed that the cost of the stadium might have been worth the benefits, but then the roof literally fell on the project.

The failure that became identified with Olympic Stadium involved its controversial roof. Olympic Stadium was designed to be the first retractable dome stadium. The roof had not been completed, however, when the building opened in 1976. Indeed, it was not finished until 1988, and its most telling feature is the mast that was designed to lift a removable roof section on and off the stadium. It was anticipated that the Expos would play their games in an open-air stadium when weather permitted, but the roof would descend to cover the field on cold and inclement days. This plan worked for only three seasons.

The mast, fifty-five stories high, is the world's tallest inclined structure and is so dominating that it overwhelms the stadium's architecture. During the years that work continued on the roof,

1976 to 1987, Olympic Stadium was an outdoor facility. In 1988, with the roof in place, the team was able to play games in an open-air and protected environment. In 1988 the team played three games with the roof off. In 1989 the roof was removed for thirteen games, and in 1991 the Expos played forty-three games with the roof removed. In 1991 the system for removing the roof was destroyed in a storm. With the stadium's cost already in excess of $1 billion, it was decided to postpone any repairs. For seven seasons Olympic Stadium became an indoor facility, with its giant mast relegated to a tourist attraction (there is an observation deck at its top) and a source of constant humor. In 1998, at a cost of $26 million, a new roof was installed, and all hoped the retractable system would again work.

The stadium's problems did not end with its roof. In September 1991, a fifty-five-ton block of concrete fell from the stadium to the street. After two months of repairs, during which time the Expos were forced to play all their games on the road, the Quebec government declared the stadium safe. The Expos returned to play in Olympic Stadium in 1992. But the image of the stadium with the roof that did not work now became the stadium that was collapsing alongside its fifty-five-story reminder of failure.

The investment in the stadium created such a substantial debt that it is still being paid off through a special property tax; the new roof in 1998 added $26 million to this debt load. Even though there is less resentment about taxes in Canada than there is in the United States, the stadium is a source of resentment, and the stadium's supporters have been forced to ask, "Can architecture be justified regardless of cost" (Marsan, 1981: 392). Why did the building cost so much? There was the common litany of overruns: the need to build a special factory for prefabrication, the importing of materials and technicians from France, and the design and shape of the mast. To support the weight of the roof, the inevitable buildup of snow, and the overhang, thousands of extra tons of concrete had to be poured at the base of the mast as a counterweight. The mast alone cost as much to construct as the Kingdome in Seattle.

THE TORONTO BLUE JAYS AND THE BUILDING OF THE "WORLD'S GREATEST ENTERTAINMENT CENTRE"

In 1977 when the American League decided to award Seattle a franchise in response to its lawsuit over the move of the Pilots to Milwaukee, adding a second team to balance the league seemed logical. The Toronto Blue Jays became that second team. By 1977, Metropolitan Toronto had a population of 2.8 million, and the Province of Ontario had more than 8.3 million people. In terms of market size, a Toronto-based team would be able to draw fans from a population base larger than what is available to the Cleveland Indians, Baltimore Orioles, Texas Rangers, and Seattle Mariners.

The team played its initial seasons in aging Exhibition Stadium, an outdoor facility located on the shores of Lake Ontario. From the moment the Blue Jays franchise was awarded, however, the city as well as the team owners envisioned a far greater playing facility: a stadium that would surpass Montreal's Olympic Stadium in aesthetics and significance and be a signature statement for Toronto.

The Blue Jays made consideration of a new stadium relatively easy even if an architectural statement and engineering marvel were not desired or deemed necessary. The Blue Jays, in a relatively brief period, went from an inept expansion team to a championship squad. In their inaugural season, similar to most expansion teams, the Blue Jays compiled the worst record in their league. The team lost 102 games in 1978; in their third year, they lost 109 games as they posted a winning percentage of .327. A few among Toronto's faithful may have feared that the Blue Jays would be perennial losers, but in only their seventh season of play, they became a winning team. In their ninth season they captured their first divisional title. From the time of their initial winning season, 1983, through 1993, the Blue Jays would win more than a thousand games, post a winning percentage of .563, and capture two World Series crowns. In only one season in the 1984–93 period were the Blue Jays *not involved* in a race for the championship of their division.

Toronto's baseball fans supported the Blue Jays in both their winning and losing seasons. Indeed, for a region where hockey is king, major league baseball has been quite well supported, and for several years one could argue that baseball overtook hockey in the hearts of Toronto's sports fans. In the Blue Jays' initial year, 1.7 million fans were attracted to games, and through each of the team's losing years, 1977 through 1980, no fewer than 1.4 million fans attended games. Attendance declined to 755,083 in the strike-plagued 1981 season, but as soon as baseball returned, attendance soared. Nearly 2 million fans attended games during the Blue Jays' first winning season, and more than 2 million went in 1984 when the team duplicated its 1983 performance. The Blue Jays consistently attracted at least 2.4 million fans, and then in 1989, playing more than half of their games at the SkyDome, the Blue Jays attracted 3.38 million fans. In 1990, 3.88 million fans attended the Blue Jays' home games. Then in 1991 the Blue Jays began a three-year streak of unprecedented attendance, attracting more than 4 million fans each year.

Building the SkyDome

Inclement weather in Toronto was always a concern, but the fact that Montreal had built a stadium with a retractable dome that did not work presented a unique opportunity for the city. If a retractable dome could be engineered, Toronto's image in Canada and the United States would be firmly established. When planning the new facility, according to one of the team's executives, the players were asked what they wanted in a new stadium. The overwhelming response was a field that could be covered on inclement days but be open by way of a removable roof for the numerous pleasant summer and fall evenings that Toronto enjoys. From that conversation and the failure of Montreal's retractable roof the ultimate challenge was born: to build a retractable dome that would work.

A three-person committee was appointed to identify the best site for the new facility, and one year later a public corporation was formed to design and construct the facility. In January 1985 a $150 million plan was proposed. Before construction work was initiated, the projected cost of the stadium had increased to $225 million. It took more than three years to build the new facility; the dome did not open until June 3, 1989. The final cost of the stadium was more than $600 million.

To outdo Montreal, a design was needed that would solve the architectural and engineering problems of a retractable dome. Ultimately, a design developed by a local firm was chosen; it involved a rotating roof pulled by an engine mounted on rails above the stadium and just below the dome itself. And while the enterprising and innovative designers would eventually be forced into bankruptcy, the ability of Metropolitan Toronto and Ontario Province to build a stadium designed by a local firm added even more prestige to the race with Montreal. The failed Olympic Stadium was designed and partially built in France. Toronto's SkyDome would be a Canadian stadium, and it would work even if the designers were financially ruined.

Toronto, similar to Montreal, Indianapolis, Cleveland, and St. Louis, also wanted to use the stadium to anchor economic downtown development. All of these communities were experiencing the slow but inevitable decentralization of economic activity to suburban areas, and Toronto had an area south and west of its business and financial centers and near Lake Ontario that was not thriving. There was a great deal of land in this area, most of it owned by Canadian-Pacific Railways. If the facility could be built near the new CN Tower, Toronto could have an an chor for this part of its downtown and shoreline. The placement of the stadium in this location also would provide a stunning visual statement since the facility would loom over the major freeway in the city. With Toronto's fixation on mass transportation, the plan for the facility did not include the development of many parking spaces. Fewer than four hundred new spaces were added because the facility is within easy walking distance of Toronto's subway system and several bus lines.

Toronto's leadership also developed a very innovative public/private partnership to build the facility. For their investments these firms secured the right to provide services at the new stadium. The public's share of the facility's cost was to be $60 million, with $30 million invested by Ontario Province and $30 million invested by Metropolitan Toronto (Reid, 1991). Thirty corporations were initially invited to invest $5 million each in the facility. These private owners would share in the profits from the stadium (which never materialized) and receive certain business opportunities related to the building and operation of the stadium. Joined together with the public's initial investment, the partnership secured $215 million of the needed $225 million. The partners agreed to cover the shortfall from operating profits to guarantee the total cost of the project. This latter point was crucial because the private-sector partners had limited liability and would not have to pay more than $5 million; therefore they would not be responsible for any additional costs. The public corporation that operated and managed the facility would have responsibility for the $10 million anticipated shortfall.

In retrospect, the estimated $10 million in extra costs would become the least of the financial problems to beset SkyDome. Six months after construction began, the stadium's management company decided to add more restaurants and recreation venues to the project. This increased the projected cost of the facility by $36 million. In April 1987 it was estimated that the SkyDome complex would cost $261 million. One month later the corporation decided to add a hotel and health club to the complex. The cost of these facilities was estimated to be $57 million, elevating the overall construction project cost to $318 million. (The actual cost of the hotel and health facility would be $112 million.) To accommodate the hotel, seats were removed from the stadium so that several rooms in the hotel would have a view of the playing field. The loss of these additional seats, estimated to be between five thousand and eight thousand, would reduce revenues to the stadium and the Toronto Blue Jays, especially during the team's championship seasons.

As the projected opening day for the stadium began to slip into the 1989 baseball season, the SkyDome's management company authorized extra overtime to complete the project. At this point, there was no public record of the entire cost of the project, but fears begin to build that the project was substantially over budget. At the end of the saga, after the transfer of the stadium's ownership to the private-sector partners, there would still be very different estimates of the cost of the stadium. Different media analysts placed the cost of the entire facility at $580 million, $600 million, and $628 million. The statement of public accounts issued by the Province of Ontario in 1993 would place the cost of the stadium at $608.9 million. With an original cost estimate of $225 million, a final cost of $580 million would mean the final price tag was 257 percent larger than anticipated. If the final cost was $628 million, the SkyDome would have cost 279 percent more than expected. The province's own estimate calculated the cost at 271 percent more than anticipated. Regardless of the final cost projection used, the project cost 2.5 times more than taxpayers were initially told.

Approximately one year after SkyDome opened, Ontario's provincial government realized that the revenues from the facility would never be sufficient to support the interest payments on the money borrowed. SkyDome cost so much that the *daily* interest was $60,000. With annual interest charges in excess of $20 million, the facility's operating profits were simply too small to support the stadium's expenses (Van Alphen, 1991). As a result, each year that the public sector retained ownership, its financial responsibilities and the cost of SkyDome increased.

With a new political party in office, different from the one that planned, developed, and built the SkyDome, the idea that the government should sell the facility to private owners began to gain considerable momentum. The problem with the suggestion was that no one was interested in paying the full cost of the public sector's investment. There also was no interest in paying the accumulated interest charges that had been accruing on the amount of money spent by the public sector. Although the facility was generating an operating profit, that profit was not sufficient to cover the debt payments for the capital construction costs. The operating revenues from SkyDome did cover the costs of maintenance. However, when the interest charges associated with the cost of the facility were included in a financial statement, together with the cost of the stadium, SkyDome operated at a deficit.

Within this fiscal environment it might seem prudent to sell the facility for as much as possible to minimize the public sector's costs. But here is where the story related to SkyDome gets even more curious. In 1990, to reduce the public sector's responsibilities for the $60,000 in daily interest charges, Ontario Province decided to pay off the SkyDome's debt. In other words, after 1990 there was *no debt* associated with the facility. When SkyDome attracted more than 6 million visitors to 256 event days in 1993, the operating profit from the facility belonged to the province. With the debt written off, the operating revenues were sufficient both to return a profit and to maintain the facility. From an accounting perspective the interest or revenue lost on the debt still was calculated, but that charge was not paid. Why sell the facility in such an environment?

Any cash that was received from the sale of SkyDome would represent income for the province and could be used to offset taxes or the province's own debt, which had escalated throughout the 1980s and 1990s. From a strictly business standpoint, with the capital cost of SkyDome settled, the operating income was returning a profit, which made a sale somewhat imprudent. The Province of Ontario's own records for the Stadium Corporation indicated an operating profit of $29.8 million in 1991 and $34 million in 1992 (see Table 6-7). In each year the government's accountants also placed approximately $18 million in a depreciation fund, leaving an operating profit of approximately $12 million in 1991 and $16 million in 1992. The Stadium Corporation also paid approximately $10 million in taxes to its public-sector owners. This represented income for the province and Metropolitan Toronto. So although it was a "cost" to the Stadium Corporation, it was another source of income for the public-sector partners. As a result, even after depreciation expenses, Sky-Dome was producing more than $15 million in income for its public-sector owners. This "profit" could have remained with the public sector had SkyDome not been sold to its private owners.

An agreement to sell SkyDome to the private-sector partners was negotiated in 1992. It would take more than two years to fi-

TABLE 6-7
Income and Expenses for SkyDome

Category	1992	1991
REVENUE		
Luxury seating	22,718,000	22,909,000
Facility rentals, concessions	13,703,000	12,299,000
Hotel, fitness club, parking	12,452,000	11,257,000
Advertising, other	8,797,000	9,083,000
SUBTOTAL	57,670,000	55,818,000
EXPENSES		
Hotel, fitness club, parking	9,739,000	10,263,000
Salaries and benefits	7,867,000	7,794,000
Operations	3,890,000	4,893,000
Administration	1,742,000	2,627,000
Marketing	395,000	399,000
SUBTOTAL	23,633,000	25,976,000
Gross Income	34,037,000	29,842,000
Depreciation	18,035,000	17,907,000
Taxes paid	10,682,000	9,740,000
NET INCOME	5,320,000	2,195,000

Source: Public Accounts, 1992–93, Stadium Corporation of Ontario, Limited, Province of Ontario.

nalize the deal because of pending lawsuits between several contractors and the Stadium Corporation. One of these lawsuits involved the Toronto partnership that designed the innovative roof system. These two engineers teetered on the verge of bankruptcy as lawsuits, charges, and countercharges were launched. When all the issues were settled, SkyDome was sold for $151 million plus $22 million in interest charges, reflecting the delay in the sale. The province would also receive 60 percent of the free cash flow from the facility after all interest charges (on the new owners' debt), property taxes, maintenance and depreciation costs, and a "base" rate of return for the owners were paid. Both sides publicly conceded this amount of money would be insignificant.

What the owners received for this payment is a facility with the potential to generate an operating profit of more than $24 million. Suppose, for example, the SkyDome were as successful in future years as it was in 1992 when it had a gross profit of $34 million and tax obligations of $10.7 million. That would leave the owners with a net income of $23.3 million before depreciation. The total investment by the private owners that enabled them to receive this income was $173 million. The $23.3 million earned, then, represents a 13.5 percent rate of return ($23.3 million divided by $173 million). The actual rate of return might be less if some money was placed in a reserve account for rebuilding the facility. However, since the private-sector investors could anticipate that replacement of the SkyDome would involve another public/private partnership, the investment of between $4 and $5 million in a capital fund each year probably would provide them with sufficient resources to forge another partnership. If $5 million was placed in a capital fund and discounted from their rate of return, the private-sector partners would still enjoy a 10.6 percent return on their investment of $173 million. Buying the Sky-Dome at that time was an excellent deal for the private-sector partners.

What did the SkyDome cost taxpayers? Ontario Province's records for 1992 indicate the final cost was $608.9 million; this figure was later revised by the province to $628 million (Van Alphen, 1994). The private-sector investors made an initial contribution of $150 million, and the public sector received an additional $173 million when the facility was sold. The total private-sector investment in the project was therefore $323 million ($150 million plus $173 million to buy the facility and assume 100 percent ownership), leaving the public-sector share at $305 million. The taxes paid by the facility prior to its sale should be subtracted from this amount. Even though the facility was owned by the public sector as a separate government corporation, it still paid taxes to Metropolitan Toronto. The Stadium

Corporation paid approximately $27 million in taxes in the three years before the sale, reducing the public sector's cost to approximately $278 million. The *Toronto Star* estimated the public sector's cost at $262.7 million, but it is unclear if the *Star*'s estimate included the court costs and legal fees associated with several disputes involving the construction of the facility. It also was not possible to verify whether the province's accountants included those legal fees in their final cost estimates. As a result, it is safe to conclude that the public sector's cost was no less than $262.7 million and may well have been $275 million for an excursion into sports wars to obtain economic development and civic pride. This money also becomes a subsidy to the private-sector investors because that group will earn a handsome return after assuming complete ownership of the facility.

To determine what that return will be, I assumed that the facility would continue to earn approximately $24 million per year and then calculated the present value of this annual revenue stream for the years 1995 through 2020. If the cost of money over those years is assumed to be 7 percent, the income lost by the public sector or gained by the private sector would be $254.3 million. In other words, had the public sector retained ownership, they would have earned $254.3 million during the years 1995 through 2020. The private sector paid $173 million to earn the $254.3 million through 2020, for a net return of 47 percent (not too shabby). If the cost of money is set at 8 percent, the present value of SkyDome's income through 2020 is $235.6 million. This would mean a return to the private-sector partners of 36.2 percent on their investment. If one used 9 percent as the cost of money, the present value of SkyDome's annual income flow is $219.1 million, for a return of 26.6 percent.

It could be argued that the public sector's total loss on Sky-Dome should include this income or the difference between what the private sector paid, $173 million, and what they will likely earn from 1995 through 2020. The public sector accepted $173 million for an income stream worth between $219.1 million and $254.3 million. What was received ($173 million) and what could have been earned ($219.1 million to $254.3 million) represents a loss of between $46.1 million ($219.1 million *minus* $173 million) and $81.3 million ($254.3 million *minus* $173 million). Some might say that the taxes the facility pays should be included as income, but those taxes would have been earned regardless of the entity that owned the stadium. When the SkyDome was owned by the Stadium Corporation, it still paid taxes. Indeed, even if the stadium had not been built, given the spectacular growth of Toronto it is likely that some other set of buildings would have been constructed on the land now used by SkyDome. To measure the total public-sector loss on SkyDome, these estimates of unrealized income have to be added to the other losses, which range from an estimated $262.7 million to as high as $275 million. Adding in this lost income, SkyDome cost the taxpayers not less than $308.8 million and perhaps as much as $356.3 million. Ah, but what did they get for this investment?

The Growth of Metropolitan Toronto

Numerous chapters of this book have made the point that the entity of sports by itself is not large enough to change economic development patterns. However, the intangible benefits that sports create can have an impact on an area's reputation and prestige, and on the impression that people have of their own community. All these impressions can subtly influence development. At the micro level, the presence of a facility as large and as popular as the SkyDome can influence the use of buildings and land. This is especially true if more than 6 million people each year visit a part of a city that they did not frequent in the past.

Did the SkyDome change the importance of Metropolitan Toronto in terms of its economic stature within Canada? Probably not. Metropolitan Toronto has enjoyed a spectacular rate of growth since the 1950s. While Canada's population increased more than 108 percent from 1951 to 1994, Metropolitan Toronto's population increased by 254 percent, or more than 2.5 times the rate of growth for the entire country. Much of this took place before the Blue Jays ever existed. Toronto has become Canada's economic center, and the presence or absence of the Blue Jays did not influence that outcome. *Financial World* has placed the economic activity of the Blue Jays at approximately $56.4 million. Although a business of that size certainly is robust, it cannot propel or even change the economy of a region with more than 4.3 million residents. If the total gross revenues of the Blue Jays are divided across the population of Metropolitan Toronto, the team's value amounts to less than the cost of a family of four eating at McDonald's. An impact of this magnitude will not change or influence overall economic development patterns. Within the city of Toronto itself, however, the impact is more substantial. In 1991 the city of Toronto had 635,395 residents. A business of $56.4 million generates a per capita figure of $88.76. For a family of four this is equivalent to an impact of $355 a year, quite a bit more than an evening at McDonald's. Yet this volume of activity is not sufficient to change economic development outcomes since the city of Toronto is the destination or focal point for a majority of the region's recreational spending. If the Blue Jays and the SkyDome did not exist, some of the revenue collected by the Blue Jays still would be spent within the city of Toronto.

In addition, Metropolitan Toronto and Ontario Province are now home to Canada's wealthiest residents. In 1985, average incomes placed Ontario's residents as the second wealthiest in Canada, but by 1990, Ontario Province had the wealthiest residents. In 1985, residents of Metropolitan Toronto had incomes below just two other metropolitan areas, but by 1990 they had the highest average incomes. Although this growth in income corresponds to the years in which the Blue Jays had their greatest success, the volume of money earned by the Blue Jays was not sufficient to account for the change. Toronto's growth in population and income was related to the spectacular expansion of its economy that included baseball, but it was not driven by baseball.

With these points in mind, does SkyDome deserve any credit for changing development patterns within Metropolitan Toronto? Although there have been no economic or demographic changes that could have been the result of the presence or absence of a baseball team and its playing facility, there is one factor that cannot be dismissed easily. The pressures for suburban development that are so apparent in U.S. cities are present in Canada and for Metropolitan Toronto. Indeed, within the Toronto region, one city, North York, has enjoyed spectacular growth at the same time that the city of Toronto has become a smaller and smaller part of the region. In 1951 the city of Toronto had 675,754 residents, and they comprised 55.8 percent of Metropolitan Toronto's population. In contrast, North York had 85,897 residents, comprising 7.1 percent of the region. North York's population was equal to 12.7 percent of the population of the city of Toronto. By the mid-1960s the city of Toronto's population had increased to 697,422, but this was just 30.5 percent of the metropolitan area's population. The city of Toronto had begun to shrink as part of its region. North York, on the other hand, continued to grow, with almost 400,000 residents, comprising 17.4 percent of Metropolitan Toronto, by 1996. By itself, North York's population was now 58.7 percent of the city of Toronto's, and by 1976, North York's population was 88.2 percent of Toronto's. In 1991 the city of Toronto accounted for just 16.3 percent of the region's population and had declined in proportion in each population count from 1956 through 1991. In the 1990s, Metropolitan Toronto had three cities with populations of at least 500,000: Toronto, North York, and Scarborough. North York, led by an aggressive mayor, was bidding to be the home of each of the region's professional sports, and its administration had proposed that it become the potential home for the Blue Jays and Maple Leafs. When the Raptors became Toronto's entry into the NBA, North York also proposed a site for a new venue to be built.

THE COST OF A CITY'S IMAGE

St. Louis, Montreal, and Toronto each assumed huge tax liabilities and provided extraordinary subsidies to teams to enhance their images. St. Louis's bid to improve its image involved a hard lesson in cartel politics. In 1987 a subsidy of approximately $90 million would have kept the NFL (the Cardinals) in St. Louis. To get the NFL back to St. Louis will cost taxpayers in excess of $300 million. In addition, St. Louis's football fans had to spend $60 million more for PSLs. The Cardinals, had they stayed in St. Louis, would have expected fans to pay higher ticket and luxury seat lease fees. However, it is reasonable to conclude that the total cost for getting back into the NFL's good graces cost St. Louis $350 million.

Playing ball with the NFL to improve one's image is a very expensive game for cities. Should any city agree to provide the level of welfare that St. Louis did just to enhance its image and redevelop its downtown area? The justification of the expenditure—to do something dramatic—does little to offset the fact that now the NFL can use St. Louis as the model of what it expects from cities. It may well be possible that the cost of the dome to the public sector can be lessened through the financial returns realized as a result of the existence of new convention opportunities. But should a successful convention center be operated to provide higher income to NFL owners and players? If the dome in St. Louis could be paid for through fees earned by the convention center, then why not let the NFL develop domed facilities that it uses for convention facilities? In that way the public sector does not have to be in the position of subsidizing the economically privileged.

Enhancing the image of a city is a laudable goal. Subsidizing professional sports teams and burdening taxpayers and fans with more than $350 million in expenses seems to establish an image of a different order. St. Louis was taken to the cleaners. It is not a "can-do" city; it is a city that the NFL used to teach other communities a very expensive lesson: Either you meet our demands, or we escalate the costs of playing football in your city.

*   *   *

The case histories of baseball in Toronto and Montreal offer some important ideas for containing the egos of elected officials who seek sports edifices at the public's expense. The public sector's financial losses in Toronto and SkyDome's clear excess were the result of the decision to make the stadium much more than a premier baseball facility. The hotel and health club facilities that were added were poorly planned decisions that generated no tangible or image benefits for the community. It may be possible to justify the value for a community of having a baseball team, despite questions about its role as an economic engine, but the presence or absence of a hotel or health club does not define a community's identity. Toronto's leadership wanted a monument and were willing to pass the costs to unsuspecting taxpayers.

Further, although one can make an argument that the existence of a stadium will bring people to the downtown area, there is certainly no data available that would support the argument that people will completely change their recreational patterns if another hotel or health club is developed in a downtown area. It may be true that a stadium in a downtown area shifts recreational patterns by moving some spending from the suburbs to a downtown area, and there may be public purpose or value to such a shift. However, changing recreational patterns has not been found to substantially alter job location or housing patterns.

If SkyDome's management team had performed a market analysis, they would have realized that both the hotel and the health club were not necessary for the project's success. Similarly, the other entertainment venues were also extravagances that could have been avoided. Ironically, had these extras been eliminated, the SkyDome would be a profitable stadium for the public sector and a model for others to replicate. Indeed, Toronto may well be that model if communities can focus on the development of multiuse facilities accommodating a mix of different events. A facility or the investment of public dollars should never, ever be undertaken without a carefully developed market study and business plan that identify what revenues are likely to be produced from the facility. North America is littered with unsuccessful hotel and entertainment projects. The market and business plans that are developed should focus on the services and facilities that can be fully developed by the private sector without any public subsidies or seed capital. Hotels and health clubs already existed throughout Toronto, and so it was clear that the private sector could build and develop these facilities in response to market demands without any participation by the public sector.

Toronto's SkyDome also offers a fine example of what I refer to as "municipal capitalism." Municipal capitalism encompasses certain market activities in which the public sector can assume a role and manage a set of financial returns to further publicly declared values. For example, in many communities, cable television firms must negotiate contracts to permit them to deploy their equipment. Some communities have required a share of revenues from the fees collected by cable companies. Some smaller-market cities have also encouraged their cable companies to broadcast basketball and hockey games as part of their basic packages. The companies must pay the teams a fee, and this fee is part of the overall rate set by city and company. The public value in this regard is hosting the team. Although some might not accept or agree that hosting a team has public benefits, there are those who do believe that using assets such as a cable system permits smaller communities to host professional sports teams.

SkyDome probably represents the best example of a community able to build a facility capable of generating a positive income flow and advancing the image and identity of the community. If Toronto had limited the project to the building of a stadium (without a hotel, health club, and entertainment facility) and had refused to authorize the extensive overtime payments, SkyDome would have been a successful public investment that had the potential of generating sufficient income to retire the public sector's debt. Had that taken place, downtown Toronto would have had its recreational and entertainment anchor, the city and region would have been able to extend its reputation and identity, and the Blue Jays would have been able to maintain their status as one of baseball's most financially successful franchises. A carefully planned facility could have been developed through a public/private partnership. This facility had the potential to generate sufficient income to repay its public-sector partner without perverse subsidies.

To a very real extent, ego and the desire for a super project were the undoing of both Montreal's and Toronto's entrances into baseball and stadium building. If both communities had built what was needed, practical dome or outdoor facilities, neither would have encountered the financial problems they did. Both communities sought signature statements or facilities that would become part of their city's logo. Large projects became grand projects, and in each community's rush to outdo the other, "breaking new ground" in design and function created financial nightmares and burdens for taxpayers. All that was needed by both communities to reach their desired goals of economic development and civic identity were baseball facilities that could also accommodate crowds for other events. Montreal needed a stadium for the 1976 Olympics. Toronto wanted a large indoor multipurpose facility. Both built palaces with unneeded and expensive accessories.

If your community is planning to build a new stadium, be sure to build only what is needed. A lesson to be learned from the experiences of both Montreal and Toronto is that wants—signature statements, grand and innovative stadiums, being the first to build a retractable dome—quickly became defined as needs. And since the public sector was paying the bill, few questioned whether all wants were really needs. Spend the public's money as if it were your own. Buy what is needed and do not plan anything unless it is really needed.

Another lesson to be learned from Montreal's experience with baseball is that culture does matter. Some things and some sports do not fit well into some cultures. Baseball may be loved by residents of Montreal and Quebec Province, but the sport will be dominated by English-speaking Americans as well as Spanish-speaking athletes from parts of Central America and the Caribbean. Those parts of the world produce the majority of the players that are likely to be on an MLB team. These individuals will have little incentive to learn another language and adapt to or adopt a new culture. Given that reality, will MLB succeed in Montreal?

If the public sector is to be involved with investments in sports, the community's leadership must be sure the sport fits the community. At the current time, several American cities are again joining with investors to launch a professional soccer league. Will this league be any more successful than previous efforts, or is American culture sufficiently dominated by baseball, basketball, football, and hockey to leave little room for another sport? Does the European, Asian, and South American fervor for soccer necessarily mean U.S. sports fans will be as attracted to the sport? And if there is this much uncertainty about its future, should the public sector be making investments in facilities to subsidize soccer teams, or should that investment be left to the private sector? These questions and issues should be raised before commitments are made. Be sure there is support within a community for the sport and that the sport and its athletes fit into the community before spending millions of tax dollars to create an image as an international city or as a city that is a continental center.

As the 1999 MLB season opened it was not clear if the Montreal Expos would remain in Canada. Quebec's provincial government had declared that it would not provide public assistance for the building of a new downtown ballpark, and the Canadian national government was also opposed to the commitment of tax dollars to help the team. Efforts to raise private capital also met with considerable reluctance, and as the last of MLB's deadlines for an acceptable plan passed in early March the Expos seemed poised to look for a new home in Washington, D.C., or northern Virginia. Supporters of a movement to bring the Minnesota Twins to North Carolina also held out hope that a plan could be developed to attract the Expos to Charlotte. Portland, Oregon, was another community that also was thinking about its future and MLB and could become a "bidder" in the effort to find a home for the Expos. Washington, D.C., might be the team's best option as RFK Stadium could serve as an interim home until a new facility was built.

Although the Toronto Blue Jays were secure in their home, the declining value of the Canadian dollar and lower attendance levels threatened the financial stability of the SkyDome and the team. In 1999 a bailout plan had to be developed to help the private-sector owners earn sufficient revenues to keep the Sky-Dome viable. The declining value of the Canadian dollar also weakened the team's ability to attract and retain the best players. Although fans continued to buy tickets with "the loonie," the Blue Jays had to pay their players in American dollars. As the quality of the team's play declined, so did attendance. In 1998 the Blue Jays finished twenty-six games behind the Yankees and attracted but 2.5 million fans. With 1.5 million fewer fans than they attracted in their pennant-winning years, the Blue Jays and the SkyDome's owners earned too little money to compete with teams south of the border for leading players. Symbolic of their position before the 1999 season began, the Blue Jays traded their most expensive player, Roger Clemens, to the New York Yankees for David Wells and younger, less expensive players.

7

Fights within the Family

Suburbs and Center Cities in a Battle
for the Intangible Benefits from Sports

During the next week, Arlington will be discovered for all the reasons that it ought to already be known. Having the All-Stars here will establish a national identity we otherwise could never have achieved.

Richard Greene, Mayor of Arlington,
Texas, site of the 1995 Major League All-Star game

The [Dallas/Fort Worth] metroplex is so intertwined that there is no one city that really stands independently anymore, whether you're talking about Dallas or Fort Worth or Arlington. The All-Stars are a good thing for all of us.

Terry Ryan, Executive Director,
Fort Worth Chamber of Commerce

There is little doubt that the presence of a team provides a substantial level of publicity for the city that hosts a franchise. Numerous officials interviewed for this book, even those who were not sports fans, commented on the improved image and feelings of civic pride that they believed were the result of the existence of teams. Some of these leaders expressed considerable surprise at the level of positive reactions received from many of their constituents. As discussed in Chapter 4, the residents of the Indianapolis region reported that their teams did help to establish the community's identity. The Pacers and the Colts were also critical to the pride that respondents expressed in living in the Indianapolis region. Professional sports, similar to other elements of the quality of life (the arts, parks, schools, universities, and so forth), do generate positive feelings. But do teams, their playing facilities, and the other intangible benefits lead to any measurable economic returns? It certainly is valuable to "feel good" about one's community and its image, but do these feelings generate positive economic impacts?

The best vantage from which to analyze the economic value of the intangible benefits of a sports team is a metropolitan area where cities have competed against each other to be the "home" for a team. The argument for image benefits is no more artfully made than when cities within the same region fight to be the home for a team that is already part of the region. It often is argued that if the team were located within a particular city, enhanced economic development would occur. If this does not take place, then the net effect of the cities' bidding is to raise the level of welfare provided to the team. A team that is already in a large market can maximize its position by having several cities in that region bid to build a facility.

Although the movement of teams between regions attracts the most national attention, numerous franchises have also threatened to move or have moved from one city to another within a metropolitan region. The willingness of public officials from suburban and central cities to provide a subsidy to a team is tied to the accepted image benefits that will result from the team's presence. Does a team's choice of one city over another within a metropolitan area change economic development patterns or the locational choices of individuals? Does the prestige, publicity, or pride that comes from hosting a team produce economic benefits?

To address these issues, economic development in the Dallas/Fort Worth region was studied. Across three decades, Dallas has fought with two of its largest suburbs, Arlington and Irving, to be home to the region's four major league franchises. Indeed, at different times it has seemed that the spirit of Texas, capitalism, and individualism mitigated against any form of regional cooperation and increased the subsidies required to keep a professional sports team within any city's boundary. What did Arlington, home to the Rangers, and Irving, home to the Cowboys, get when they became "major league cities"? What did Dallas gain when it remained home to the Mavericks and Stars?

CIVIC PRIDE AND THE BATTLE FOR PROFESSIONAL SPORTS TEAMS

During the last three decades suburban communities repeatedly have tried to convince teams to leave their region's center city. Boston, Buffalo, Chicago, Cincinnati, Cleveland, Detroit, Kansas City, Los Angeles, Miami, Minneapolis, New York, Philadelphia, St. Louis, Toronto, and Washington, D.C., have all had to compete with other cities (or states) in their region to host a professional team. In the Dallas/Fort Worth region, no fewer than four cities have battled to host the Cowboys, Rangers, Mavericks, and Stars. This competition has led each city to promise increasingly higher levels of subsidies to teams. Recently, even New York City has entertained a $1 billion proposal for a new Yankee Stadium that would require the city to invest $700 million in the new ballpark to keep the Yankees from joining the Giants and Jets in New Jersey.

Staying in an existing metropolitan area but orchestrating a competition between cities within that area has a number of attractions for owners and players. First, without going through all the public ridicule and political battles that accompany moves to other regions, team owners can receive the subsidies they want by simply suggesting they have an interest in moving to another city within their market area. Team owners can reap substantial profits and not risk the ire of other owners or fans that moves to other regions generate. Second, staying within a region eliminates the risk of losing existing lucrative local cable, television, or radio contracts. Yankee fans throughout Metropolitan New York would still want to receive telecasts and broadcasts even if the Bronx Bombers were the Manhattan Maulers or the Jersey Jolters. Third, movement within a region does not require league approval and frequently reduces the likelihood of any legal challenges.

Why do suburban cities compete for teams? Simply put, smaller cities have always sought status or a level of acceptance equal to that accorded center cities. Many suburban leaders believe "major league" city status can be obtained only by hosting an NFL, MLB, NBA, or NHL team. Many believe that this status will attract businesses and residents who want to be associated with a major or big league community. Can any city within a region that hosts a team capture the "image benefits" that teams supposedly generate? Through an analysis of growth and development in the Dallas/Fort Worth area it will be demonstrated that the intangible benefits from a team's presence do not create any economic returns that can be captured by a host community. Fights between cities in a region to host a team do nothing more than increase taxes and the subsidies provided to teams.

THE DALLAS/FORT WORTH "METROPLEX"

The Dallas/Fort Worth "metroplex" has been one of the nation's fastest-growing areas and, as a result, a hotbed for sports. In 1970 the region had 2.4 million residents; by 1980 the population had increased by 20.8 percent, to 2.9 million. Another decade of growth in the 1980s, a 34.5 percent increase, brought the region to 3.9 million inhabitants by 1990. Today, the market area served by the region's television stations includes 5.1 million residents.

In terms of its image, the region has adopted the name "the Dallas/Fort Worth metroplex." The term "metroplex" is used to describe a triplex set of cities in the region. The end points of the metroplex are the region's two center cities, Dallas and Fort Worth. Unlike the Minneapolis/St. Paul area, however, these cities can hardly be described as "twins." They are more like feuding cousins that have spawned even more feuding family members.

At the region's eastern pole is the central city of Dallas, in Dallas County. There are two large suburbs to Dallas's east, but in terms of the concept of a metroplex, it is useful to think of Dallas as one end of the region. Approximately forty miles to the west is the region's other center city, Fort Worth. Far smaller than Dallas, with less than five hundred thousand residents, Fort Worth is the central city of Tarrant County. There are a few small communities to Fort Worth's west, but none is as large as Dallas's eastern suburbs. In the middle are several suburban and emerging central cities (Arlington and Irving). Some important and growing cities can also be found to the north of this corridor. These all represent the three-tier structure of the region, or a sort of triplex of cities in a single metropolitan area (hence metroplex). With Arlington and Irving emerging as central cities, the region may well need another new term to describe itself.

Metroplex cities have a history of competing against one another for economic activity, and this lack of regional cooperation has created a very fertile environment for sports teams. The feuding among cities in this region, though sometimes bitter and sometimes comical, is always present. The initial fighting for economic dominance of the region occurred between Dallas and Fort Worth, but Arlington and Irving have now joined the feud. The competition is partly based on the very different images the two center cities have of each other and of themselves.

For Dallasites, Fort Worth is a sleepy, provincial, and backward-looking west Texas "cow town." Dallas's old-time residents take great pleasure in a story that had one of their leaders venturing into the "frontier" of downtown Fort Worth, only to find it so quiet that a panther was sleeping on Main Street. Some still refer to Fort Worth as the Panther City. In later years Fort Worth was able to capitalize on this reputation with a restored stockyards section that has since become a popular tourist attraction. An old "drovers' house" has been refurbished as a restaurant, and a hotel was restored to its nineteenth-century grandeur. Several bars and western clothing and saddle shops are also part of this section of Fort Worth. However, when Dallasites speak of it as a cow town, they are attempting to denigrate Fort Worth.

Fort Worth's citizenry "see" Dallas as eastern, not unlike New York City and the Northeast of the United States. These attributes, of course, are frequently described in disparaging terms and are contrasted with Fort Worth's western and more community-oriented values. Amon Carter, Fort Worth's civic and economic icon, countered the sleeping panther tale by carrying his own lunch to Dallas whenever he had to attend meetings. He argued there was no restaurant in the city able to satisfy his dining needs.

As the Dallas/Fort Worth area has grown to a region of more than 5 million people, the competition between cities has expanded. At first the competition was at a more distant or secondary level, with growing suburban cities fighting with one another to be "the" bedroom community and to attract some of the area's largest employers to their business parks. As the region and its suburbs began to grow, however, new "giants" were created in the area between Dallas and Fort Worth and to Dallas's north. These suburban cities then sought to enhance their images and become "big league" cities in their own right.

The city that decidedly changed the urban competition between Dallas and Fort Worth into a three-way battle, especially for sports teams, was Arlington. A nineteenth-century stagecoach stop and a sleepy home to a small military academy in the early part of the twentieth century, Arlington, even in 1970, was little more than a footnote to the Dallas/Fort Worth area. Located virtually midway between Dallas and Fort Worth, its population in 1970 was less than one-fourth of the population of Fort Worth. In the early 1970s, Arlington was not even the biggest suburban city in the region; but the seeds for Arlington's growth had been planted and cultivated years earlier with the election of Thomas Vandergriff as mayor. To foster development, the young mayor, who was to lead the city for three decades, helped secure the political support for building a large lake within the city and on its western border with Fort Worth. Having secured access to water, a necessity for any city in Texas that wishes to thrive, Arlington was able to attract a large General Motors assembly plant. Since then, Arlington's growth has been nothing short of spectacular.

Arlington was the beneficiary of several assets that have sustained its decades-long growth spurt. First, there was Arlington's location. At the virtual midpoint of the region, two interstate highways crossed Arlington from east to west. Two north-south state highways linked the city to the Dallas/Fort Worth Regional International Airport, and one of these roads eventually became a limited access freeway.

Second, Arlington's political and community leadership was well organized and produced several dynamic leaders. Two mayors held sway over tightly knit growth machines and a regime for more than forty years. Tom Vandergriff's persistence brought MLB to Texas and Arlington, and Richard Greene led the effort to build the Ballpark in Arlington.

Third, Tom Vandergriff did not stop his efforts to build Arlington with the establishment of Lake Arlington or the attraction of the GM plant. With these successes under his belt, he next focused on enhancing Arlington's educational resources. When it became apparent that the state would create a University of Texas system with a campus in the Dallas/Fort Worth area, Mayor Vandergriff was able to use the competition between Dallas and Fort Worth and his own substantial political acumen to "suggest" Arlington as a possible compromise site. In 1967, Arlington State College became the University of Texas at Arlington (UTA); today, more than twenty-five thousand students attend UTA. Other companies also sought locations in the expanding Arlington area, including Bell Helicopter. With new corporate and educational resources, Arlington was on an economic development roll.

Fourth, Mayor Vandergriff shifted his economic development focus to recreational enterprises as a way to further elevate Arlington's image. The Six Flags (over Texas) amusement park opened in Arlington, as did an unsuccessful marine-life park. Mayor Vandergriff also was able to convince the Washington Senators to move to the city (this will be discussed in greater detail later in this chapter), and when the Dallas/Fort Worth Regional Airport opened to Arlington's north, Arlington became far more than an edge or suburban city. With an expanding affluent population attracted to the city's largely homogeneous neighborhoods, Arlington became a retail and urban center for the Dallas/Fort Worth metroplex.

Fifth, Arlington is the largest city in the United States without any form of public transportation. This policy, robustly supported by the residents and their elected officials, minimizes the number of lower-income people who can live in the city. Even today the city has refused to join any of the region's transportation districts. Although this would appear to be a limitation as opposed to an asset for attracting sports teams, the less than friendly environment that the lack of transportation creates for lower-income households protects Arlington's fiscal stability and status.

Sixth, with its central location, Arlington has become a prime location for retail development. Retail trade in Arlington produced $57.1 million in sales tax revenues for the city in 1998.

Seventh, surrounded by unincorporated land, Arlington has been able to annex all the property it needs for residential and retail development.

Finally, Arlington's mayors (and the city councils) hired leading professionals as city managers to propel Arlington's image as a sophisticated and efficiently managed community. A series of excellent city administrators ensured the stability of the political leadership through the efficient delivery of services. A small example of this technical expertise is projected by Arlington's home page on the World Wide Web; its presentation on the information highway is substantially more sophisticated than the home pages designed by most other cities in the metroplex.

Arlington's success is best illustrated by the meteoric rise of its population. From 1970 to 1995, Arlington attracted more new residents to its boundaries than did any city in the Dallas/Fort Worth region. During this twenty-five-year period, 189,371 people moved to Arlington. In contrast, 185,749 people moved to Dallas despite its larger geographic size, and Fort Worth's population increased by just 77,125 people. In 1995, Arlington's total population of 279,600 made it the largest suburban city in the region, the seventy-first largest city in America, and the seventh largest city in Texas. Recent projections indicate that the city has more than 300,000 residents. From just another "burb,"

Arlington, at the cusp of the twenty-first century, has become major league in every way. It was and is a major competitor for economic development with Dallas, Fort Worth, and every other city in Texas and the southwestern United States.

Arlington was not the only suburban city to emerge as a major competitor of Dallas and Fort Worth. Though perhaps not as large as Arlington, four communities in Dallas County also became important players in the economic destiny of the region. The population of Irving, located immediately west of Dallas and adjacent to the Dallas/Fort Worth International Airport, grew from 97,260 to 165,950 in 1995. Of greater significance for the development of Irving, however, was the building of the Las Colinas office and residential complex. A virtual "edge city," or city within a city, Las Colinas became the home office for several of the Dallas/Fort Worth region's largest employers. Complete with a canal, hotels, a golf course, and luxury housing, and with close proximity to the airport, Las Colinas is a prime location for financial and computer technology firms. Approximately 30,000 people now work in the Las Colinas "edge city" complex. In 1997 the city of Irving received $33.8 million in sales tax revenues, and that figure is on track to grow to $36 million in 1998. Richardson, north and east of Dallas, saw its population increase by 62 percent from 1970 to 1995. The home of the University of Texas at Dallas, Richardson now has 78,200 people. Plano, a prime residential suburb north of Dallas, increased its population by a whopping 845 percent, from 17,872 in 1970 to 168,900 in 1995. Plano was easily the region and state's fastest-growing city, while Garland, an older suburb to Dallas's east, remains quite large. In 1970, Garland had 81,437 residents; in 1995, 192,200 people called this suburb home.

Each of these suburbs has attracted some of the region's wealthier residents, concentrating lower-income people in both center cities. In 1989, 14.7 percent of all households in Dallas had incomes at or below the poverty level; 13.6 percent of all households in Fort Worth had incomes this low. In contrast, just 3.1 and 2.2 percent of the populations of Richardson and Plano, respectively, had incomes this low. In Arlington, 5.7 percent of the households had incomes at or below the poverty level. This unequal distribution of lower-income households meant that the center cities, as is typical in many metropolitan areas, had a greater challenge in terms of attracting and retaining businesses and residences while also generating the revenues needed to provide inducements that would attract or retain professional sports teams. These teams would be naturally attracted to fast-growing and wealthy suburban areas.

The competitive environment of the metroplex is now defined by battles to entice businesses and sports teams. To be sure, there are some important examples of regional cooperation. The North Central Texas Council of Governments produces a series of reports and analyses helpful in managing the region and fostering its economic development. Both Dallas and Fort Worth fought to be the site of the airport that became the Dallas/Fort Worth Regional International Airport. After the federal government intervened to specify the site, both cities worked together to develop the facility that has become the nation's second busiest airport. These examples of cooperation, however, do not minimize the competition that characterizes the relationships among and between the cities in the Dallas/Fort Worth region. Perhaps the spirit of Texas and the emphasis on rugged individualism contribute to the difficulty in developing regional perspectives and more intensive and extensive examples of cooperation.

SPORTS AND THE METROPLEX

The Dallas/Fort Worth region's history with major league professional teams began in 1960. The upstart AFL targeted rapidly

growing areas that did not have teams and placed one of its char-
ter franchises, the Texans, in Dallas. The NFL, in an effort to protect potential markets, quickly responded and created the Dallas
Cowboys. The NFL, with more prestige and popular teams
(Chicago Bears, Green Bay Packers, New York Giants, and others), was far more successful in the new market. In 1963 the Texans moved to Missouri and became the Kansas City Chiefs.

Dallas, with the region's only NFL-caliber stadium, became the
home for the first major league franchises. Arlington, however,
was the home to the region's minor league baseball team, and in
1971 it would use its existing baseball facility to attract the Washington Senators. Arlington first tried to secure a baseball team
when the National League expanded in the late 1960s. The Dal-
las/Fort Worth area was "in the running" for a team when the
Montreal Expos and San Diego Padres were created. With Houston already home to a National League team, the Dallas/Fort
Worth area seemed more likely to be an attractive site for an
American League team. Since expansion was not planned by that
league, the area had to attract an existing team. Tom Vandergriff,
with the support of all cities in the region, began the arduous
process of persuading an existing team to move. In 1971, Mayor
Vandergriff was able to persuade Bob Short to relocate his floun-
dering Washington Senators to the center of the Dallas/Fort
Worth region. In 1972 the Texas Rangers began play in Arlington
Stadium, a minor-league facility but adjacent to Interstate 30 and
at the geographic and transportation center of the region. As part
of the agreement with the Washington Senators and Bob Short,
Arlington agreed to expand its minor league stadium to accommodate fifty thousand fans. Arlington would never be able to fulfill that part of its original contract with the team, and that failure
would affect all future negotiations between the team and the
city.

The NBA made its appearance in the Dallas/Fort Worth area with the awarding of the Dallas Maverick's team franchise in 1980. The team has played in Reunion Arena in downtown Dallas since its inception. Reunion Arena, built for an NBA team, was opened in 1980 and provided the city with its initial "first-class" enclosed facility capable of competing with Fort Worth's Tarrant County Convention Center (located at the opposite end of Interstate 30 in downtown Fort Worth). Dallas built Reunion Arena for the Mavs, and although the facility does not have any suites or luxury seating, the team only pays rent equal to $10,000 per game plus 5 percent of gross ticket revenues in excess of $324,000. If receipts are less than this amount, the team pays per game 7 percent of the gross or $10,000, whichever is less. The team also receives a small portion of all advertising and concession income. In 1997 the team's demand for a new arena would lead to a sports battle within the region and a public subsidy of more than $100 million.

The NHL did not come to the Dallas/Fort Worth region until the 1990s. In 1994 the Minnesota North Stars moved to Reunion Arena and began play as the Dallas Stars. The Stars received a lease that was virtually identical to the one given the Mavericks.

Obtaining the Dallas Cowboys, Texas Rangers, Dallas Mavericks, and the Dallas Stars was seen as major image and economic development coups for the Dallas/Fort Worth region. Sports provided a conduit through which a new image could be shaped, and the success of the Cowboys certainly helped create other perspectives of Dallas. Although Dallas's attachment to the Cowboys and the extensive fan following is a result of the team's two sustained periods of success, there may well be other reasons that Dallas cherishes its relationship with "America's team." The popularity of the Cowboys during their first period of substantial success coincided with the aftermath of the assassination of President John F. Kennedy and the death of Lee Harvey Oswald. The success of the Cowboys seemed to have the potential for changing the image of Dallas. In the 1960s the name "Dallas," for many people, rekindled their memories of the murder and chaos associated with President Kennedy's assassination. It was a perspective or view the region wanted to change; the Cowboys and their success was a first step in that effort.

The relocation of the Washington Senators, at about the same time that the region opened the Dallas/Fort Worth Regional International Airport, continued the process of redefining the city and region's image. The entire region now seemed to be on the move and destined for substantial economic growth. As the Cowboys became America's team, the metroplex came to typify the growth and expansion that embodied so much of America's view of itself. With the Cowboys winning, a new airport, new sports teams, and expanding economic growth, one could hardly wait for tomorrow, for it was destined to be better than today. All these accomplishments spotlighted the region's success and provided the whole metroplex with an image and swagger that the teams, and the Cowboys in particular, emulated. When the Cowboys added their cheerleaders to the equation, the entire region was seen as beautiful, brash, and successful, hardly the dreary, backward section of America where a president was murdered.

WANDERING EYES AND IMAGE BENEFITS

When any of the cities in the region first attempted to bring a new sports franchise to the metroplex, there was a high level of cooperation to ensure that the team would come to the area. As soon as any of the teams began to cast a wandering eye about the region for a better stadium or arena, however, cooperation gave way to a battle to achieve a "major league image." In the same order they appeared in the region, the teams began to seek improved stadiums and arenas, and to encourage competition among the cities.

The Cowboys played their home games at Dallas's historic but aging Cotton Bowl. This facility lacked many of the amenities that teams and fans sought. In addition, the Cotton Bowl is located in a declining, predominantly minority neighborhood that suffers from high crime levels and economic disinvestment. In the late 1960s the Cowboys and the city of Dallas exchanged ideas and plans for a new downtown facility or a facility north of downtown. Four separate plans were developed, but none was supported by all parties. Frustrated with the pace of negotiations and the city's seeming lack of concern or appreciation for the needs of the team, the Cowboys began to look for alternatives. When no agreement could be reached with the city of Dallas, the team initiated negotiations with the city of Irving. Although some of Dallas's leadership could hardly imagine a football team in Irving, the Cowboys and Irving reached an agreement for the building of Texas Stadium; the Cowboys have played there since 1971. As had so many other teams of that era, the Cowboys left the center city for the suburbs. The actual site of the stadium was less than half a mile from Dallas's city limits, but the new location was in the midst of a suburban area and far removed from the inner-city world of the Cotton Bowl's neighborhood.

In contrast to some of today's stadium deals, the city of Irving acquired the Cowboys for a bargain price. The cost of Texas Stadium was $35 million; in 1998 this would be the equivalent of $140.4 million. Municipal bonds were sold to season ticket holders; each seat required the purchase of a $250 bond. This raised $15 million. The city paid $10 million for the land, and the balance of the money, $10 million, was raised by selling a municipal bond to the owner of the Cowboys (Rosentraub, 1988). The city of Irving retired all these bonds from their general revenues. All revenues from Texas Stadium were assigned to the team, but the Cowboys do pay a small rental charge each year to the city of Irving. Irving, then, got itself into the professional sports business for a total investment of $140.4 million (1998 dollars), with the team paying nothing toward the capital cost of the facility.

The Texas Rangers and the city of Arlington had a long history of problems with Arlington Stadium. Designed to serve a minor league team, the stadium was small and had inadequate food and beverage facilities, and a large proportion of its seats were outfield bleachers. The city made two major sets of innovations, including the construction of a new upper deck that provided more seating around home plate, but the facility never could seat the promised fifty thousand fans. With only 42,500 seats—and more than one-third of these outfield bleachers—the revenue potential for the team was extremely limited.

Without a large cable television contract, the Rangers were dependent on stadium revenues for their fiscal success. If the team was to survive, a new stadium with far more revenue potential was needed. Such a decision had substantial implications because the city of Arlington had yet to retire all the bonds sold for the expansion of Arlington Stadium. In addition, the failure of the city to provide a stadium of the size agreed to in 1972 created a weakened bargaining position for Arlington. Since the team had never received what it was promised, Arlington, if it was to keep the team, had little choice but to build a signature statement stadium that both the team and the city would enjoy. The Rangers, of course, engaged in a series of tactics to ensure the city's cooperation in this effort, including the review of potential sites for a new ballpark in Dallas. Arlington's robust fiscal status and wealth also meant that building the facility would not be a major financial problem. These factors combined to create a situation ripe for the provision of a substantial set of incentives and welfare payments that would increase the wealth of the team's owners and players.

In the early 1990s the Rangers began to explore their options: a new facility in Arlington, a stadium in Dallas, a stadium in one of Dallas's northern suburbs, or a possible move to St. Petersburg, Florida, and its Sun Coast Dome. (The Florida city had built the dome stadium without a commitment from any team. The Rangers and the Chicago White Sox both used the threat of a move to the Sun Coast Dome to secure new facilities [Mier, 1993].) The Rangers were unlikely to want to leave the nation's eighth largest media market. Although flirting with Florida was designed to increase Arlington's flexibility, the team's attention was focused on Arlington, Dallas, and Dallas's northern suburbs.

Initially Dallas wanted to discuss three sites with the team. One site, located about five miles east of downtown and south of Texas Stadium, within the city of Dallas, was at the nexus of an east-west freeway (Interstate 30) and a north-south state highway. A second site was in an area close to the home of the Mavericks and Stars, just west of the downtown core area. The third site was east of downtown. All these sites had locational disadvantages and would have required substantial infrastructure improvements. It was also possible that environmental problems would make one or more of them unacceptable or impractical. A location in one of Dallas's northern suburbs would have moved the team far from its fans in Arlington and Fort Worth. More important, the transportation links to these northern suburbs were not as convenient as those that existed in Arlington. The best outcome for the team was to remain in Arlington, but the best deal could be negotiated only if Arlington thought the team might leave.

Negotiations between the Rangers and the city of Arlington eventually developed into the plans that led to the Ballpark in Arlington, a facility widely proclaimed as one of the finest in America. The deal that was negotiated, summarized in early chapters, involved the investment of $21 million by the team (present value). In addition, the Rangers pay the city of Arlington $2 million per year as their rental fee for the use of the stadium. The city of Arlington agreed to spend $135 million for the new stadium, to be raised via a 0.5 percent increase in the local sales tax. When the electorate was asked to ratify this proposal, more than two-thirds of the voters supported it.

When the new stadium financing proposal was on the ballot, voter turnout was the largest in Arlington's history. A report issued by the State of Texas's comptroller assured voters that as much as 60 percent of the sales taxes collected in Arlington was to be paid by nonresidents. This helped convince the voters to support the proposed financing program. As a retail center, Arlington is able to export a great deal of its sales taxes to nonresidents because they pay the sales for the stadium each time they buy anything in the city of Arlington. As such, although the public sector did pay for a large portion of the Ballpark in Arlington, that public included residents from all cities and communities in the Dallas/Fort Worth region. Arlington has been so successful in financing its commitment through this sales tax that the bonds sold will likely be paid five years sooner than anticipated. This success meant that the city had the tax capacity to consider other investments—a factor that became quite important when the Mavericks and Stars sought a new home.

Although Arlington has been successful in retiring its debt earlier than anticipated, it is still doing that with taxes and not revenues earned from the stadium itself. As is typical in most deals involving cities and teams, after the initial year, the Texas Rangers retained virtually all revenues generated at the stadium including 100 percent of all advertising and parking revenues, 100 percent of all luxury seating revenues, and all concession profits. The team's stadium management group is responsible for all maintenance, leaving the rental payment as an increment to the city's revenues. However, since the facility is owned by the city, the stadium is tax exempt. Had the land been developed instead, it is quite likely the city would have received more in property tax revenues than it earns in rental fees.

The team's ability to retain virtually all revenues from the stadium substantially increased its value. By 1998 the Texas Rangers were the seventh (worth $254 million) most valuable MLB franchise despite having appeared in just two postseason series. The team's lack of success on the field, only reversed in 1996, did not detract from its financial value.

The competition among cities in the region for the Rangers set the stage for another round of sports wars involving the Mavericks and Stars. Reunion Arena, though relatively new, does not have the luxury suites and club seating that have increased the profitability of several NBA and NHL teams. In addition, the arena's capacity is less than in the newer facilities that several cities have developed. Indeed, indoor arenas now frequently have more than twenty thousand seats or are at least 15 percent larger than Reunion Arena. In 1993 the Mavericks' ownership began to explore the possibility of a new arena with the city of Dallas. At the same time, the team's owner purchased land in a northeast suburb in an effort to consider a move from Dallas to the city of Lewisville. The voters in Lewisville narrowly defeated a proposition to implement a local sales tax to support their investment in the arena. Soon afterward, Arlington signaled its interest in building a new arena for the Mavericks and Stars by hiring a consulting firm to perform a feasibility study. This study would determine whether an indoor arena located near the Ballpark in Arlington was a viable enterprise. The favorable results were released to the media and discussed at a city council meeting that was covered extensively by the region's television and radio stations and newspapers.

Although the city of Arlington's official position was that it would not make a proposal to the Mavericks and Stars until such time as a deal was not feasible in Dallas, Arlington's officials did nothing to conceal their excitement about attracting both teams. In the first half of 1995, then, a sports war broke out in the Dallas/Fort Worth region for the Dallas Mavericks and Stars. In late 1995 it seemed as if the Mavericks would indeed land in Arlington. However, when the team was sold to an ownership group that included Ross Perot Jr., Dallas's fortunes improved. A two-year process was initiated that led to a proposal for an investment of $120 million by the city of Dallas in a new arena to be built a few miles north of Reunion Arena. Less than 51 percent of the voters approved this proposal, and in 1998 construction began on a new home for the Mavericks and Stars in Dallas. Many voters conceded that their support for a subsidy was based on their fear that if the proposal failed, the teams were bound for Arlington.

SPORTS FRANCHISES AND THE BENEFITS FROM BEING A "MAJOR LEAGUE CITY"

Each city that provides incentives to attract or retain teams does so with the hope and expectation that the enhanced image and status acquired by hosting the teams will result in economic benefits. If these benefits are indeed a product of the team's presence, then one would expect to find higher levels of population growth and economic development, and a higher concentration of high-income and high-skill occupations in cities that are "major league."

Population Growth

The population growth rates in Dallas, Arlington, and Irving were compared to all other communities in the region, and there were no statistically significant differences in the rate of growth in these cities. Several other cities in the Dallas/Fort Worth region grew at considerably higher rates than the cities that invested in sports. In terms of both nominal percentage changes and net local growth (that is, nominal growth less the national growth of cities of the same size class), the region's non-investor cities did better on average than the investor cities. From 1970 to 1980, Arlington grew considerably, but four other suburbs grew at a higher rate; from 1980 to 1990, six non-investor suburbs grew at a higher rate than Arlington (see Table 7-1). From 1970 to 1980, Irving ranked thirteenth among all seventeen cities examined here but did manage to exceed the rate of growth in six of the non-investor cities in the 1980s. Overall, however, the data do not support the proposition that sports franchises attract people to the "host" investor city faster than to non-investor cities within the same region.

Comparative Fiscal Benefits

Many cities that attain major league status by attracting a team expect to enjoy improved local finances. Because sports-related

TABLE 7-1
**Population Change, by City and Sports Investor Class,
Dallas/Fort Worth Metropolitan Area, 1970–80 and 1980–90**

	Pop. 1970 (1)	Pop. 1980 (2)	Pop. Change 1970–82 (3)	Nat'l Percentage Change (4)	Nat'l Growth by City Size% (5)	Net Local Growth% (4-5)	Pop. 1990 (6)	Pop. Change 1980–90 (7)	Nominal Percentage Change 1980–90 (8)	Nat'l Growth by City Size% (9)	Net Local Growth% (8-9)
Investor Cities											
Arlington	90,229	160,113	69,884	77.5	8.6	68.9	261,717	101,604	63.5	15.1	48.4
Dallas	844,401	904,078	59,677	7.1	-16.1	23.2	1,007,618	103,540	11.5	-7.3	18.8
Irving	97,260	109,943	12,683	13.0	8.6	4.4	155,037	45,094	41.0	15.1	25.9
Average Growth				32.5		32.2			38.6		31.0
Non-Investor Cities											
Bedford	10,049	20,821	10,772	107.2	12.5	94.7	43,762	22,941	110.2	2.6	107.6
Euless	19,316	24,002	4,686	24.3	12.5	11.8	38,149	14,147	58.9	8.9	50.0
Farmers Branch	27,492	24,863	(2,629)	-9.6	17.2	-26.8	24,250	(613)	-2.5	2.6	-5.1
Fort Worth	393,455	385,164	(8,291)	-2.1	12.4	-14.5	447,619	62,455	16.2	20.3	-4.1
Garland	81,437	138,857	57,420	70.5	8.6	61.9	180,635	41,778	30.1	15.1	15.0
Grand Prairie	50,904	71,462	20,558	40.4	8.6	31.8	99,606	28,144	39.4	20.5	18.9
Grapevine	7,049	11,801	4,752	67.4	9.0	58.4	29,198	17,397	147.4	2.6	144.8
Hurst	27,215	31,420	4,205	15.5	17.2	-1.7	33,574	2,154	6.9	8.9	-2.0
Lewisville	9,264	24,273	15,009	162.0	9.0	153.0	46,521	22,248	91.7	8.9	82.8
Mesquite	55,131	67,053	11,922	21.6	8.6	13.0	101,484	34,431	51.3	20.5	30.8
N. Richland Hills	16,514	30,592	14,078	85.2	12.5	72.7	45,895	15,303	50.0	8.9	41.1
Plano	17,872	72,331	54,459	304.7	12.5	292.2	127,885	55,554	76.8	20.5	56.3
Richardson	48,405	72,496	24,091	49.8	17.2	32.6	74,840	2,344	3.2	20.5	-17.3
Southlake	2,031	2,808	777	38.3	9.0	29.3	7,082	4,274	152.2	0.7	151.5
Average Growth				69.7		57.7			59.4		47.9

Note: National growth by city size (cols. 5 and 9) is total population growth in all U.S. cities of this size class during the period.

Sources: North Central Texas Council of Governments, annual population estimates, 1970–1991; U.S. Statistical Abstract, various years.

facilities often are fixed-capital investments, city officials anticipate higher property values around such sites, which in turn are
expected to generate more property taxes for the municipality.
However, city officials *voice* less attention to the debt impacts of
sports facilities. Investments in sports facilities require the imple-
mentation of public debt, so we might also speculate that investor cities exhibit higher levels of debt. On the other hand,
because these fixed investments bring in fans and presumably
create entertainment complexes around stadiums, more sales tax
revenue might be expected from investor cities. Finally, investment in sports facilities is expected to affect the operating expenditures of investor cities; that is, if higher property taxes and sales
tax revenues are being generated, there may be more revenues to
support higher levels of public municipal spending. Conversely,
if revenues are not increased, the expenditure requirements of
sports franchises and their fixed investments may reduce the
sums available for general government services. Either way, we
expect to see different spending patterns by investor versus non-
investor cities (see Table 7-1).

In a previous study of the 1970 to 1978 period in Dallas/Fort
Worth, it was found that Arlington and Irving were not able to
capture a larger share of the fiscal benefits after the movement of
the Rangers and Cowboys (Rosentraub and Nunn, 1978). As the
new suburban franchise locations matured during the 1980s,
however, new entertainment and business complexes may have
resulted in comparatively better fiscal performance in the two
suburban cities. The same may be hypothesized for the city of
Dallas because of the Dallas Mavericks franchise.

As shown in Table 7-2, differences in fiscal performance from
1980 to 1991 do indeed exist, but not always in the direction expected for the investor cities. Investor cities do have statistically
higher levels of per capita debt—nearly 20 percent higher on average among Dallas, Arlington, and Irving—than non-investor

TABLE 7-2

Mean Per Capita City Finances, by City and Sports Investment Class, Dallas/Fort Worth Metropolitan Area, 1980–1991

	Assessed Property Value	Property Taxes	Sales Taxes	Total Debt	Total Expend.
All Cities	51,162	196	152	1,083	818
Investor Cities	43,445	207	160	1,246	806
Arlington	32,341	162	127	1,479	726
Dallas	50,804	266	200	1,449	1,009
Irving	47,190	194	155	811	683
Non-Investor Cities	53,119	193	150	1,042	821
Euless	24,806	120	79	484	389
Farmers Branch	106,790	432	400	1,201	1,362
Fort Worth	28,705	226	133	1,325	1,001
Garland	31,649	149	74	1,323	1,278
Grand Prairie	35,778	164	101	875	671
Grapevine	57,853	219	214	1,435	1,317
Hurst	31,695	155	184	463	542
Lewisville	36,723	168	110	1,195	501
Mesquite	29,491	142	116	643	638
N. Rich and Hills	28,873	122	108	846	574
Plano	77,256	219	111	1,171	785
Richardson	144,917	201	173	1,545	794
F-score	1.69	0.75	0.41	3.97	0.04
Probability	ns	ns	ns	0.05	ns

Notes: (1) All figures expressed in constant 1992 dollars. (2) All figures represent 12-year averages for each city, except for Grand Prairie, which reflects a ten-year average. (3) F-score and probability refer to differences between investor and non-investor city groups (ns=not significant).

Sources: U.S. Census, City Government Finances, various years; Moody's Municipal and Government Manual, various years.

cities. Arlington's per capita debt is exceeded only by the city of Richardson. Since Dallas, Arlington, and Irving were not the fastest-growing cities in the region (see Table 7-1), these higher debt levels were not driven by population growth. Other factors including the fixed asset financing and service requirements of professional sports facilities underlie these debt figures.

Although no other statistically significant differences exist, the nominal per capita differences are intriguing. First, non-investor cities had higher per capita assessed property valuations than investor cities. Second, in terms of property and sales tax revenue per capita, the investor cities did somewhat better than non-investors, although the differences are not statistically significant. Furthermore, seven non-investor cities exhibited a higher average annual property tax per capita than did Arlington, while five non-investors collected more sales tax per capita on average. Irving did somewhat better in these two revenue categories, but a number of cities without franchises still exceeded its twelve-year averages.

Overall, this fiscal comparison lends additional empirical support to the proposition that investor cities cannot prevent the leakage of public tax and revenue benefits of sports investment to other cities in the region. In terms of these fiscal indicators, there is not a great deal of differentiation between investor and non-investor cities, or at least very little that is statistically significant. This suggests that if the presumed fiscal largesse of the sports franchises is real, the region as a whole appears to share in it, even though the costs of the sports investments are borne by the investor cities. Although some may argue that Arlington exports a portion, 60 percent, of its sales taxes to nonresidents, this is still a cost because these funds, in the absence of a stadium, would be available for other municipal functions or lower property taxes.

It also was possible to secure updated reports on the sales tax revenues received by the investor and non-investor cities in the Dallas/Fort Worth region for the years 1992 through 1997 from the comptroller's office for the State of Texas. Focusing on sales taxes alone in this time period permits inclusion of the potential benefits of Arlington's new Ballpark for the Texas Rangers. Again, however, there was no significant difference in the sales tax revenues earned by investor cities when compared to non-investor cities. Separate comparisons were also made between Arlington and other suburban cities since it was the city that made the most recent investment. For no pairing of cities could any statistically significant difference be found. Table 7-3 illustrates the per capita sales tax revenues received by cities in the Dallas/Fort Worth region in the years 1992 through 1997.

Comparative Attraction of High-Skill Employment

Many advocates of the value and importance of professional sports teams point to the image and prestige effects of sports franchises; the familiar refrain is that these benefits are important to a city because of the people that will want to live in the community. Thus one is hoping not just that there will be an improvement in the "quality of life" per se when competing for professional sports teams but that these teams will lure highly skilled, highly paid employees to the host (investor) cities. This proposition can be tested by examining the proportion of each Dallas/Fort Worth city's occupational workforce that is classified as executive/administrative/managerial, professional, or technical. Of all the standard labor force occupational classifications, these reflect the "high-skill" occupations that presumably seek the high quality of life to which professional sports are believed to contribute. (Based on U.S. Census data, the categories of occupations include the following: (1) executive, administrative, and managerial, (2) professional specialty, (3) technicians and related support, (4) sales, (5) administrative support, (6) private household, (7) protective service, (8) services, (9) farming, (10) precision production, (11) machine operators, (12) transportation, and (13) handlers and laborers. The first three categories listed

TABLE 7-3
Per Capita Sales Tax Revenues by City, 1992 through 1997

City	1997	1996	1995	1994	1993	1992
Irving	193	178	179	176	151	136
Arlington	186	178	180	178	160	145
Dallas	166	160	149	143	134	124
Fort Worth	119	113	112	106	96	89
Euless	160	126	121	114	81	59
Garland	81	73	73	69	64	60
Farmers Branch	475	450	410	395	332	323
Grand Prairie	165	148	139	131	106	85
Grapevine	191	162	155	146	130	123
Hurst	234	233	236	229	173	159
Lewisville	216	192	208	172	142	125
Mesquite	194	187	188	179	162	103
N. Richland Hills	197	193	26	25	23	22
Plano	157	153	184	164	149	121
Richardson	253	246	220	185	171	173

here were summed and classified as "high-skill occupations" for the purposes of this analysis.)

Changes in high-skill occupations in the Dallas/Fort Worth region, classified by city and sports investment class, are shown in Table 7-4. Once again, several non-investor cities in the Dallas/Fort Worth area fared as well as and often better than Dallas, Arlington, and Irving. Looking only at the average proportion of high-skill employment, the investor cities exceeded non-investors in 1970 only, and by 1990 non-investor cities averaged a 35 percent high-skill workforce, compared to 33 percent in the investor cities. On an individual basis, non-investor cities such as Plano, Richardson (home to the University of Texas at Dallas and several computer firms), Garland, and Farmers Branch consistently have had proportions of high-skill occupations similar to the investor cities. Of the investor cities, however, Arlington has maintained the proportion of high-skill

TABLE 7-4

Changes in High Skill Occupations, by City and Sports Investment Class,
Dallas/Fort Worth Metropolitan Area, 1970–1990

	1970		1980		1990		Percentage change in high-skill occupations	
	Number in high-skill occupations	As percentage of city's employment	Number in high-skill occupations	As percentage of city's employment	Number in high-skill occupations	As percentage of city's employment	1980	1990
Investor Cities (mean)		29.8		26.9		32.9	45.2	75.2
Arlington	15,689	39.1	27,149	31.2	51,805	35.4	73.0	90.8
Dallas	91,431	24.4	122,570	26.4	162,567	31.8	34.1	32.6
Irving	11,047	25.8	14,190	23.3	28,668	31.4	28.5	102.0
Non-Investor Cities (mean)		26.6		27.8		35.3	131.4	113.4
Euless	1,908	24.4	3,156	23.4	7,631	33.0	65.4	141.8
Farmers Branch	2,767	23.9	3,981	27.7	4,274	32.2	43.9	7.4
Fort Worth	29,524	18.4	41,616	23.2	60,644	29.3	41.0	45.7
Garland	8,865	25.8	20,418	27.9	31,451	32.0	130.3	54.0
Grand Prairie	4,599	21.5	6,730	19.3	14,107	27.8	46.3	109.6
Grapevine	645	22.8	1,753	26.8	6,942	41.6	171.8	296.0
Lewisville	879	21.6	3,081	24.6	9,451	34.2	250.5	206.8
Mesquite	4,301	19.5	6,294	18.2	16,163	29.7	46.3	156.8
N. Richland Hills	2,036	29.7	4,594	28.5	8,493	33.3	125.6	84.9
Plano	2,777	37.4	15,026	42.3	34,688	48.2	441.1	130.9
Richardson	9,280	47.8	17,019	44.2	19,269	46.7	83.4	13.2

Notes: (1) "High-skill occupations" include executive/administrative/managerial, professional, and technicians. (2) "City's employment" refers to employment of the individual city only.

Source: U.S. Bureau of the Census, "General Social and Economic Characteristics, Texas," various years.

occupations at approximately one-third of its labor force, exceeding both Dallas and Irving in 1970, 1980, and 1990. In 1990, Arlington ranked fourth behind Plano, Richardson, and Farmers Branch. (Arlington is also home to the University of Texas at Arlington.) Similar findings are exhibited in terms of the decade-by-decade growth of high-skill employment. Several non-investors (such as Plano, Lewisville, Grapevine, and Euless) indicate more growth than in the investor cities. This certainly was true in 1970 to 1980 and 1980 to 1990 when comparing the *average* growth in high-skill occupations between the investor and non-investor cities as two separate groups. Moreover, individual non-investor cities had ten-year growth rates far exceeding the investor cities. With respect to attracting and keeping high-skill occupational classes, then, the investor cities in the Dallas/Fort Worth region do not show clear evidence of doing a better job than many of the non-investor cities.

THE TANGIBLE REWARDS FROM SPORTS TEAMS

The experiences of Arlington, Irving, and Dallas clearly indicate that if there are tangible benefits from hosting a team, they do not accrue to any single city. If Arlington, Dallas, and Irving became "major league" because they invested in facilities that helped support professional sports teams, then they did not receive any more returns or benefits than other cities that did not invest. It is possible that benefits accrued to the entire region and that Arlington, Dallas, and Irving shared in the economic and social gains that all communities enjoyed. However, the outcomes in the metroplex clearly indicate that no one city captured an image or quality-of-life benefit that led to economic gains. These benefits, if they exist at all, are available to all communities in a region. The decentralized and integrated nature of America's urban economies makes it impossible for any single city to capture a disproportionate share of these benefits. At a minimum, then, if any investments are to be made in sports facilities, they should be shared by an entire region and should not be the responsibility of any single community.

LESSONS LEARNED FROM THE DALLAS/FORT WORTH REGION

The spending at stadiums does not increase wealth in investor cities.

There seems to be little doubt that there are intangible benefits from the presence of a team. Civic pride probably increases for many people, and there is undoubtedly a substantial amount of publicity generated from the team for a city. Do any of these intangible benefits attract business, economic development, or people? If the experiences of the investor cities in the Dallas/Fort Worth area are any indication, economic gains do not accrue to investor cities. Do sports teams make cities "major league"? If major league means attracting more people or investment, the answer is no. No single city in a region will be able to capture a disproportionate share of any economic activity generated by a team.

If an area wants to include sports, it should use a regional tax.

With no city able to contain the economic or image benefits from a team's presence, any area that wants to subsidize a team should use a regional tax. Arlington's sales tax approximates such a tax because it is a regional shopping center. However, most of its shoppers are from the western half of the region. In that sense, then, those who live in the eastern half of the region pay less for the benefits than those people who shop in Arlington. Of course, residents of the region can avoid any payment for the stadium by simply refusing to shop or dine in Arlington. The point here is that the best possible approach for financing a regional effort is through a tax paid by all or most residents of the region, not a tax paid by residents of a single city. The tax used by Arlington comes far closer to creating a balance between the liability for the costs and the sharing of benefits. In contrast, Irving residents pay for their investment through their property tax; therefore, a larger proportion of the tax is paid by the residents and businesses of Irving.

If it quacks, it is still a duck.

The success Arlington has had in financing its shiny new ballpark and the regional nature of the tax does not obscure the conclusion that the city and taxpayers across the region are subsidizing wealthy owners and players. Sales taxes paid by lower-income people produce excess profits that are divided between players and owners, all of whom enjoy salaries that most taxpayers can only dream about. A subsidy spread across hundreds of thousands of people amounts to a small charge each year. It is still, however, a transfer of wealth from the lower and middle classes to the upper class. It is still welfare in a state that abhors life on the dole. It is still a subsidy in a state that defends capitalism and the spirit of the free market. Arlington may well have found the least offensive tax, but it is still a tax and it is still welfare for the rich. And since Arlington and Irving secure no tangible or intangible benefits from the presence of a team, each city is providing welfare. Perhaps it is time to see if other investments (such as in schools, public safety, and family recreation) could make a city "major league" and produce the same or a higher level of tangible benefits to the community.

8

Can Small Regions Afford Professional Sports? Who Is Responsible for the Viability of Small-Market Teams?

I've heard a lot of concerns from the public—things like whether Andy Van Slyke will get a $4 million salary next year. But I think residents realize that having a baseball team keeps us as one of the Number 1 cities in the United States.

Councilman Joe Cusick, Pittsburgh,
explaining his support for a municipal loan to the Pirates

If there is a financial crisis in professional sports, it involves the viability of small-market teams. Each league has struggled to find a revenue-sharing formula that permits teams in smaller markets to earn sufficient revenues to attract and retain the best players. There is, of course, an inherent conflict for any league that attempts to share revenues among its members. Those teams that earn more money want to share as little as possible. In addition, those owners who paid dearly for their franchise are far less interested in revenue-sharing than other owners.

The NFL has taken the greatest strides toward achieving a degree of financial parity through the sharing of its largest single revenue source. However, even sharing the $17.6 billion television contract among the teams has led to some critical revenue differences between large- and small-market teams. The NFL does not share stadium-related revenues; therefore, the income earned by teams from luxury seating, naming rights, advertising, and concessions has led to critical revenue differentials. For example, in 1996, the Dallas Cowboys earned $26 million more than any other team. Eliminating the Cowboys and the Dolphins from the comparison still leaves a gap of $15 million between the "haves" and "have-nots." Although the league's hard salary cap minimizes some of the advantages of the high-revenue teams, as already noted, there are experts in cap economics that have permitted some teams to use their excess revenues to attract and retain better players.

The revenue differential or gaps are far larger in the three other sports. In 1996 the Yankees earned more than three times the gross income of the Pittsburgh Pirates. There was a $25 million gap in revenues earned between the eight MLB teams that had the largest revenues and the eleven teams with the smallest revenues. In 1996 six teams earned more than $70 million while thirteen earned less than $50 million. In the NHL, while thirteen teams earned less than $40 million, six earned more than $50 million. In the NBA, six teams earned more than $75 million in 1996 while fourteen earned $50 million or less.

The common refrain when critics point to revenue differentials of this magnitude is that local communities in smaller markets have to develop financing plans to help their teams. In some instances, very wealthy community residents have done just that. Some team owners have been willing to accept losses to ensure that their community has a team. The civic contributions by such families as the Rooneys, Kauffmans, Krocs, and Simons represent substantial additions to the quality of life in cities like Pittsburgh, Kansas City, San Diego, and Indianapolis. In several other situations, however, the expectation is that the public sector will provide a subsidy by building a new stadium and arena and allowing the team to retain most of the revenue generated by the new facility. Each of the leaders of the four sports leagues has visited communities from coast to coast to lecture them on the sacrifices they must make to close the revenue gaps that exist between their team and those that earn far more money. These lectures never include any discussion of the leagues'

1. responsibility for a substantial portion of these revenue gaps;
2. ability to reduce the revenue gaps themselves; or
3. responsibility to live up to the commitments they have made to the U.S. Congress and various courts to ensure the viability of small-market teams.

Before detailing in the conclusions how the fiscal problems of small-market teams can be eliminated and the sports welfare system ended, a more complete understanding of the fiscal plight facing small-market teams is needed. For more than ten years the city of Pittsburgh has wrestled with the small-market problems that have defined its battle to keep the Pirates. Although the Pirates have played in the city for more than one hundred years, the lack of meaningful revenue sharing has placed this team at a decided disadvantage in its efforts to recruit and retain the best players. The team and MLB have argued that the Pirates simply need a new stadium and more fan support to make the team competitive and financially viable, and given the team's current debt, the public sector would have to be responsible for building the new facility. In Indianapolis, despite the sharing of the NFL's lucrative television contract, the Colts demanded a change in their lease for use of the RCA Dome to make them more competitive. The Colts, like the Pirates, play in one of their leagues' smaller markets, and without extensive public support, they, too, found themselves at the bottom of the revenue heap. How much does it cost small markets to host professional sports teams? Who should pay for the extra costs required to keep small-market teams competitive? These issues are explored against the backdrop of the experiences of the Pirates and Pittsburgh and the Colts and Indianapolis.

SAVING BASEBALL IN
A SMALL METROPOLITAN REGION

The future of one of the oldest teams in MLB has been threatened by the economics of baseball. Although it is hard to imagine the sport without the Pittsburgh Pirates, the team is now a small-market franchise. This is somewhat ironic given the history of the team and city. Founded in 1887, the Pirates have played within the city limits of Pittsburgh for 112 years. The Pirates played in the first World Series (1903), losing to the Boston Red Sox. They won their first title in 1909 and have appeared in seven World Series, but none more memorable than the 1960 series in which Bill Mazeroski's ninth-inning home run defeated the Yankees, 4 games to 3. Never before had a World Series been decided by a home run in the final at-bat by a team in the seventh game, and the image of Bill Mazeroski leaping around the base paths remains one of MLB's most endearing and enduring memories. The Pirates also were the team for which two of baseball's most distinguished citizens played. Willie Stargell defined the spirit of the team in the 1970s, and Roberto Clemente's image still shines as an example of what an athlete can represent for a community.

Although these memories are both kind and warm, Pittsburgh's demographic realities paint a very stark and cold vision in terms of the economics of baseball. The city of Pittsburgh lost 135,539 residents from 1970 to 1990. More important for the economics of baseball and efforts to retain a team, Metropolitan Pittsburgh also is shrinking. In 1970 the region had 2,556,000 residents; by 1990 it had lost 12.2 percent of its residents and was now home to 2,243,000 people (see Table 8–1). In 1970 more than one-fifth of the state of Pennsylvania's population lived in the Metropolitan Pittsburgh region. By 1990 the Pittsburgh region accounted for 18.9 percent of the state's population. When the Pirates began to play in the latter part of the nineteenth century, Pittsburgh was one of America's most important economic centers. By 1990, Pittsburgh was the nineteenth largest metropolitan region, a shrinking giant.

CAN THE PIRATES SURVIVE IN PITTSBURGH?

The Pirates have been in a perpetual state of fiscal crisis since 1985. After two consecutive poor seasons and a stark analysis of the Pittsburgh market, the team's owner sought to sell the franchise. When no local buyers could be found, a consortium of local institutions joined with the city of Pittsburgh to ensure that the team would remain in western Pennsylvania. The Pittsburgh Associates agreed to buy the team for $26 million. This group included the following:

AlCoA Service Corporation
APT Holdings (Mellon Bank)
Carnegie Mellon University

TABLE 8-1
Population Changes in the Pittsburgh Region

	1990	1980	1970
Pittsburgh			
City	366,852	423,959	502,391
Metropolitan area	2,243,000	2,423,000	2,556,000
Pennsylvania	11,882,000	11,864,000	11,801,000
Pittsburgh's Population as a Percentage of:			
Metropolitan area	16.4	17.5	19.7
State of Pennsylvania	3.1	3.6	4.3
Metropolitan Pittsburgh's Population as a Percentage of:			
State of Pennsylvania	18.9	20.4	21.7

Eugene Litman
John McConnell
National Intergroup
PNC Financial Corporation
PPG Industries
Ryan Homes
Frank Schneider
USX Corporation
Harvey Walken
Westinghouse Electric

By 1993 Eugene Litman, Harvey Walken, and Ryan Homes were no longer part of the Pittsburgh Associates. In addition, the city of Pittsburgh agreed to lend the team $25 million to increase its operating funds. Only $20.8 million of the promised $25 million was ever transferred to the team by Mayor Richard Caliguiri's administration, and the remaining $4.2 million would become part of a lawsuit the team would bring against Pittsburgh. In any event, at the conclusion of 1985, the Pirates were saved, and the city was part of a thirteen-member public/private partnership that kept the team in Pittsburgh.

In spite of the fact that such a management structure would seem to be a prescription for disaster, the Pirates actually thrived. After failing to draw a million fans in 1985, the team's play improved and attendance soared. In 1991 the Pirates sold 2.3 million tickets, and, through the cessation of play in 1994, had attracted 1,222,520 fans (see Table 8-2). In the early years of the 1990s, the Pirates had the best record in baseball. The Pirates were Eastern Conference Champions in 1990, 1991, and 1992, but in each year they lost the championship series. The 1992 and 1993 losses to Atlanta created some of baseball's best memories of the decade but failed to produce a pennant for the team with the best cumulative record during those three seasons.

The collection of partners that had purchased the Pirates created neither a management nightmare nor a poorly performing team, but the financial record of the team was another matter. The team lost money in eight of the nine seasons from 1986 through 1994. During this period the team's net loss was $44.6 million (see Table 8-2). These losses were in addition to the $20.8 million loan from the Urban Redevelopment Authority. Including the loan in an accounting of the team's finances would push the Pirates' debt to $66 million. In the fall of 1994 the *Pittsburgh Business Times* placed the team's debt at $49.1 million (Elliott, 1994), while the *Pittsburgh Post-Gazette* in September 1994 estimated the debt to be greater than $60 million (Halvonik, 1994). Another estimate by the *Pittsburgh Post-Gazette* placed the debt at $62 million (Schmitz, 1994). Although figures were unavailable for 1995, the team attracted fewer than 1 million fans, making it safe to assume that the team's debt has surpassed $65 million if the funds lent by the city of Pittsburgh are included in the total and are to be repaid.

TABLE 8-2

Attendance at Pirate Games and Operating Profits and Losses

(attendance and tickets in thousands; profit/loss in millions of dollars)

Category	1986	1987	1988	1989	1990	1991	1992	1993	1994	1995
					Season					
Attendance	1,001	1,161	1,867	1,374	2,050	2,065	1,829	1,651	1,223	906
Tickets	1,220	1,429	2,160	1,876	2,304	2,376	2,063	1,800	N. A.	N. A.
Profit/loss	−3.4	−1.8	+2.8	−2.0	−7.1	−7.6	−11.8	−5.0	−6.1	N. A.

Sources: Heltzel, 1991; Ruck, 1993; Ozanian, 1995.

To reduce their staggering debt and declining revenues the Pirates' owners asked the city for additional fiscal help. At the same time, however, the city of Pittsburgh was encountering its own budgetary shortfalls and was dealing with the very real possibility of raising taxes, eliminating workers, or reducing services. In such an environment it is not surprising that tempers flared and the city and team were in open conflict with each other.

The first confrontation between the team and the city was in 1981 when John Galbreath, the owner of the franchise at that time, asked for a revised lease for use of Three Rivers Stadium. When the city refused to change the lease, the team sued the city, arguing that they should be released from their obligations to pay the current level of rent because Pittsburgh had failed to honor two commitments to the team: The land adjacent to the stadium had never been developed to help make the area more of an attraction and more likely to bring more fans to games, and the city had failed to make needed highway repairs to improve overall access to the Three Rivers Stadium. To "spice up" the lawsuit, team officials met with the management of the Louisiana Superdome in a deliberate effort to create the impression that if Pittsburgh was not responsive to the team's needs, perhaps it was time for the Pirates to consider another home. The team's meeting with officials from New Orleans led to a separate lawsuit against the city of New Orleans by the city of Pittsburgh. Pittsburgh argued that New Orleans was "tampering" with its team and a franchise that held a valid lease with the city for the use of Three Rivers Stadium. In due course all the conflicting lawsuits were settled when Pittsburgh's City Council agreed that the city would assume more responsibility for the operation and maintenance of Three Rivers Stadium, thus reducing the team's costs and increasing the revenue flows to the franchise. The Pirates agreed, as part of the settlement, to end their conversations with the city of New Orleans and to remain in Pittsburgh. The first crisis had ended, but the seeds for future conflicts had been sown.

In 1991 another series of heated exchanges took place. The Pirates' owners declared they lost $7.1 million during the 1990 season. The team's management repeated their desire to remain in Pittsburgh, but they were also careful to point out that the team's value to other communities was probably in the range of $100 million. In other words, if they could leave Pittsburgh, they could make a great deal of money. However, to be profitable in Pittsburgh, a new stadium was needed. As the 1991 baseball season was coming to an end and the Pirates were in the process of clinching their second straight Eastern Conference Championship, Pittsburgh's mayor proposed building a new $100 million baseball-only facility. This stadium proposal survived less than a fortnight. On September 18, 1991, confronted with a $35 million deficit in the city's operating budget, the City Council rejected the mayor's proposal, calling it ill-timed and impossible in a year in which workers would be fired and taxes increased.

After the 1991 baseball season ended, the Pirates announced that they wanted their lease revised if no new stadium was to be built. The basis for this request was the city's failure to provide all the funds ($25 million) promised when the current owners bought the team. When there was no progress on these negotiations, the Pirates sued. Since the city was in "default" on its payment to the team, the Pirates believed they did not have to make their final lease or rental payment. The Pirates withheld $1.1 million in rental payments against the $4.2 million that the team believed it was owed and filed a lawsuit to get the remaining money. The team's action struck a harsh blow to its relations with the city. Mayor Sophie Masloff declared that "the team is taking a wrecking ball to the public-private partnership" that preserved the team for Pittsburgh. Her executive secretary, Joseph Sabino Mistick, proclaimed the lawsuit "a slap in the face to taxpayers and baseball fans in the city. This is the thanks they get for standing by the Pirates all these years." The Pirates' lawsuit did not end with their demands for the money that they were promised. The team also claimed that the stadium was in need of substantial repairs to maintain the first-class appearance promised in the lease. The Pirates' owners reaffirmed their desire to stay in Pittsburgh, but they argued that their fans needed better facilities.

Negotiations to resolve the dispute dragged on through the summer of 1993, and the city responded with a proposal to renovate Three Rivers Stadium and to improve the terms of the team's lease to increase revenues. In 1994 the city also proposed a second loan of $8 million to provide the team with additional operating capital. In exchange for this loan, however, the City Council wanted an additional seat on the team's board of directors and an agreement that the team would stay in Pittsburgh for another twenty years. Since the city was considering the infusion of cash as a loan, interest would be charged, 8.69 percent, sinking the team further into debt. Lastly, the city also wanted assurance that it would receive 53 percent of the net revenues from any sale of the team.

The team reviewed the city's offer but rejected the proposal in favor of an ultimatum that Pittsburgh had six months to find a new owner. If the city could not find an acceptable owner, the existing ownership group would put the team on the open market. An action of that nature could have meant the Pirates were bound for another city. During the ensuing six months the city was able to identify several potential owners, but none came forward with a bona fide offer to purchase the team. Faced with a possible move of the team, Pittsburgh asked for additional time. The Pirates granted the city an extension, but to reduce their operating deficit many of the best players were traded or their contracts were allowed to expire. These steps illustrate the owners' intent to reduce their losses and to put pressure on the city to either find a buyer or present a plan to increase revenues. The strategy of trading one's best players led to a sharp decline in attendance. In 1995 the team attracted fewer than 1 million fans and finished the season thirty-two games out of first place.

In 1996 a new ownership group was constructed consisting of twenty-two individuals and corporations. This new partnership, Pirates Acquisition, Inc., included the *Pittsburgh Post-Gazette*, the H. J. Heinz Company, one of the city's leading law firms, and several other local corporations and wealthy individuals. Led by Kevin McClatchy, who invested $10 million, the partnership would pay $85 million for the team and assume the $60 million debt. The net to the existing owners would be $25 million. As part of the deal, a local bank also agreed to provide the team and its new owners with a $50 million line of credit, and the city of Pittsburgh agreed to $9 million in stadium lease concessions and to support the concept of a new stadium for the Pirates. The governor of Pennsylvania also was recruited to give his public support for a new Pirates stadium.

The Pirates' performance has not changed substantially under new ownership. In 1996 the team lost eighty-nine games and finished fifteen games out of first place. In 1997 the team still lost more games than it won but finished five games out of first place

in the division. In 1998 the Pirates finished thirty-three games behind division champion Houston. Not coincidentally, the Pirates
have also consistently finished last in earnings. In 1996 with gross
revenues of $39.9 million, the Pirates earned $26 million less than
the average of all teams. What will it take to make the Pirates
profitable in Pennsylvania? How much does the community and
the state have to pay to subsidize a new stadium if MLB assumes
no responsibility for the plight of small-market teams?

WHAT WOULD SAVING
THE PIRATES COST A SMALL-MARKET CITY?

In 1999 a successful MLB will need revenues of approximately
$135 million to be profitable and competitive. Teams with gross
revenues below this level and not owned by media conglomerates
will be at a competitive disadvantage. What would it take to raise
the Pirates' revenues from the $49 million they earned in 1997 to
at least $135 million?

In 1996 the Pirates earned $17.7 million from media sources (lo-
cal and share of the national contract for the World Series and
playoffs). Measured against the region's population, this revenue
was equal to $7.89 for every resident, a very competitive figure
when contrasted with other teams. The Yankees, even with their
very large cable contracts, earned less than half of this figure, and
the Pirates' earnings exceeded the Philadelphia Phillies and Houston Astros. If the Pirates returned to their winning ways, it is likely
they would earn more media revenue. It is quite unlikely, however,
that they would ever earn enough to produce additional revenues
to equal the gross revenues of the upper tier of MLB teams. In 1997
the Cleveland Indians reported local and national media earnings
of $32 million. That figure also includes all income from MLB. The
Pirates could expect that much money but that would still mean

saving the team must involve increasing their revenues from a new stadium. Yet if the facility has to generate an additional $50 million for the Pirates (the team earned $49 million and with $32 million in media revenue approximately $50 million would still be needed to field a competitive team), how much could the team afford to pay for the stadium, and how much would the fans and/or public sector have to pay?

How much is a stadium going to cost that can produce the level of revenues needed by the Pirates? Jacobs Field in Cleveland cost in excess of $185 million. The total cost of the Ballpark in Arlington was approximately $195 million. Although there has been some discussion in Pittsburgh about building a stadium with fewer than forty thousand seats, it seems prudent to antici- pate a total stadium cost of approximately $225 million to $250 million in today's dollars.

The city of Arlington's obligation for the Ballpark in Arlington was limited to $135 million. The team was responsible for $65 million, and the Rangers committed 115 percent of the first year's lease of luxury suites and 5 percent of these revenues in years two through four of the stadium's operations. Luxury leases generated approximately $11 million in income for the Rangers during their first year, producing $12.7 million for the stadium (Greene, 1995). In the second year of operations, however, the team received about half of that amount (Much and Friedman, 1996). Five percent of that figure for years two through five would yield $670,000 (in present-value terms). With these ap- proximate figures, the first component of the team's *cash* invest- ment in the stadium was $12.4 million (present value).

There was a second component to the team's investment in the capital cost of the Ballpark in Arlington. The Rangers pay $1.5 mil- lion each year (in addition to their annual rent) to the city of Ar- lington until the bonds for the stadium are retired. The fixed rental charge for use of the stadium is $2 million for the period 1994 through 2024. The present value of the entire *cash* investment by the Rangers in building the Ballpark in Arlington, using a discount rate of 8 percent, is approximately $21 million. This figure does not include the base rent that the team pays, and the team is also responsible for maintaining and operating the stadium.

The Cleveland Indians also provided a portion of the funds to support Jacobs Field. The initial investment by the team was $20 million, and the club agreed to pay $2.9 million annually, for a portion of the facility's debt. The present value of this contribution to the stadium's construction is $31 million. The team's owner also agreed to an annual fee for the naming rights to the stadium; the present value of these annual payments is $5.8 million. In sum, then, the Cleveland Indians will invest a total of $53.9 million in Jacobs Field. Although it could be argued that the expenditure by the team's owner for naming rights was an optional decision and involves an advertising benefit, the team's investment was $20 million plus an annual payment of $2.9 million to retire $31 million of the stadium's debt.

Both the Indians and Rangers generate revenues within the target range of $135 million. It would seem, then, that financing a new stadium in Pittsburgh could be based on a set of financial arrangements similar to those developed by the cities of Arlington and Cleveland. As such, could the city of Pittsburgh expect an investment of between $20 million and $54 million from the team? Well, there is one other factor to consider.

The Pittsburgh franchise has substantial financial debts that must be retired. For the team to remain competitive it must be able to pay this debt, and that may limit the Pirates' contributions toward building and maintaining a new stadium. If the Pirates were to pay a debt of $60 million over a period of twenty-five years and a 7 percent loan could be secured, the team's annual payments would be $5.2 million. If the debt grows to $65 million and none of it is forgiven, the team's annual cost could be as much as $5.8 million.

To estimate the potential attendance and gate revenues the Pirates could earn with a new stadium, the experiences of the Texas Rangers and Cleveland Indians again are good models. Although both teams play in markets that are larger than the one served by the Pirates, both teams have created a substantial level of excitement for MLB in their communities. In many ways the problems faced by the Pirates in terms of attendance levels are similar to the ones encountered by the Rangers and Indians. In spite of the Pirates' smaller fan base, they have had a far more competitive team than either the Indians or Rangers. For example, since 1970 the Pirates have appeared in postseason play nine times (1970, 1971, 1972, 1974, 1975, 1979, 1990, 1991, 1992). The Pirates have appeared in more postseason series than any National League team. The Rangers appeared in the playoffs in 1996, and they are again poised to be in a very competitive race for the playoffs in 1998. The Indians won the American League pennant in 1995 and 1997, and are also likely to be one of the teams in the 1998 playoffs.

With a successful team in Jacobs Field, the Cleveland Indians have attracted more than 3.4 million fans (all eighty-one games have been sold for the past four years), and the Rangers have attracted 2.9 million fans. If the success of past Pirate teams is achieved and a new stadium is built, it seems reasonable to expect that approximately 2.8 million fans will be drawn to games on a regular basis. This figure assumes a level of success equal to that of the Rangers and Indians in a slightly smaller market, coupled with the inevitable few seasons when the team fails to make the playoffs. In other words, there would likely be seasons when as many as 3 million tickets are sold; in other years, attendance might fall below 2.8 million. If the average ticket price to attend a

Pirate game matches what the Indians charged in 1998, $15.29, the Pirates would earn at least $42.8 million in ticket revenues. If they could draw 3 million fans, they would earn $45.9 million.

Media revenues for the Pirates are expected to continue at their current levels, as will revenues shared with other MLB teams, bringing the franchise approximately $33 million. It is also assumed that the Pirates will earn $41 million in revenues from stadium operations if they are as successful as the Indians. These stadium revenue figures include the income from the sale of luxury seating and all food and beverages as well as income from advertising and other concessions. With these figures in mind, the gross revenues available to the Pirates would be approximately $117 million ($33 million in media and shared revenue, $42.8 million in ticket revenue, plus $41 million in revenues from stadium operations).

If the Pirates were able to generate those revenues, they still would have to repay their loan. If those payments were approximately $5.5 million a year, the team would have gross earnings of $111.3 million. Even if the Pirates contribute nothing to the cost of a new ballpark they will not be able to generate enough money to field a competitive team.

If the facility could be built for $250 million and financed for a period of thirty years, the cost to the taxpayers (assuming an interest rate of 6.25 percent) would be $18.7 million per year. Recently the State of Pennsylvania agreed to pay $180 million for a new ballpark. If Pittsburgh needed $170 million, its costs would be $12.7 million per year. How much of a tax increase would this be? In 1991, Allegheny County collected $289.6 million in taxes from residents. To raise an additional $12.7 million, taxes would have to increase 4.3 percent. The city of Pittsburgh collected $238.9 million in taxes. As a percent of these taxes, $13.4 million would amount to a tax increase of 5.3 percent. If the city and county's tax collections were joined together, both units of government would have collected $528.5 million. A $12.7 million annual subsidy to build the stadium would amount to 2.4 percent of the combined 1991 tax collections of the county and city (excluding school tax collections). Based on a 1990 county population of 1.34 million, the $12.7 million annual subsidy would amount to a payment of $9.48 for every person in the county to keep the Pirates in Pittsburgh.

It should be remembered that this subsidy would still leave the team with a shortfall of at least $23 million relative to revenue needed to field a competitive team. If the city of Pittsburgh and the county also accepted responsibility for the team's debt, the cost to taxpayers for the team would increase from $9.48 per person each year to approximately $15. If local governments or the state also decided to provide operating income for the team, as was done in the past or as the State of New York recently did for the Buffalo Bills, this tax bill would be higher. It also must be remembered that the residents of the area would also need to be prepared to buy up to 2.8 million tickets for the games in addition to their tax payments.

INDIANAPOLIS AS A TWO-TEAM MARKET

Indianapolis has two major league sports teams. While Pittsburgh struggles to be a home for the Steelers, Penguins, and Pirates, the Colts and Pacers are Indianapolis's major league teams. Both cities are also fortunate to have one of their franchises owned by a family with long-standing ties to the community. The Rooneys have owned the Steelers since they were founded in 1933. The Simon brothers have owned the Pacers since 1983 when they responded to the call of Indianapolis's mayor to save the team for the Hoosier capital. Both the Rooneys and the Simons have been committed to keeping their teams in Indianapolis and Pittsburgh, and each family's businesses, not the teams, are the primary sources of their wealth. This has afforded both cities and teams options as both families have been willing to accept a level of financial losses or smaller profit levels to keep their teams competitive and in their hometowns. For example, the Simons have endured losses in excess of $10 million on the operation of the Pacers to keep the team competitive. In recent years they made it clear, however, that losses of this magnitude were no longer possible, and the city of Indianapolis responded with the construction of a new arena. The Steelers remain in Three Rivers Stadium although the team has mentioned the desirability of a new facility.

James Irsay owns the Indianapolis Colts franchise. He inherited the team from his father, who engineered the relocation of the franchise from its legendary home in Baltimore. The team represents the primary source of wealth for James Irsay. As such, he does not have available to him some of the options that are available to the Simons and the Rooney family. In addition, although the Irsay family is very comfortable in Indianapolis and an active participant in the civic life of the community, Indianapolis does not represent for the Irsay family what it does for the Simons. As a result, relocation of the franchise is probably not as unappealing for James Irsay as it is for the Simons or Rooneys. Consequently, Indianapolis has to make sure that the Colts are as profitable for the Irsay family in the Hoosier capital as they would be in another location.

Ensuring the viability of small-market franchises has been a hallmark of the NFL, and the league's lucrative contract with several different television networks has been the cornerstone of the plan that makes sure that teams from Green Bay can compete for players with those in New York and Chicago. Early in his tenure as commissioner of the NFL, Pete Rozelle realized that without substantial revenue sharing the teams in the largest metropolitan areas would dominate. Unbalanced competition of this nature would lead, he believed, to declining attendance levels. In the 1950s and early 1960s, MLB, dominated by the Yankees, was already suffering from a lack of competition and declining attendance levels. Although the NFL aggressively shared revenues from fans attending games (visiting teams received 10 percent of all ticket money), each team retained all revenue from the telecast of their games. This meant that teams in the larger markets earned more money. In addition, some small-market teams were concerned that a network might decide to televise a game involving a large-market team instead of their game. This would further reduce the revenues earned by small-market teams and their ability to attract and retain the best players.

Prior to 1961 the NFL was prohibited from bargaining as a single entity with any television station or network. In the 1950s a court ruled that the NFL would violate antitrust provisions if it bargained as a single entity. Commissioner Rozelle believed that a truly competitive league with viable small-market teams would increase the profits of every team in the NFL. By 1961 he was able to convince all owners of the value of a truly competitive league and the benefit of pooling television revenues. Rozelle then led the effort to secure an exemption from Congress from the Sherman Act, permitting the NFL to bargain with the television networks as a single entity and give each team an equal share of whatever revenue was raised. Congress granted the NFL and each of the other sports leagues the right to bargain as a single entity and then to divide these revenues without fear of violating any aspects of the federal government's antitrust laws. As the popularity of the NFL increased and the league absorbed the AFL, the number of networks involved with the broadcast package increased. In 1997 the NFL startled the sports world when it was able to announce an eight-year, $17.6 billion package for the broadcast of its games by the Fox Network, CBS, ABC, and ESPN. This contract guarantees each team more than $73 million for each season from 1998 through 2005.

Despite this incredible bonanza, several NFL teams are still at a severe fiscal disadvantage relative to their competitors. Although the NFL provides equal shares to each team from its national broadcast contacts and from NFL properties (from the sale of merchandise), and although visiting teams receive 40 percent of the revenue from the sale of tickets, there are some very large sources of revenue that are not shared. Each NFL team is permitted to retain its "in-stadium" or "stadium-related" income. As we have seen, these revenues include income from the rental or sale of luxury seating (suites and club seats), advertising, sponsorships, naming rights, parking, permanent seat licenses, and food and beverages. When fans buy luxury seating, their payments are divided into a charge for the luxury seat or suite and a fee for the ticket to the game. Visiting teams receive 40 percent of all ticket sales but do not receive any of the income from luxury seat or suite charges, which can sometimes exceed $100,000. These arrangements and agreements have led to some very large revenue differentials between teams, and in 1996 and 1997 the Indianapolis Colts found themselves one of the "have-nots" with regard to in-stadium revenues.

Ironically, Bob Irsay was lured to Indianapolis from Baltimore by a lease for the use of a new domed stadium that he saw as capable of increasing the amount of money he would earn. The Colts had been trying to get a new stadium or substantial improvements to their existing home in Baltimore for several seasons. Indianapolis had just built a new domed facility as an annex to its convention center and agreed to a lease that would cost the team only $25,000 per game. For this fee the team could not only sell the more than sixty thousand seats but could also receive 50 percent of the revenue from ninety luxury suites. Although the public sector retained all revenues from parking, naming rights, and in-stadium advertising, access to suite revenue was still a substantial enhancement to the Colts' finances. Access to this revenue was seen as so vital that the team accepted a 5 percent ticket tax to help pay for the dome. The Colts were also permitted to retain all revenue from the sale of programs and other football-related merchandise, but the public sector retained the profits from all food and beverage sales. The lease signed by the team committed the Colts to the city of Indianapolis through the 2006 season.

The lease signed by the Colts for 1984 certainly represented a bonanza of sorts for the team and Bob Irsay. However, the economics of football were about to change, and within a decade the lease was obsolete, leaving the Colts at the bottom of the NFL's revenue pyramid. The team did earn in excess of $3 million from stadium-related sources, but several other teams were earning much more. In 1996, for example, the Dallas Cowboys earned $41.5 million from in-stadium revenues, more than any other team. Nevertheless, seven other teams earned at least $9 million from in-stadium revenues, and eleven other teams had commitments for new stadiums or new lease packages that would guarantee them no less than $9 million in in-stadium revenues. By the 1998 season, if there were no changes in their lease, the Colts would confront a situation in which nineteen of the NFL's teams would be in a position to earn as much as 300 percent more from in-stadium revenue sources.

Although the Colts' owner maintained that he did not want to leave Indianapolis, Mr. Irsay also made it clear that without some changes in the lease and capital improvements to the dome, the team could not be competitive. The NFL's commissioner went to

Indianapolis to underscore the league's interest in keeping the Colts in Indiana's capital city, but he insisted that the city had to help the team remain competitive. The bottom line was that the team wanted to retain far more of the revenue produced by the dome; it wanted the public sector to construct club seats so that the team could enhance its revenue position even more. In essence, the Colts wanted a lease that matched the revenue potential other teams had received from their host cities since 1984.

The problem for Indianapolis, however, was that some of the funds the Colts now wanted were being used to meet the public sector's debt obligations for the capital construction of the dome. In addition, no source of cash was available to make the capital improvements to the facility if the public sector did not have access to some of the revenue produced by the new club seats. Indianapolis's challenge, then, was to try to find additional revenue for the team without jeopardizing its own fiscal situation. If the Colts were permitted to retain the funds currently being used to retire the debt on the facility and maintain it, then the public sector would have to use tax revenues to offset the monies given to the Colts. This presented Indianapolis's mayor, Stephen Goldsmith, with a particularly unpleasant dilemma. If the revenue available to the Colts was not improved, it was clear that he faced losing the team. But he did not want to be placed in a position of raising taxes for professional sports at a time when he was advocating lower taxes and fewer government programs.

Even if Indianapolis was willing to divert revenues to the team and create an entirely new lease, there were other challenges relative to the team's ability to earn the same as other franchises. Indianapolis is one of the NFL's smallest markets, and the income levels of households in the region are far more modest than those of fans in other cities. In terms of total population in the market area for media and entertainment, Indianapolis is ranked twenty-five out of the twenty-nine markets with NFL teams. There are twenty-six markets with NFL teams that have a larger concentration of high-income households, and twenty-three markets have a greater number of high-income households. Lastly, in terms of the presence of large firms that would be prime candidates to purchase luxury seating, the Indianapolis market has 179 businesses with five hundred or more employees. There are twenty-one NFL markets with a larger number of firms with five hundred or more employees.

After more than a year of discussions, the public sector agreed to assign virtually all game-related income from the dome to the Colts. The public sector would also be responsible for the maintenance and operation of the facility. Under the new lease the Colts would receive 100 percent of the revenue from all suites, but the public sector would be responsible for the staff that attends to the fans in these suites. The Colts would receive all advertising revenue (except for onetime events) and all revenue from naming rights after the current contract with RCA expires. In addition, the Colts were empowered to establish new advertising or naming fixtures and to retain all revenue they are able to secure as a result of these new fixtures and opportunities. For the 1998 season the Colts also had the right to sell or use 555 parking spaces, and in 1999 and all subsequent seasons the team would be given 1,400 parking spaces. The public sector also committed itself to helping the club receive game-day revenues from the State of Indiana's parking facility located across the street from the dome.

The RCA Dome, opened in 1983, does not have any club seats. The Colts want the option to have this form of luxury seating, and as a result of the negotiations the public sector agreed to remodel the facility to accommodate thirty-one hundred club seats. The cost for this capital construction project was estimated at $6 million. The public sector is to receive the fees for these seats for *one* season in exchange for providing 100 percent of the construction funds. It is not clear how much money the public sector will earn. The prices charged by teams for club seats varies across the NFL, from $45 (Detroit Lions) to $297.50 (for selected seats by the Ravens and Panthers). These prices include both a ticket charge and the luxury fee. The public sector will receive the income only from the luxury-seating fee. If all club seats were sold for the first season with a luxury fee of $50 per game (total ticket price of approximately $85), the public sector would earn approximately $1,550,000. With a luxury fee of $75 and a total ticket price of approximately $125, then the public-sector share would be approximately $2,325,000. It seems unlikely that the public sector would be able to recoup even 50 percent of its capital construction cost for the new club seats, further increasing its subsidy of the team's operations. Finally, the public sector agreed to build six new kiosks for the Colts to permit the team to have more places to sell souvenirs.

It was generally believed that if the Colts could lease all suites and club seats at rates comparable to those in other NFL markets, the team's in-stadium revenues would increase by $8.9 million per season. Under the new lease, then, the Colts would have the potential to earn $12.1 million from these revenues. Although this would be considerably less than the amounts earned by the Cowboys and Dolphins, the Colts would still move into the upper quarter of in-stadium revenue earners (based on projections for the 1998 season). Of course there was no guarantee that other cities or newer facilities would not provide other teams with more revenues, and the Colts might then need to reopen this version of their lease.

This new lease created a small revenue problem for the city of Indianapolis. First, revenue that was received and used to retire the bonds sold to build the dome was now assigned to the team. Second, there would be at least $6 million in new capital construction costs. These two changes left the public sector with a revenue shortfall relative to the bonds for the dome, the expenses for maintaining the facility, and the funds required for the new construction. To meet these obligations a tax on the short-term renting of cars was passed. It also appears likely that a portion of the hotel room occupancy tax will be needed to help the public sector meet its new and continuing obligations at the dome. The mayor strongly opposed to new taxes and committed to making government smaller eventually had to accept additional taxes and greater public commitments to the Colts to keep the NFL in Indianapolis. Indeed, despite many social needs, the only time Indianapolis raised taxes during Stephen Goldsmith's administration was to meet the needs of a professional sports team.

Although the new lease certainly establishes the potential for the Colts to realize far more revenue, the saga of professional sports and the small market has not yet concluded in Indianapolis. The Colts will substantially increase the price for luxury suites (in 1997 the average price was below $35,000; the Colts hope to double this price over the next few seasons) and sell club seats at levels that match the fees charged by other NFL teams. At the same time, the city's NBA franchise will be opening a new arena (for the 1999–2000 season) that will have sixty-five suites and two thousand club seats. At the current time the Indiana Pacers play at Market Square Arena, which has no suites or club seats. As a result, there are currently 155 luxury suites and as many as 5,100 club seats available for sale in Indiana.

The central Indiana market is also the prime source of revenue for several other major sports events and the programs of several universities. For example, both Purdue and Indiana universities draw a substantial amount of their support for their football and basketball teams from the same market as the Pacers and Colts. The Indianapolis 500 and the Brickyard 400 are also part of this same market, and the track where these events are held also markets luxury seating to businesses and families in the region. In addition, there are several other smaller university-based athletic programs that look to the Indianapolis market for their support, as do a minor league baseball team and a minor league hockey team.

Is there sufficient wealth in the central Indiana market to purchase this entire supply of sports tickets and luxury seating? The Knicks and Nets in the NBA and the Jets and Giants in the NFL divide a market of 19.8 million people, with more than 205,000 households that have incomes in excess of $150,000. In addition, more than 1,000 businesses in the New York market have at least 500 employees. In central Indiana, the Pacers and Colts, Boilermakers and Hoosiers, and the Indianapolis 500 and Brickyard 400 are trying to sell their seats in a market with approximately 3.2 million people, 179 firms with more than 500 employees, and 13,098 households with incomes in excess of $150,000.

CONCLUSIONS

The saga of the Pittsburgh Pirates and Indianapolis Colts provides two examples of the impact of the power of the leagues on smaller markets. For the Pittsburgh community, even if taxes are increased and residents buy almost 3 million tickets and the same amount of luxury seating as the Indians sell, the team will not earn enough to field a competitive team. The State of Pennsylvania has agreed to provide $80 million toward the cost of a new ballpark for the Pirates. If the public sector in Pittsburgh agreed to pay the remaining costs for the new ballpark and repaid the team's debt, taxes would increase $15 per person per year for thirty years. And this would still leave the team with a revenue shortfall of at least $23 million in its quest to field a competitive team.

In Indianapolis the public sector will have to assign all in-stadium revenues to the Colts and build the team club seats in an effort to increase the franchise's potential profitability. The revenues now assigned to the Colts increase the public sector's debt and tax obligations as those funds were being used to repay the debt associated with the building of the RCA Dome. A new tax on the short-term rental of cars was passed to permit the transfer of revenues to the Colts. And after raising taxes, assuming responsibility for additional costs related to stadium operations, and building thousands of new club seats, Indianapolis will still have to hope that taxpayers and businesses will be interested in purchasing all of the luxury seats at the new prices charged by the Colts. If the Colts are not successful in raising these revenues, Indianapolis can expect another set of calls for increased subsidies to prove it is interested in being a major league city.

Today the professional sports leagues are again on the verge of creating minor leagues out of their smaller markets and forcing smaller markets to provide unreasonable subsidies to their teams. In addition, if larger communities decide to subsidize playing facilities, smaller markets will need to provide even larger subsidies. This endless loop will continue until there is either a substantial form of revenue sharing among teams in all sports or market forces are allowed to work to create more teams in the largest markets.

9

Ending the
Great Sports Welfare System

Virtually every community that hosts a professional sports team has used tax dollars to pay for all or most of the costs of the stadium or arena used by its home team. In those rare instances where an owner pays for the entire cost of his or her team's facility, the public sector usually is expected to make infrastructure improvements to help make the arena or stadium a success or to reduce the taxes paid by the team's owners. If state and local governments and their taxpayers benefited from these expenditures to the same extent as team owners and players, the sports business would operate in everyone's best interests.

Unfortunately, as the case studies of cities and sports illustrate, this is not what happens. Taxpayers and the public sector frequently are left with the bills for stadiums and arenas while team owners and their players receive the benefits from the tax dollars spent for the new sports palaces replete with luxury suites, club seats, and fine restaurants. Cities and states have been unable and unwilling to resist the demands made by team owners and the four major sports leagues because these groups have absolute control over the supply of franchises. It is the four major sports leagues that decide which communities will have teams and which will not. As elected officials across the continent have learned, if you do not meet the demands of team owners you lose your team. A legalized form of extortion thrives across North America and its power to control the number of franchises has lead to the creation of the great sports welfare system. Cities and their taxpayers have been turned into major league losers by this system, and it is now time to reduce the tax burdens on all residents of North America. Just as with new proposals for social welfare, a welfare-to-work system is needed for the four major sports leagues.

Five separate reforms will be discussed in this final chapter. The proposals range from ending the leagues' monopolistic control over the number of teams that exist to permitting city and state governments to increase the number of teams that exist regardless of any league's objections. New approaches for financing stadiums and arenas are also needed to eliminate the use of broad-based taxes and taxes on tourists; this too is discussed in this chapter.

In discussing these reforms some people might ask, "Why bother?" Sports are simply entertainment and a diversion. If fans and taxpayers do not like the current system they can vote against the rascals who push for tax subsidies and refuse to attend and watch games. On the surface this would appear to be a sensible position. It does, however, ignore the importance of sports in life, an importance that has continued for several thousand years. Some may believe that an exaggerated importance is placed on sports, but it is difficult to deny that hundreds of millions of people play, watch, and enjoy sports. Holiday celebrations include sporting events; political statements are made through sporting events; the social calendars of adults, teenagers, and children are filled with sporting events. Sports teams also generate pride in one's community, and it is clear that the identity of different communities is defined to some extent by sports. The celebrations that accompany victories are, for the most part, extremely positive parts of civic life. The importance suggests that if one group was able to seize inappropriate control of the institutions of sports they could extract excess profits and subsidies from the large number of people that enjoy this component of life. In North America this is exactly what has happened, and society needs to examine different ways of ensuring that sports institutions operate to benefit owners, players, fans, and taxpayers without subjugating any one group to the whims of others.

1. Increasing the Supply of Teams

Changing the sports welfare system will require the creation of more teams. Although the four major sports leagues try to convince taxpayers and sports fans that there are already too many teams, there are actually too few. The population and wealth of North America has increased far more quickly than the number of teams. Using the ratio of teams to the population of the United States from the 1950s and 1990s, one would conclude that as many as 40 or 45 baseball teams could exist. There could be as many as 42 football teams.

Sports fans have been told that there are too few quality athletes to play for these teams. That too simply is not true. Today there actually are fewer players per 100,000 people than there were in the 1940s and 1950s, and all leagues now draw talent from all racial groups and from many different countries. The pool of athletic talent from which players are drawn is far larger today than it was in the 1940s and earlier. Some of baseball's loyalists enjoy ridiculing this position by repeatedly pointing to the absence of quality pitching as evidence of too few players.

However, in a comparison of pitchers that Babe Ruth faced in his sixty-home-run season and those faced by Mark McGwire in 1998, *Sports Illustrated* found that the modern-day pitchers had lower earned-run averages. In addition, when any fan is asked to identify the best teams of all time in any sport, virtually everyone points to modern-day teams.

With the population of North America able to support far more teams, an **undersupply** exists, increasing the subsidies cities are willing to provide to have a team. MLB, the NFL, the NBA, and the NHL are the OPEC of the 1990s, at least as far as taxpayers and professional sports teams are concerned. Just as the oil-producing nations held the oil-consuming nations hostage to high prices in the 1970s, the sports leagues and their players are holding cities and their taxpayers hostage by controlling the number of franchises that exist.

How could the leagues be forced to add more teams? If the leagues continue to fail to expand then the Congress needs to separate the leagues back into their competing components. Just as AT&T was divested of some of its component parts, the major sports leagues can be divided to increase the competition for markets. Instead of having one baseball, football, or basketball league, a "breakup" strategy would create at least two leagues where now only one exists. The NFL could be forced to revert back to its pre-1966 status with an AFL and NFL. The NBA could become the NBA and the ABA. MLB also could become two leagues again with independent American and National Leagues. Each sport could still have its Super Bowl, World Series, or championship series, but with two leagues competing for revenues and markets, cities that want teams would be able to work with local investors and seek admission to either league.

The existence of competing leagues does not ensure that any community with appropriate investors could secure a team or that areas with teams in both leagues would get an additional franchise. Yet, in the long run, competing leagues would lead to an interest in expanding revenues by placing teams in markets where excess profits existed. For example, the Dallas Cowboys are able to attract the largest revenues of any football team because of their success in a region that adores football. But if the Cowboys were in a two-league system, the other league might well decide to place a second team in this lucrative and expanding market. Similarly, either the AFL or the NFL might decide to increase its revenues in the New York area by adding a second franchise on Long Island or in a new sports complex planned by the city of New York for Manhattan.

The existence of competing leagues offers several other interesting possibilities. Suppose, for example, that both groups of owners acting independently decided not to create additional franchises. What could cities do that still wanted teams? Those cities without franchises could bring legal action arguing a restraint of trade if their communities did not receive teams but had willing owners and a sufficient level of commitments from fans to purchase season tickets. If the leagues set unfair franchise admission fees, the cities again could sue on the grounds of unfair price fixing practices. If the leagues failed to increase the number of teams in large-market areas or share revenues with smaller-market teams, cities that were forced to provide operating subsidies could bring legal actions, indicating that the failure to increase the number of teams was leading to higher taxes.

Splitting each league into at least two competing entities would move the sports leagues closer to a market-based system. Removing protections from market forces will lead to more teams, fewer subsidies, lower taxes, and, in the long run, lower ticket prices. However, changes of this magnitude will require a great deal of political support in the Congress, and with the leagues willing and able to fight these changes, fans and taxpayers, and well as state and local officials, will have to work together to implement these changes. Taxpayers and sports fans, as well as state and local leaders, must demand action to undo the sports welfare system. However, if the political environment is not conducive to such changes, then perhaps allowing cities and states to participate in the establishment of the number of franchises that exists could bring some tax relief.

2. Putting State and Local Governments in the Franchise Game

There is a great deal of irony in contrasting what happens to state and local governments when they negotiate with a professional sports team and when a community is willing to host a casino. Many investors interested in establishing gaming facilities not only commit to build facilities without any public subsidies, but they offer the state and local communities impressive payments for the right to build a casino. Communities as small as Evansville (Indiana) have received a new hotel, a redeveloped downtown theater, and a substantial contribution of $200,000 to the local United Way for a franchise to build a riverboat for gaming. In East Chicago (Indiana) the firm that received a permit for a riverboat pledged 1 percent of the casino's gross revenues. The city of East Chicago worked with their casino operator to fund a mortgage guarantee program to permit new housing starts for lower-income families in a section of the city that had been ignored by developers for decades. Likewise, Rising Sun (Indiana) received several million dollars from the investors who received a license for a riverboat and used these funds to establish a health center (the town did not have a doctor prior to the existence of the casino) and a senior citizens center. Each of these communities also receives annual fees paid by users of the casinos, and no one of these communities provided any taxpayer funds to support development of the casinos (Felsenstein, Klacik, and Littlepage, 1998).

Contrast these outcomes with those for taxpayers in Cleveland, Indianapolis, Montreal, Toronto, Arlington, Dallas, St. Louis, and so forth, when those areas attracted or retained teams. Instead of receiving inducements from the teams, the taxpayers were expected to provide substantial incentives. Why are these outcomes so different? In the case of gaming facilities, it is cities and their states that control the supply of franchises. In the case of the professional sports leagues, the leagues control the supply of franchises. Can some of the power the public sector has to control the supply of gaming franchises be extended to the world of professional team sports? There may be several ways to do this, and some other countries already have experimented with one option that may be particularly interesting to public leaders in North America.

In Italy, for example, investors and any community or city can start a soccer franchise by holding an open competition and signing an appropriate number of players. This new team then is placed in the lowest division—a minor league of sorts. Each year, the top two teams in each league are promoted to the next higher league, with the two teams with the worst records being demoted. New investors who are willing to pay the best players could, over a period of three to four years, have a team capable of winning a sufficient number of games to be promoted to the premier league. In this fashion, then, new teams can be created in any community and if the team proves to be of sufficient quality, it could be "major league" in a very short period of time.

Such a system could be adapted to fit the structure of MLB, the NHL, and the NBA. There are minor leagues in each of these sports, and teams that had the best records could be promoted to the next highest level. To be sure, there are substantial hurdles that would have to be cleared to implement such a system in North America. For example, MLB baseball teams actually employ most of the minor league players in the AAA, AA, and A–level leagues. But that could be changed as NBA and NHL teams do not employ most of the minor league players in basketball and hockey. There is of course no minor league in professional football, but one could be established. Although these changes might be too severe relative to implementing a simple plan to give cities and states greater control over the supply of franchises, they do lead to other ideas.

For example, suppose cities were given the right to work with local investors to establish teams that would have to be admitted to any of the four existing sports leagues. The requirements for team ownership used by the four leagues could be maintained. Owners of new teams would be expected to pay an admission or franchise fee equal to the average value of all teams in the league and to meet the same requirements for ownership expected of existing franchise holders. In this manner the public sector would have the ability to authorize franchises in a league, and no community able to find an interested entrepreneur could be denied a team.

How could such a process or reform be justified? After all, the leagues are private associations, so how could the Congress impose its will or ideas on these leagues? The Congress could argue that restricting the availability of teams limits the ability of any city to enhance its reputation and attractiveness through the hosting of a professional sports franchise. Although the economic benefits of a team may be small, permitting a small group of owners to control the number of franchises works against the public's interests and the clear preferences of a large number of citizens and communities to have teams.

What would happen if such a process existed? The number of teams in each of the professional sports leagues would increase to meet the demand. More teams could exist in the largest market areas and investors might be attracted to markets the size of New York and Los Angeles that had but one or two teams. Would this lead to a proliferation of teams? There would be more teams, but not necessarily a proliferation. New teams would be created only if the investors were able to pay a franchise fee equal to the average value of all teams in the league; as a result, substantial investments would be required to gain admission to a league. For example, if the values established by *Forbes* were used to secure a MLB franchise, investors would need approximately $200 million (average 1997 value of all MLB teams). An NBA franchise would require more than a $150 million dollar investment; an NFL could cost as much as the $535 million paid for a new Cleveland franchise. After paying this fee, investors still would need money to pay players and a staff, establish offices, and develop playing facilities. Investing in a professional sports team is a $300 million to $600 million investment, and is definitely not for the faint of heart because a great deal of risk and a large amount of capital are required. Therefore, there would be more teams, but not necessarily a plethora of teams flooding the market.

This proposal also would protect existing team owners. Each team that is admitted to the league would provide league owners with a substantial amount of income (franchise fees would be divided equally among existing team owners). That money would remain with the owners even if the new teams failed. Further, while the new teams would be permitted to draft one player from the existing teams, each team could protect a number of players following the same procedures that are currently used when the leagues expand. Team owners would be required to share league resources with the new teams, but the franchise fees are payments for those income flows.

If this system were adopted in North America, the power of the leagues to declare which cities or regions could have teams and how many teams could exist in any region would be eliminated. With more teams, a form of price competition would emerge as the newer franchises begin to attract fans. With more teams and price competition, the profit levels of the existing teams would decline; however, the franchise fees received by those teams would compensate them for lost profits (profits that only existed because the unfair cartels).

As the profitability of each individual team declined and price competition emerged, teams would have fewer dollars to pay individual players. The inflated salaries of some players would decline as well, creating some lost income opportunities. To offset these losses, existing players should be permitted to share in the income from the franchise fees paid by new teams. In much the same way that players share in the revenues earned by the leagues today, these franchise fees should be added to the revenue pool. For example, if a league currently pledges that players receive 52 percent of all income earned by the teams, that formula should include income from franchise fees. In that manner, both the existing players and owners would receive windfall income from the increase in the number of teams. As this income offsets the loss in future income, players and owners would be compensated for the change to a market-based system.

Under this system the current players and owners would be protected from excessive losses as they receive income from the franchise fees paid by new team owners. Cities and states would be freed from paying unneeded welfare-reducing taxes, and working with investors could help secure a team for their region without capitulating to the extortion now demanded by the leagues for a new team. If cities and investors create teams, fans would benefit from lower ticket prices, players would have more realistic salaries, and sports fans and cities would enjoy more teams. Fans, players, owners, and taxpayers all gain under this system.

3. Sharing the Wealth Created

It also is essential for communities to share in the wealth their tax dollars and support have created. As the example of Governor Bush's profits when the Texas Rangers were sold illustrates, when taxes are used for the construction of a stadium, the financial gain realized by team owners is enormous. Taxpayers should share equally in the profits made from the sale of a team, given their substantial investment in the team and facility. If a community agrees to pay for a portion of the cost of a new arena or stadium, they should be entitled to that proportion of the increment in a team's value. When new facilities are constructed, complete with luxury seating, the value of most teams increases. Since a substantial portion of that increased value is a function of the revenue sources built into the facility, the public sector should share in the wealth created. If state and local governments paid 50 percent of the cost of a new facility, then they should be entitled to receive 50 percent of the increase in the team's value if the team is ever moved. Prior to the opening of the Ballpark in Arlington, the Rangers were worth approximately $106 million. They were sold for $250 million in 1998 and the sales tax paid for 70.7 percent of the construction cost. The taxpayers should be entitled to 70.7 percent of the increased value of the team, or $101.8 million.

This return to the public sector could be described as asset valuation financing. For participating in the financing of the stadium or arena the public sector receives a *proportionate* share of the value it generates in relationship to its share of the cost of a new playing facility. The public sector, however, would not receive its share of the wealth unless the team is sold and provides a net gain for the existing owners.

4. *Protecting Communities*

If a team threatens to leave a community, and the public sector has paid at least 50 percent of the cost for constructing or rebuilding the playing facility used by the team, the public sector should have the right of first refusal to purchase the team. What's the rationale for this proposal? With communities spending in excess of $200 million to build playing facilities for professional sports teams, public entities have substantial financial interests in a team's continued presence in a community. In addition, fans have a substantial emotional investment in a team. After making these investments, if a team still elects to leave, the city should have the right to purchase the team to ensure its continued presence in the community and at the facility. The team still would be managed by professionals in much the same manner as are many other public assets, including port authorities, airports, water companies, and the Green Bay Packers.

This proposal presents an opportunity for substantial symmetry in terms of the benefits it provides for communities and team owners. This proposal protects a community against a possible move and the payment of any foregone rent by another city. When the Browns franchise moved to Baltimore and the Rams moved to St. Louis, both teams fulfilled their financial obligations, but both Cleveland and Anaheim lost their teams. The dollars for these rent payments came from the new home cities that were only too happy to subsidize the move to immediately have a team in their community.

5. Financing Facilities Without Broad-Based Taxes

The way in which stadiums and arenas are financed also needs to be changed. Many communities have relied upon sales and property taxes, lottery proceeds, and taxes on tourists to finance facilities. Taxes of this nature are inherently unfair as they are not directly related to the benefits created by a team's presence. In addition, those people who do benefit from a team are not asked to pay for the full costs of a stadium and arena. Ironically, it would be quite simple to ask those who gain the most from a team to pay for the costs of a stadium or arena. When financing a facility, two simple questions should be asked. *First*, who benefits from a team's presence? *Second*, can these people be assessed a fee to pay for the costs of a stadium and arena? The answer to both questions is yes.

Those who benefit most from the presence of a team either work at or near a proposed facility or attend or watch events. These "users" or beneficiaries can be assessed small fees by thinking of the immediate area surrounding a stadium or arena as a small tax district. In these very small districts, user charges, fees assessed for the broadcast of games, and income taxes paid by those employed by teams or earning income from activities in the facilities would ensure that the principal beneficiaries from the presence of facilities and teams pay for the benefits generated. Could such a district help generate sufficient funds to pay for a facility needed by a team?

The revenues raised within this tax district should be compared to the resources needed to build a facility. For example, if thirty-year financing were acceptable, a $275 million facility, at an interest rate of 7 percent, would require annual payments of approximately $22.2 million. Arenas for hockey and basketball teams can be built for less than that figure (typically $175 million to $200 million; $14.1 million per year to $16.1 million per year).

Income Taxes or User Charges from Players

Currently, nineteen states collect income taxes from players. Local governments in these areas collect income taxes from the athletes as well. The taxes apply to players from both the home teams and from the visiting teams (commuters' income tax). The existence of these taxes has not discouraged the location of teams as these taxes are collected in states with some of the most valuable and popular franchises. Likewise, leagues have expanded into states that collect these taxes (e.g., Arizona, North Carolina, and Ohio), and have relocated to states that tax the income of players (Arizona and Maryland). The revenues collected by state and local governments from these taxes in 1996 are summarized in Table 9-1.

States that do not collect income taxes could collect a locker-room fee equal to the average tax revenues collected by the nineteen states (and their communities that administer income taxes) to be sure that they do not forego this source of income. The locker-rooms fees that would need to be collected are identified in Table 9-2.

Charging the Fans Who Attend Games for the Cost and Maintenance of Facilities

Those who attend events are among the most central beneficiaries of a team's presence. User charges should be assessed on tickets purchased to help defray the costs of operation and of building a facility. Although this has been done in many instances, the funds frequently are collected by the teams to offset

TABLE 9-1
State and Local Income Taxes Paid by Athletes

Sport	Average Annual Taxes Collected	Average Player Salary	Average Team Salary
Football	1,922,917	603,057	34,294,135
Basketball	1,992,814	2,057,725	28,897,619
Hockey	883,989	966,631	24,331,667
Baseball	1,819,553	1,194,675	29,866,868

Note: Averages are based on figures for nineteen states.

TABLE 9-2
**Needed Per-Locker Fees to Offset the Revenues
Foregone by States Without Income Taxes**

Sport	Per-Game and Per-Player Locker Fee
Football	2,000
Basketball	1,600
Hockey	650
Baseball	898

the owner's investment (or as a revenue enhancement). The public sector also should have the ability to assess a per-ticket charge to defray its investment costs in a facility's construction and operations (maintenance).

Table 9-3 provides the attendance levels for each of the major sports franchises in Texas for the most recent seasons. Various ticket charges were calculated from the typical fees assessed by ticket services to slightly higher fees.

These fees would represent a tax on the team; however, in the absence of the charge, the teams still would charge the highest possible price to maximize their revenues. As a result, the fans are not paying this charge as they would pay the same price for the ticket regardless of the existence of the fee. With the team receiv-

TABLE 9-3
**The Revenue Potential from Per-Ticket Charges
for Facility Construction and Maintenance**

Team	Recent Attendance Level	Per-Ticket Facility Cost Charge		
		$4.00	*$5.00*	*$6.00*
Dallas Mavericks	541,541	2,166,164	2,707,705	3,249,246
Dallas Stars	655,878	2,623,512	3,279,390	3,935,268
Texas Rangers	2,945,228	11,780,912	14,726,140	17,671,368
Dallas Cowboys	511,767	2,047,068	2,558,835	3,070,602
Houston Rockets	666,685	2,666,740	3,333,425	4,000,110
Houston Astros	2,046,811	8,187,244	10,234,055	12,280,866
Houston NFL team	320,000	1,280,000	1,600,000	1,920,000
San Antonio Spurs	783,455	3,133,820	3,917,275	4,700,730

ing less revenue, the net effect on the tax would be to have fewer dollars available for player salaries and owner profits. Fans, however, would not pay a higher price

Assessing Fees for the Broadcast and Telecast of Games

Fans enjoy games that are broadcast by television and radio stations in much the same way as do those who attend the games at the stadium or arena. In addition, the broadcast and telecast of games create substantial revenues and profits for teams, players, the stations involved, and advertisers. A fee based on the number of households that watch and listen to games could be assessed by cities that build facilities. These charges would lead to higher advertising costs or additional commercials, but no additional fees to the fans that listen to or watch games.

To illustrate the revenue potential from these fees for stadium and arena construction, a per-household charge was calculated. The charge would be assessed against the stations broadcasting games based on the actual rating levels achieved by Texas's major league teams. Households' exposure (points) is the way in which advertisers assess value and pay for their commercial time. Several different combinations of charges are illustrated in Table 9-4; the highest rate would be $1.50 per household for televised games and $0.75 for games broadcast by radio stations. The market-share data are the latest available from advertising companies at the time of this writing. Games broadcast refers to home games only and uses numbers to reflect current practices (games televised). For example, it was assumed that an NFL team in Houston would televise only four games whereas the Texas Rangers would continue to televise all of their home games.

Franchise Fees for In-Stadium and In-Arena Advertising and Concessions

New facilities provide substantial opportunities for income from advertising and the sale of food, beverages, and souvenirs. An option for all communities that build facilities would be to administer a 10 percent or 15 percent concession fee or tax on sales and advertising. This rate is larger than those proposed for other businesses (e.g., car rental, hotels, etc.) when some cities seek to tax tourists to build sports facilities, but this tax is focused on direct consumers of sporting events. To provide a valid estimate of the revenue potential from a new arena for the Spurs, Rockets, Mavericks, and Stars, the income realized by the Cleveland Cavaliers at their new home, Gund Arena, is included in Table 9-5. Any sales taxes collected on the purchase of products (food, beverages, and souvenirs) would be in addition to the concession fees. Those receipts could provide or establish additional revenue to support a stadium or arena.

TABLE 9-4

**Anticipated Revenues from the Broadcast of
Games Involving Professional Teams in Texas**

Team	Average Rating	Television Market Size	Consumers	Games	Fee Per Household Per Game Season Revenue Total $1.50/Game Revenue	$1.00/Game Revenue	$.50/Game Revenue
Mavericks	3.5	1,763,400	61,719	30	2,777,355	1,851,570	925,785
Stars	2.0	1,763,400	35,268	30	1,587,060	846,432	529,020
Rangers	6.0	1,763,400	105,804	81	12,855,186	6,856,100	4,285,062
Cowboys	42.0	1,763,400	740,628	8	8,887,536	4,740,020	2,962,512
Rockets	17.0	1,452,000	246,840	30	11,106,000	5,924,160	3,702,600
Astros	8.0	1,452,000	116,160	50	8,712,000	4,646,400	2,904,000
NFL team	15.0	1,452,000	217,800	4	1,309,500	873,000	436,500
Spurs	4.5	584,900	26,321	30	1,184,424	631,692	394,808

Team	Average Rating	Radio Market Size	Consumers	Games	$.75/Game Revenue	$.50/Game Revenue	$.25/Game Revenue
Mavericks	1.2	1,763,400	21,161	41	650,697	433,798	216,899
Stars	2.4	1,763,400	42,322	41	1,301,388	867,592	433,796
Rangers	3.2	1,763,400	56,429	81	3,428,049	2,285,366	1,142,683
Cowboys	8.2	1,763,400	144,599	8	867,594	578,398	289,199
Rockets	4.5	1,452,000	65,340	41	2,009,205	1,339,470	669,735
Astros	2.5	1,452,000	36,300	81	2,205,225	1,470,150	735,075
NFL team	3.5	1,452,000	50,820	8	304,920	203,280	101,640
Spurs	2.0	584,900	11,698	41	359,715	239,810	119,905

Potental Media Revenue That Could be Raised by Team	Fee Combinations, TV/Radio $1.50/.75	$1.00/.50	$1.50/.25
Dallas Mavericks	3,428,052	2,285,368	1,142,684
Dallas Stars	2,888,448	1,714,024	962,816
Texas Rangers	16,283,235	9,141,466	5,427,745
Dallas Cowboys	9,755,130	5,318,418	3,251,711
Houston Rockets	13,115,205	7,263,630	4,372,335
Houston Astros	10,917,225	6,116,550	3,639,075
Houston NFL team	1,614,420	1,076,280	538,140
San Antonio Spurs	1,544,139	871,502	514,713

Note: Market size and viewers are in number of households.

Source: Ratings information from Allyn and Company, Dallas, Texas.

TABLE 9-5
**Potential Revenue from Concession Fees at
Stadiums and Arenas in Texas**

| Team | Facility Revenue | Concession Fee Rate | |
		10%	15%
Dallas Cowboys	43,700,000	4.4 million	6.6 million
Texas Rangers	22,800,000	2.3 million	3.4 million
Houston Astros	16,800,000	1.7 million	2.5 million
Houston Rockets	7,000,000	0.7 million	1.1 million
Houston NFL team	4,500,000	0.45 million	0.7 million
Dallas Mavericks	5,300,000	0.5 million	0.8 million
San Antonio Spurs	7,900,000	0.8 million	1.2 million
Dallas Stars	4,200,000	0.4 million	0.6 million
Cleveland Cavaliers	17,600,000	1.8 million	2.6 million

Source: Some of the data in this table are extracted from *Financial World* magazine.

The Revenue from Users
Available to Finance a Facility

The data in Table 9-6 summarize the revenue that could be raised
for sports facilities through a variety of user charges. It should be
noted that there are other revenue sources that could be used, including parking fees. However, in planning for the development
and operation of a successful facility, the public sector needs to
ensure that there will be adequate revenues from which players
can be paid and owners can earn a fair return on their investments.

For multiuse arenas that serve as home to more than one team,
the projected annual incomes would be combined. For instance,
the Mavericks and Stars will share a new arena in Dallas; their
combined revenues under these fees would total approximately
$17.5 million. There also would be substantial income from con-
certs and shows because the teams need the facility for no more
than a maximum of 110 dates. A new facility likely would cost no
more than $16 million per year. The income from all user charges

TABLE 9-6
Annual Revenues from Selected Fees
(in millions of dollars)

Team	Income Tax/ Locker Fee	$6 Ticket Charge	Media Income	Concession Fee, 15%	Annual Income
Dallas Cowboys	1.9	3.2	9.8	6.6	21.5
Texas Rangers	1.8	17.6	16.3	3.4	39.1
Houston Astros	1.8	12.3	10.9	2.5	27.5
Dallas Mavericks	2.0	3.2	3.4	0.8	9.4
Dallas Stars	0.7	3.9	2.9	0.6	8.1
Houston Rockets	2.0	4.0	13.1	0.7	19.8
Houston NFL team	1.9	1.6	1.6	0.5	5.6
San Antonio Spurs	2.0	4.7	1.5	1.2	9.4

and the income from the additional events would support the entire cost of construction and the fees associated with the maintenance of the facility. Although Dallas's voters did support increased taxes for the new arena, user fees could have supported the costs of the facility. Similarly, a new baseball or football stadium would cost approximately $22 million per year. The Cowboys could comfortably handle that cost without any broad-based or tourist taxes, and the Texas Rangers easily could have paid for the Ballpark in Arlington without the sales tax dollars provided from shoppers in Arlington. The Houston Astros also do not need any assistance from taxpayers for their new stadium, but they are going to get it.

This analysis clearly indicates the substantial potential that exists for communities to ask those who benefit from the presence of teams to pay for the needed facilities. In some instances there may be a shortfall in securing the needed revenues. However, there are other revenue sources that could be used, including extending a sports district tax area to include businesses located within one or two blocks of a stadium and arena. Businesses this close to a facility typically enjoy economic gains from the crowds that attend events. Although there will not be sufficient revenue to build and maintain a facility in every instance, the figures based on the teams in Texas indicate far less in taxes is needed to build a stadium then some have argued. In addition, most if not all, arenas can be constructed without any broad-based or tourist taxes. Following the very basic principle of charging users for the benefits they enjoy would eliminate the need for most if not all taxes for stadiums and arenas.

Sports can be survived. None of the recommendations made here will be easy to implement, but they are necessary steps. An excessive welfare system has been created and it transfers large sums of money to the most economically privileged groups in our society. It can be stopped. It should be stopped. We live in an era in which people want more individual responsibility and less taxes; sports should not be excluded from the "reinvention" process that is so much a part of today's politics and business world. Sports subsidies must be "downsized." After all, the examples we set through sports seem to attract a great deal of attention.

We cannot continue to let the interest in and "hype" generated by sports take money from taxpayers. Sports, like other business, can financially support itself and does not deserve welfare. Cities should not be held hostage to demands issued by team owners for subsidies that do not make sporting events more available to citizens but simply increase profits and salaries. It is time for cities, their taxpayers, and their civic leaders to recognize the leagues for what they are. Leagues are cartels that ensure profits and salaries at the public's expense.

REFERENCES

Ahmad-Taylor, Ty. "Who Is Major Enough for the Major Leagues?" *New York Times*, April 2, 1995, p. E5.

Ahmadi, Mossoud. "Economic and Fiscal Impacts of Baltimore Orioles' 1992 Season in Maryland." Office of Research, Maryland Department of Economic and Employment Development, State of Maryland, Baltimore, Maryland, unpublished mimeo, 1992.

Ahmed, Safir. "Escape from St. Louis." *The Riverfront Times*, January 24–30, 1996a, No. 903, pp. 18–21.

———. "Phantoms of the Opera House." *The Riverfront Times*, February 7–13, 1996b, No. 905, pp. 20–23.

Applebaum, Rhonda, David Casey, Michael Grant, Kristin Hahn, Phil McGivney, Barton Phillips, Damon Shanle, Dominic Wiker, Lamar Willis, and Patrick Larkey. *Ballpark Systems Synthesis Project, Final Report*. Pittsburgh: H. John Heinz III School of Public Policy and Management, Carnegie Mellon University, 1995.

Arthur Andersen and Company. "Economic Impact: Report on Target Center." Report for the City of Minneapolis, 1994.

Associated Press. "Browns' Modell Indicates Team Will Move to Baltimore." *Indianapolis Star*, November 4, 1995, p. B7.

Austrian, Ziona, and Mark S. Rosentraub. "Cleveland's Gateway to the Future." In Roger G. Noll and Andrew Zimbalist, eds., *Sports, Jobs, and Taxes: The Economic Impact of Sports Teams and Stadiums*. Washington, DC: Brookings Institute, 1997, pp. 355–384.

Baade, Robert A. "Professional Sports as Catalysts for Metropolitan Economic Development." *Journal of Urban Affairs* 18:1 (1996), 1–17.

———. "Stadiums, Professional Sports, and City Economics: An Analysis of the United States Experience." In John Bale and Olaf Moen, eds., *The Stadium and the City*. Keele, England: Keele University Press, 1995.

————. *Stadiums, Professional Sports, and Economic Development: Assessing the Reality.* Heartland Policy Study, Number 68. Chicago: The Heartland Institute, April 4, 1994.

Baade, Robert A., and Richard F. Dye. "Sports Stadiums and Area Development: A Critical Review." *Economic Development Quarterly* 2:4 (1988), 265–275.

Bale, John. *Sports Geography.* London and New York: E. & F. M. Spon, 1989.

Barnekov, Timothy, and Daniel Rich. "Privatism and the Limits of Local Economic Development." *Urban Affairs Quarterly* 25 (1989), 212–238.

Barnes, Tom. "Council, Bucs Reach Loan Accord." *Pittsburgh Post-Gazette*, June 28, 1994, p. 1.

Bartik, Timothy J. *Who Benefits from State and Local Economic Development Policies?* Kalamazoo, MI: W. E. Upjohn Institute, 1991.

Bartimole, Roldo. "Gunds Sandbag Politicians." *Cleveland Free Times*, August 16, 1995a, p. 3.

————. "$600,000 Gund Gateway Apartment." *Point of View* 28:2 (July 29, 1995b), 1–4.

————. "Gateway Cost: $750,000,000." *Point of View* 26:15 (March 26, 1994), 1–4.

Beauregard, Robert A., Paul Lawless, and Sabrina Deitrick. "Collaborative Strategies for Reindustrialization." *Economic Development Quarterly* 6:4 (November 1992), 418–430.

Becker, Bob, and Lou Mio. "Baseball Chief Opposes City Losing Indians, but Says Move Is Possible." *Cleveland Plain Dealer*, May 3, 1990, pp. 1, 10.

Bennett, C. "Moving Can Be Hell." *The Times-Picayune*, May 12, 1994, p. C12.

Birch, David, et al. *Entrepreneurial Hot Spots: The Best Places in America to Start and Grow a Company.* Cambridge, MA: Cognetics, 1993.

Blum, Debra E. "Sports Programs Continue to Lose Money, Survey Finds." *Chronicle of Higher Education* 41:2 (September 7, 1994), 58.

Bodley, Hal. "Baseball Payrolls Increase by Only 1.8%." *USA Today*, April 5, 1996, pp. C1, 14.

Bowen, Ezra. "Blowing the Whistle on Georgia." *Time* (February 24, 1986), 65.

Brace, Pete. "Blockbuster Wins 'Special District.'" *PA Times* 17:11 (November 1, 1994), 1.

Broadway, Michael J. "Montréal's Changing Tourist Landscape." *Canadian Journal of Urban Research* 2:1 (June 1993), 30–48.

Brown, Gerry, and Michael Morrison, eds. *ESPN 1999 Information Please Sports Almanac.* Boston: Information Please, LLC, 1998.

Buchanan, James. "Principles of Urban Fiscal Strategy." *Public Choice* 4 (1971), 1–16.

Burstein, Melvin L., and Arthur J. Rolnick. "Congress Should End the Economic War Among the States." *The Region* 9:1 (March 1995), Special Issue.

Cagan, Joanna, and Neil deMause. *Field of Schemes: How the Great Stadium Swindle Turns Public Money into Private Profit.* Monroe, ME: Common Courage Press, 1998.

Carter, Gary, with Ken Abraham. *The Gamer.* Dallas: Word Publishing, 1993.

CCRC, First Annual Report St. Louis: Civic Center Redevelopment Corporation, 1963.

Chass, Murray. "Yanks to Pay $4.4 Million in Luxury Tax." *New York Times*, December 25, 1997, p. C18.

———. "Baseball Owners Approve Revenue-Sharing Plan." *New York Times*, March 22, 1996, p. B17.

———. "Budig Sees New Parks in 6 Cities." *New York Times*, June 7, 1995a, p. B10.

———. "Pirates Left at Gate in Many Ways." *New York Times*, May 16, 1995b, p. B11.

City of Arlington, Texas, Office of the City Manager. "Questions and Answers About the Sales Tax Referendum and Proposed Texas Rangers Stadium." City of Arlington memorandum, 1991.

Cobb, Steven, and David Weinberg. "The Importance of Import Substitution in Regional Economic Impact Analysis: Empirical Estimates from Two Cincinnati Area Events." *Economic Development Quarterly* 7:3 (August 1993), 282–286.

Colcord, Frank C., Jr. "Saving the Center City." In Elliot Feldman and Michael A. Goldberg, eds., *Land Rites and Wrongs: The Management, Regulation and Use of Land in Canada and the United States.* Cambridge, MA: Lincoln Institute of Land Policy, 1987, pp. 75–124.

Coopers & Lybrand. "Analysis for a Proposed Multi-Purpose Arena in Arlington." Report prepared for the Arlington City Council, 1994.

———. "Review of the Sources and Uses of Funds for the Development and Operation of the Gateway Sports Complex, Cleveland, Ohio." Cuyahoga County: Auditors Office, 1992.

———. "City of St. Louis: An Analysis of Net New Fiscal Benefit Generated from the Construction and Operation of the Expanded Cervantes

Convention Center." Prepared for the St. Louis NFL Corporation, Dallas, Texas, February 27, 1991a.

————. "State of Missouri: An Analysis of Net New Fiscal Benefit Generated from the Construction and Operation of the Expanded Cervantes Convention Center." Prepared for the State of Missouri, February 27, 1991b.

Cosell, Howard. *I Never Played the Game*. New York: William Morrow, 1985.

Cox, William A., and Dennis Zimmerman. "Baseball, Economics, and Public Policy." Washington, DC: Congressional Research Service, Library of Congress, 1995.

Crothers, Tim. "The Shakedown: Greedy Owners Are Threatening to Move Their Teams if Demands for New Stadiums, Betters Lease Deals, etc., Aren't Met." *Sports Illustrated* 82:24 (June 19, 1995), 77–82.

Cummings, Scott, C. Theodore Koebel, and J. Allen Whitt. "Redevelopment in Downtown Louisville: Public Investments, Private Profits, and Shared Risks." In Gregory D. Squires, ed., *Unequal Partnerships: The Political Economy of Urban Redevelopment in Postwar America*. New Brunswick, NJ: Rutgers University Press, 1989, pp. 202-221.

Cuyahoga County. "Cuyahoga County Commissioners Approve Financial Package for the Economic Development of the Central Market Gateway Project." Press Release, March 21, 1990.

Danielson, Michael N. *Home Team: Professional Sports and the American Metropolis*. Princeton, NJ: Princeton University Press, 1997.

Dayton Daily News. "Marge Disgusted by Stadium Report." *Dayton Daily News*, February 12, 1995, p. D12.

DeLater, Laurie. "It's Official—Cavs Would Play at Gateway." *Cleveland Plain Dealer*, May 3, 1990a, pp. 1, 10.

————. "Big Profits Prove Hard to Come by for New Stadiums." *Cleveland Plain Dealer*, April 29, 1990b, pp. 1–2.

Dion, Stephanie. "The Dynamic of Secession: Scenarios After a Pro-Separatist Vote in a Québec Referendum." *Canadian Journal of Political Science* 28:3 (September 1995), 533–551.

Doeringer, Peter B., and David G. Terkla. "Japanese Direct Investment and Development Policy." *Economic Development Quarterly* 6:3 (August 1992), 255–272.

Drier, Peter. "Economic Growth and Economic Justice in Boston Populist Housing and Jobs Policies." In Gregory D. Squires, ed., *Unequal Partnerships: The*

Political Economy of Urban Redevelopment in Postwar America. New Brunswick, NJ: Rutgers University Press, 1989, pp. 35–58.

Dvorchak, Robert. "It's State Against State in a Battle for New Jobs." *Indianapolis Star,* October 4, 1992, pp. 1–2.

Edwards, Harry. *Sociology of Sport.* Chicago: Dorsey Press, 1973.

Eisinger, Peter K. *The Rise of the Entrepreneurial State.* Madison: University of Wisconsin Press, 1988.

————. "State Economic Development in the 1990s: Politics and Policy Learning." *Economic Development Quarterly* 9:2 (1995), 146–158.

Elliott, Suzanne. "City Willing to Share $6 Million to Keep Pirates at Three Rivers." *Pittsburgh Business Times,* October 10–16, 1994, p. 1.

Euchner, Charles C. *Playing the Field: Why Sports Teams Move and Cities Fight to Keep Them.* Baltimore: Johns Hopkins University Press, 1993.

East-West Gateway Coordinating Council (EWCGG). *Where We Stand.* St. Louis: EWCGG, December 1992a.

————. *How We See It.* St. Louis: EWCGG, May 1992b.

Farber, Michael. "Stars Are Out." *Sports Illustrated* 82 (April 17, 1995), 32, 35.

Felsenstein, Daniel, Drew Klacik, and Laura Littlepage. "Casino Gambling as Local Growth Generation: Playing the Economic Development Game in Reverse?" Indianapolis: Center for Urban Policy and Environment, Indiana University, 1998.

Financial World. "Team Values." Financial World Website.

Gagnon, Alain, and Mary Beth Montcalm. *Quebec: Beyond the Quiet Revolution.* Ontario: Nelson, 1990.

Gateway Economic Development Corporation. "Lease and Management Agreement by and Between Gateway Economic Development Corporation and Cavaliers Division of Nationwide Advertising Service, Inc.," December 20, 1991a.

————. "Lease Agreement by and Between Gateway Economic Development Corporation and Cleveland Indians Baseball Company Limited Partnership," July 3, 1991b.

George, Thomas. "Rams Get Green Light to Proceed to St. Louis." *New York Times,* April 13, 1995, p. B7.

Ginsburg, David. "Modell Bids Cleveland Goodbye." *Indianapolis Star,* November 7, 1995, pp. C1, 10.

Gittell, Ross. "Dynamic Development Cycles and Local Economic Management." *Economic Development Quarterly* 6:2 (May 1992), 199–210.

Gorman, Jerry, and Kirk Calhoun. *The Name of the Game: The Business of Sports.* New York: John Wiley, 1994.

Goyens, Chrys, and Allan Turowetz. *Lions in Winter.* Toronto: McGraw-Hill Ryerson, 1994.

Grabowski, John J. *Sports in Cleveland.* Bloomington: Indiana University Press, 1992.

Greco, Anthony L. "Sports Value More Myth Than Reality." *Standard and Poor's Creditweek,* July 26, 1993.

Greene, Richard. Personal correspondence between Richard Greene, mayor of the city of Arlington, and the author, 1995.

Halvonik, Steve. "Rooneys Looking to Buy Pirates." *Pittsburgh Post-Gazette,* September 16, 1994a, p. A2.

————. "Pirates' Lease Their Own Fault." *Pittsburgh Post-Gazette,* August 30, 1994b, p. 1.

Hamilton, Arnold. "Bricktown Boomtown." *Dallas Morning News,* March 5, 1995, p. 41.

Hellinger, Daniel. "Most Reporters Were Uncritical Promoters of Stadium Financing." *The St. Louis Journalism Review* 25:177 (June 1995b), 1ff.

————. "Finally Flim-Flam Football." *The St. Louis Journalism Review* 25:176 (May 1995a), 1ff.

Heltzel, Bill. "Pirates Lose $7.6 Million, Say They'll Stay." *The Pittsburgh Press,* February 1, 1991, p. 1.

Helyar, John. "A City's Self-Image Confronts Tax Revolt in Battle on Stadiums." *Wall Street Journal,* March 19, 1996, p. 1.

————. "Pro Basketball Loses Its 'Feel Good' Image in Nasty Labor Dispute." *Wall Street Journal,* August 7, 1995a, p. 1.

————. "Newly Cool NHL Skates on Some Thin Ice." *Wall Street Journal,* January 19, 1995b, p. B6.

————. "Canadian Clubs Appear to Skate on Thin Ice Amid Hockey Lockout." *Wall Street Journal,* November 15, 1994a, p. 1.

————. *Lords of the Realm: The Real History of Baseball.* New York: Ballantine Books, 1994b.

Higgins, Benjamin. *The Rise and Fall of Montréal.* Moncton: Canadian Institute for Research on Regional Development, 1986.

Hirsch, Werner. *Urban Economic Analysis.* New York: McGraw-Hill, 1973.

Hudnut, William H., III. *The Hudnut Years in Indianapolis, 1976–1991.* Bloomington: Indiana University Press, 1995.

Humber, William. *Diamonds of the North: A Concise History of Baseball in Canada.* Toronto: Oxford University Press, 1995.

Industrial Development Authority of the City of St. Louis. "Preliminary Official Statement" for bond issue dated October 27, 1992. Prudential Securities Incorporated.

Johnson, Arthur T. "Rethinking the Sport-City Relationship: In Search of Partnership." *Journal of Sport Management*, forthcoming.

————. *Minor League Baseball and Local Economic Development.* Chicago: University of Illinois Press, 1993.

————. "Local Government, Minor League Baseball, and Economic Development Strategies." *Economic Development Quarterly* 5:4 (1991), 313–323.

Johnson, Chuck. "Montréal, Alou Rebuild—Again." *USA Today*, March 11, 1996, p. 4C.

Kearns, Gerry, and Chris Philo, eds. *Selling Places: The City As Cultural Capital, Past and Present.* New York: Pergamon Press, 1993.

Keating, Dennis W. "Cleveland and the 'Comeback' City: The Politics of Redevelopment Amidst Decline." Cleveland: Levin College of Urban Affairs, Cleveland State University, 1995.

Keating, Dennis W., Norm Krumholz, and John Metzger. "Cleveland: Post-Populist Public-Private Partnerships." In Gregory D. Squires, ed., *Unequal Partnerships: The Political Economy of Urban Redevelopment in Postwar America.* New Brunswick, NJ: Rutgers University Press, 1989, pp. 121–141.

Kieschnick, M. *Taxes and Growth: Business Incentives and Economic Development.* Washington, DC: Council of State Planning Agencies, 1981.

Kissling, Catherine L. "Gateway Arena Costs Soaring." *Cleveland Plain Dealer*, May 26, 1994, pp. 1, 11.

————. "Details About Gateway Plans Still Sketchy." *Cleveland Plain Dealer*, April 15, 1990, p. 16A.

Klacik, Drew, and Mark S. Rosentraub. *The Economic Importance and Impact of IUPUI as a Major Urban University for Indianapolis and Central Indiana.* Indianapolis: Center for Urban Policy and the Environment, School of Public and Environmental Affairs, Indiana University–Purdue University, 1993.

Koff, Stephen. "Gateway Financial Disclosure Sought." *Cleveland Plain Dealer*, December 15, 1994, p. 1B.

Koff, Stephen, and Evelyn Theiss. "Mayor Offers Fourth Stadium Plan." *Cleveland Plain Dealer*, June 2, 1995, p. 1.

Kotler, Philip, Donald H. Haider, and Irving Rein. *Marketing Places.* New York: The Free Press, 1993.

Kruckemeyer, Thomas J. *For Whom the Ball Tolls.* Jefferson City, MO: Kruckemeyer Publishing, 1995.

Land Clearance for Redevelopment Authority (LCRA). St. Louis bond issue prospectus. Prudential Securities Incorporated, 1992.

———. "Downtown Sports Stadium Project Redevelopment Plan." St. Louis: LCRA, revised July 1965.

LaPointe, Joe. "Red Wings' Rebirth Helps Enliven Detroit." *New York Times,* June 18, 1995, p. 18.

Larkin, Brent. "No Threat, Just Facts from Jacobs." *Cleveland Plain Dealer,* April 17, 1990, p. 1D.

Lederman, Douglas. "Do Winning Teams Spur Contributions? Scholars and Fund Raisers Are Skeptical." *Chronicle of Higher Education* 34:18 (January 13, 1988), 1–2.

Levine, Marc V. "The Politics of Partnership: Urban Redevelopment Since 1945." In Gregory D. Squires, ed., *Unequal Partnerships: The Political Economy of Urban Redevelopment in Postwar America.* New Brunswick, NJ: Rutgers University Press, 1989, pp. 12–34.

Lipsyte, Robert. "Why Sports Don't Matter Anymore." *New York Times Magazine,* April 2, 1995, pp. 51–57.

———. *SportsWorld: An American Dreamland.* New York: Quadrangle Books, 1977.

Logan, John R., and Harvey L. Molotch. *Urban Fortunes: The Political Economy of Place.* Berkeley: University of California Press, 1988.

Lund, Leonard. *Locating Corporate R&D Facilities.* Washington, DC: The Conference Board, Inc., 1986.

MacAloon, John J. "Missing Stories: American Politics and Olympic Discourse." *Garnett Center Journal* 1:2 (Fall 1987), 111–142.

Marsan, Jean-Claude. *Montréal in Evolution: Historical Analysis of the Development of Montréal's Architecture and Urban Environment.* Montréal and Kingston: McGill-Queen's University Press, 1981.

McKenna, Brian, and Susan Purcell. *Drapeau.* Toronto: Clarke, Irwin and Company, 1980.

McNabb, David. "TCU Football Program Faces Loss of 25 Scholarships over Two Years." *Dallas Morning News,* April 24, 1986, B1.

Meserole, Mike, ed. *The 1996 Information Please Sports Almanac*. New York: Houghton Mifflin, 1995.

———. *1995 Information Please Sports Almanac*. Boston: Houghton Mifflin, 1994.

Michener, James A. *Sports in America*. New York: Random House, 1976.

Mier, Robert. *Social Justice and Local Development Policy*. Newbury Park, CA: Sage Publishers, 1993.

Miklasz, Bernie. Commentary. *St. Louis Post Dispatch*, January 22, 1995, p. 1f.

Miller, James Edward. *The Baseball Business: Pursuing Pennants and Profits in Baltimore*. Chapel Hill: North Carolina University Press, 1990.

Miller, Laura. "Why Dallas Shouldn't Replace Reunion Arena." *The Dallas Observer*, October 20–26, pp. 17–29.

Miller, W. S., and Alan Friedman, eds. *Inside the Ownership of Professional Sports Teams*. Chicago: Team Marketing Report, 1998.

Mills, Edwin S. "Should Governments Own Convention Centers?" Chicago: The Heartland Institute, January 21, 1991.

Milward, H. Brinton, and Heide Newman. "State Incentive Packages and the Industrial Location Decision." *Economic Development Quarterly* 3:3 (1989), 203–218.

Miranda, Rowan, Donald Rosdil, and Sandy Yeh. "Growth Machines, Progressive Cities, and Regime Restructuring: Explaining Economic Development Strategies." Unpublished paper presented at the 88th Annual Meeting of the American Political Science Association, Chicago, Illinois, 1992.

Molotch, Harvey. "The Political Economy of Growth Machines." *Journal of Urban Affairs* 15 (1993), 29–53.

———. "The City as a Growth Machine." *American Journal of Sociology* 82:2 (1976), 309–330.

Montréal Expos. *Guide 1995*. Montreal: 1995.

Morgan, Jon. *Glory for Sale: Fans, Dollars, and the New NFL*. Baltimore: Bancroft Press, 1997.

Much, Paul J., and Alan Friedman. *Inside the Ownership of Professional Sports Teams*. Chicago: Houlihan, Lokey, Howard, and Zukin, 1998.

———. *Inside the Ownership of Professional Sports Teams*. Chicago: Team Marketing Report, 1996.

Mullin, Bernard J., Stephen Hardy, and William A. Sutton. *Sports Marketing*. Champaign, IL: Human Kinetics Publishers, 1993.

Nader, George. *Cities of Canada*. Vol. 2. Toronto: Macmillan of Canada, 1976.

Neft, David S., and Richard M. Cohen. *The Sports Encyclopedia: Baseball, 1996.* New York: St. Martin's Griffin Press, 1996.

New York Times. "Angry Fans See a Game and Maybe a Team Lost." *New York Times,* November 6, 1995a, p. B5.

———. "In Nashville, a Beer Ban Ends," *New York Times,* June 8, 1995b, p. B8.

Noll, Roger G. "Professional Basketball: Economic and Business Perspectives." In Paul D. Staudohar and James A. Morgan, eds., *The Business of Professional Sports.* Chicago: University of Illinois Press, 1991, pp. 18–47.

Noll, Roger G., and Andrew Zimbalist. "Build the Stadium—Create the Jobs." In Roger G. Noll and Andrew Zimbalist, eds., *Sports, Jobs, and Taxes: The Economic Impact of Sports Teams and Stadiums.* Washington, DC: Brookings Institute, 1997a, pp. 1–54.

———. "The Economic Impact of Sports Teams and Facilities." In Roger G. Noll and Andrew Zimbalist, eds., *Sports, Jobs, and Taxes: The Economic Impact of Sports Teams and Stadiums.* Washington, DC: Brookings Institute, 1997b, pp. 55–59.

Norton, Erle. "Football at Any Cost: One City's Mad Chase for an NFL Franchise." *Wall Street Journal,* October 13, 1993, p. A1.

O'Connor, Michael. "Officials' Ratings of Local Improvements Underscore Importance of Quality of Life." *Site Selection* 32:4 (August 1987), 778–784.

Oates, Wallace. *Fiscal Federalism.* New York: Harcourt Brace Jovanovich, 1977.

Ozanian, Michael K. "Selective Accounting," *Forbes* 162:2 (December 14, 1998), 124–134.

———. "Suite Deals: Why New Stadiums Are Shaking Up the Pecking Orders of Sports Franchises." *Financial World,* May 9, 1995, pp. 42–56.

Piraino, Thomas A., Jr. "The Antitrust Rationale for the Expansion of Professional Sports Leagues." *Ohio State Law Journal* 57:5 (1996), 1677–1729.

Peck, John E. "An Economic Impact Analysis of South Bend's Proposed Class A Baseball Stadium." South Bend: Bureau of Business and Economic Research, Indiana University at South Bend, 1985.

Penne, Leo R. *Art Spaces and Economic Development: Experiences in Six Cities.* Washington, DC: Partners for Liveable Places, 1986.

Perkins, Dave, "It's Time to Cut SkyDome Losses and Walk Away." *Toronto Star,* January 5, 1994, p. C1.

Peterson, Iver. "The Mistake Wakes Up, Roaring." *New York Times,* September 10, 1995, p. 9.

Peterson, Paul. *City Limits.* Chicago: University of Chicago Press, 1981.

Picard, Andre. "Bouchard Vows Not to Raise Taxes When He's Premier." *The Globe and Mail,* December 7, 1995a, p. A5.

————. "Expos Win Big in the Courtroom." *The Globe and Mail,* September 2, 1995b, p. A19.

Piraino, T. A., Jr. "The Antitrust Rationale for the Expansion of Professional Sports Leagues." *Ohio State Law Journal.*

Porter, Michael E. *The Competitive Advantage of Nations.* New York: The Free Press, 1990.

Post, Paul W. "Origins of the Montréal Expos." *The Baseball Research Journal* 22 (1993), 107–110.

Price Waterhouse. "1994 Arena and Stadium Managers' Annual Report." Vol. 2. Tampa, FL: Price Waterhouse Sports Facilities Advisory Group, 1994.

Quirk, James, and Rodney D. Fort. *Pay Dirt: The Business of Professional Team Sports.* Princeton: Princeton University Press, 1992.

Radich, Anthony J. *Twenty Years of Economic Impact Studies of the Arts: A Review.* Washington, DC: National Endowment for the Arts, 1993.

Reese, Laura A. "Local Economic Development in Michigan." *Economic Development Quarterly* 6:4 (November 1992), 383–393.

Regional Commerce and Growth Association (RCGA). "Annual Economic Impact of the NFL Rams on the St. Louis Region." St. Louis: RCGA, March 28, 1996.

Reid, Susan. "Toronto Seeks Public Inquiry into Financing of SkyDome." *Toronto Star,* September 18, 1991, p. 2.

Richler, Mordecai. *Oh Canada! Oh Canada!: Requiem for a Divided Country.* New York: Alfred A. Knopf, 1992.

Rosentraub, Mark S. "Does the Emperor Have New Clothes?" *Journal of Urban Affairs* 18:1 (1996), 23–31.

————. "Public Investment in Private Businesses: The Professional Sports Mania." In Scott Cummings, ed., *Business Elites and Urban Development.* New York: State University of New York Press, 1988, pp. 71–96.

Rosentraub, Mark S., and Samuel Nunn. "Suburban City Investment in Professional Sports." *American Behavioral Scientist* 21 (1978), 393–414.

Rosentraub, Mark S., and David Swindell. "Fort Wayne, Indiana." In Arthur T. Johnson, ed., *Minor League Baseball and Local Economic Development.* Chicago: University of Illinois Press, 1993, pp. 35–54.

———. "Just Say No? The Economic and Political Realities of a Small City's Investment in Minor League Baseball." *Economic Development Quarterly* 5:2 (May 1991), 152–167.

Rosentraub, Mark S., David Swindell, Michael Przybylski, and Daniel R. Mullins. "Sport and Downtown Development Strategy: If You Build It, Will Jobs Come?" *Journal of Urban Affairs* 16:3 (1994), 221–239.

Rubin, Herbert J. "Shoot Anything That Flies; Claim Anything That Falls: Conversations with Economic Development Practitioners." *Economic Development Quarterly* 2:2 (May 1988), 236–251.

Ruck, Rob. "Bye, Bye Baseball?" *Pittsburgh,* August 1993, pp. 38–43.

Rushin, Steve. "The Heart of a City." *Sports Illustrated* (December 4, 1995), 59–70.

St. Louis Regional Convention and Sports Complex Authority. *1994 Annual Report.* St. Louis: Sports Complex Authority, 1995.

Sandomir, Richard. "Devils Plan to Stay in New Jersey for a Year." *New York Times,* July 14, 1995a, p. B11.

———. "New Jersey Working to Keep the Devils." *New York Times,* May 17, 1995b, p. B10.

———. "Yankees Cool to Stadium Renovation." *New York Times,* March 9, 1995c, p. B8.

Schaffer, William A., Bruce L. Jaffee, and Lawrence S. Davidson. *Beyond the Games: The Economic Impact of Amateur Sports.* Indianapolis: Chamber of Commerce, 1993.

Schmenner, Roger. *Making Business Location Decisions.* Englewood Cliffs, NJ: Prentice Hall, 1982.

Schmitz, Jon. "Ballpark May Be the Key to a Deal." *Pittsburgh Post-Gazette,* August 4, 1994, p. A1.

Scully, Gerald W. *The Market Structure of Professional Team Sports.* Chicago: University of Chicago Press, 1995.

———. *The Business of Major League Baseball.* Chicago: University of Chicago Press, 1989.

Seymour, Harold. *Baseball: The Early Years.* New York: Oxford University Press, 1989.

Shanahan, James L. *The Arts and Urban Development.* Akron, OH: Center for Urban Studies, University of Akron, 1980.

Sperber, Murray. *College Sports, Inc.* New York: Henry Holt, 1990.

Squires, Gregory D., ed. *Unequal Partnerships: The Political Economy of Urban Redevelopment in Postwar America.* New Brunswick, NJ: Rutgers University Press, 1989.

Stainer, Harry. "Gateway, Indians Produce Agreement." *Cleveland Plain Dealer,* December 9, 1990, pp. 1–2.

Stein, David Lewis. "Selling Off Our St. Peter's Basilica Is Profane." *Toronto Star,* April 6, 1994, p. 23.

Stephenson, M. O., Jr. "Whither the Public-Private Partnership." *Urban Affairs Quarterly* 27 (1991), 109–127.

Stevens, John. "The Rise of the Sports Page." *Garnett Center Journal* 1:2 (Fall 1987), 1–11.

Stuteville, George. "Lugar Labels Himself Ripken of GOP Field." *Indianapolis Star,* September 10, 1995, p. 1.

Suskind, Ron. "How the Inner Circles of Medicine and Sports Failed a Stricken Star." *Wall Street Journal,* March 9, 1995, pp. A1, A14.

Swanstrom, Todd. "Semi-Sovereign Cities." *Polity* 21 (Fall 1988), 83–100.

———. *The Crisis of Growth Politics: Cleveland, Kucinich, and the Challenge of Urban Populism.* Philadelphia: Temple University Press, 1985.

Swindell, David. *Public Financing of Sports Stadiums: How Cincinnati Compares.* Dayton, OH: The Buckeye Center, 1996.

Swindell, David W., and Mark S. Rosentraub. "Issues Involved in the Selection of Tools for Public Policy Analysis." *Economic Development Quarterly* 6:1 (1992), 96–101.

Taylor, Humphrey. "Evaluating Our Quality of Life." *Industrial Development* 32:4 (March/April 1987), 299–300.

Thompson, Lyke, and Mark S. Rosentraub. "Growth Poles and Lending Patterns in a Conventional Mortgage Market." *Social Science Journal* 17:1 (1980), 73–86.

Tiebout, Charles. "A Pure Theory of Local Expenditures." *Journal of Political Economy* 65 (1956), 416–424.

Turner, Dan. *The Expos Inside Out.* Toronto: McClelland and Stewart, 1983.

U.S. House of Representatives. Professional Football League Merger, Subcommittee Number 5 of the Committee on the Judiciary, October 13, 1966.

U.S. Senate. "Authorizing the Merger of Two or More Professional Basketball Leagues, and for Other Purposes." Report Number 92–1151, 92nd Congress, 2d Session, 1972.

Van Alphen, Tony. "Final Dome Tally: $263 Million Lost." *Toronto Star*, September 29, 1994, p. 1.

————. "How SkyDome's Debt Soared Through the Roof." *Toronto Star*, August 2, 1992, pp. 1, 10.

————. "Public Will Never Know Final Score on SkyDome." *Toronto Star*, November 25, 1991, p. B1.

Verducci, Tom. "A Farewell to Skinny Arms." *Sports Illustrated* 88:12 (March 23, 1998), 62–71.

Warren, Robert. "National Urban Policy and the Local State." *Urban Affairs Quarterly* 25 (1990), 541–561.

Weber, Michael J. *Industrial Location*. Beverly Hills, CA: Sage Publications, 1984.

Whitford, David. *Playing Hardball: The High Stakes Battle for Baseball's New Franchises*. New York: Doubleday, 1993.

Whitt, J. Allen. "The Role of Performing Arts in Urban Competition and Growth." In Scott Cummings, ed., *Business Elites and Urban Development: Case Studies in Critical Perspectives*. Albany: State University of New York Press, 1988, pp. 49–90.

Will, George. "Baseball Owners Abuse Their Power." *Dallas Morning News*, December 30, 1994, p. 25A.

Williams, Dick, and Bill Plaschke. *No More Mr. Nice Guy: A Life of Hardball*. San Diego: Harcourt Brace Jovanovich, 1990.

Williams, Huntington. "The News in Network TV Sports." *Garnett Center Journal* 1:2 (Fall 1987), 25–38.

Wilson, John. *Playing by the Rules: Sport, Society, and the State*. Detroit: Wayne State University Press, 1994.

Wolff, Alexander. "Broken Beyond Repair." *Sports Illustrated* 82:23 (June 12, 1995), 20–26.

Wolman, Harold. "Local Economic Development Policy: What Explains the Divergence Between Policy Analysis and Behavior." *Journal of Urban Affairs* 10: (1988), 19–28.

Zimbalist, Andrew. *Baseball and Billions*. New York: Basic Books, 1992.

Zimmerman, Dennis. "Public Subsidy of Stadiums." *NTA Forum* (Newsletter of the National Tax Association), March 1998.

Ziniuk, Dan, and Daniel Westreich. "L'Equipe de Denis Boucher: The Montréal Expos and Nationalism in Québec." Paper presented at the Cooperation Symposium on Baseball and American Culture, Cooperstown, New York, June 8–10, 1994.

INDEX

Note: Please refer to pages 18–22 for a list of major league teams.